D1191861

KNOXVILLE

CUBA, 1753-1815

Crown, Military, and Society

ALLAN J. KUETHE

THE UNIVERSITY OF TENNESSEE PRESS

Frontispiece: Volunteer, Cavalry Regiment of Havana (AGI)

The paper used in this book meets the minimum requirements of the American National Standard for Permanence of Paper for Printed Library Materials, Z39.48-1984. Binding materials have been chosen for durability.

Library of Congress Cataloging-in-Publication Data
Kuethe, Allan J., 1940–
  Cuba, 1753–1815

  Bibliography: p.
  Includes index.
  1. Cuba—History. 2. Cuba—History—British
occupation, 1762–1763. 3. Spain. Ejército—History.
I. Title.
F1779.K84 1986   972.91'04   85-17844
ISBN 0-87049-487-2 (alk. paper)

for Lourdes

————————————————————————

Contents

MAPS

ILLUSTRATIONS

TABLES

Preface

Cuba was a special colony. Located on the principal naval routes into and out of the Gulf of Mexico and the point of departure for vessels leaving the Caribbean, the island commanded a military significance far greater than its own economic resources could justify. During the eighteenth century, and particularly during the reigns of Charles III (1759–1788) and Charles IV (1788–1808), the Spanish crown spent huge sums on fortifications and manpower for its defense. By reason of Cuba's strategic importance and their relatively easy access to Spain, the island's inhabitants, above all the creole patriciate of Havana, enjoyed a level of intimacy with the royal administration that escaped American elites located in the distant inland centers of colonial life. Trooping to and from court in impressive numbers, *habaneros* understood the workings of royal politics well; they sometimes knew His Majesty's ministers personally; and they were uncommonly adept at exploiting their access to Madrid for both personal and collective advantage. The military basis for this special relationship, as seen through the workings of the military reform, is the subject of this book.

Despite the rapidly growing volume of literature on the Bourbon reforms, Cuba has been relatively neglected. Many years ago, William Whatley Pierson completed an institutional study on the Cuban intendancy, and more recently, Bibiano Torres Ramírez contributed a pioneering work on the *visita* of Alejandro O'Reilly as did Jaime Delgado on the parallel administration of the Conde de Ricla, the reformist captain general.[1] Franklin W. Knight, Pablo Tornero, and Manuel Mor-

1. William Whatley Pierson, Jr., "Institutional History of the *Intendencia*," *James Sprunt Historical Studies* 19 (Chapel Hill, 1927), 74–133; Bibiano Torres Ramírez, *Alejandro O'Reilly en las Indias* (Seville, 1969), 1–52; Jaime Delgado, "El Conde de Ricla, capitán general de Cuba," *Revista de historia de América*, nos. 55–56 (1963), 41–138.

eno Fraginals, while not addressing the formation of commercial policy as such, have traced the spectacular development of the sugar industry and the emergence of the planter elite during this same period.[2] The lack of research on Cuba has left an unfortunate void in the current understanding of the imperial reform process, for the island served as the testing ground for the colonial reorganization initiated by Charles III and perpetuated by his son.

Following his grave reverses in the Seven Years' War, Charles III resolved to place his American empire on a competitive military footing through an expansion of the regular, or veteran, garrisons and the introduction of the disciplined militia system that had been developed in Spain. Cuba, the scene of Spain's greatest humiliation, hosted the initial experiment in military reform and, in conjunction with that undertaking, far-reaching innovations in the areas of finance, administration, and commerce. To support the enlarged military establishment, Charles's dominant minister, the Marqués de Esquilache, increased taxation and introduced the intendent system of administration to improve fiscal management and to control illegal commerce more effectively. To mollify offended taxpayers, to stimulate economic growth and thus enlarge the royal revenue base, and to woo Cuban commerce to Spanish ports, the Esquilache government structured a "free trade" policy for the island in the same process, broadening the legal outlets for Cuban produce and rationalizing the levies on commerce. In that these military, financial, administrative, and commercial initiatives were all part of the same package, this study reaches beyond the limits of the military institution, advancing new insights into the larger process of reform.

When speaking of the colonial reorganization under Charles III in his work on miners and merchants in Bourbon Mexico, D.A. Brading asserted: "In some sense, the Bourbon dynasty reconquered America. It entirely transformed the system of government, the structure of the economy and the order of society which had prevailed in the colonies since the days of the Hapsburgs."[3] Brading saw this reconquest in terms of a reordering and tightening of administrative authority, harsher and more effective revenue collection, an attempt to draw the colonies into a tighter mercantilistic dependence on Spain, a restructuring of the privileged orders, and an attempt to purge the colonial governments,

2. Franklin W. Knight, "Origins of Wealth and the Sugar Revolution in Cuba, 1750–1850," *HAHR* 57 (May 1977), 231–53; Pablo Tornero, "Hacendados y desarrollo azucarero cubano (1763–1818)," *Revista de Indias*, nos. 153–154 (July–Dec. 1978), 715–37; Tornero, "La participación de Cádiz en el comercio exterior de La Habana (1776–1786)," *Jornadas de Andalucía y América* (Huelva, 1981), I, 85–103; Manuel Moreno Fraginals, *El ingenio: Complejo económico social cubano del azúcar,* 3 vols. (Havana, 1978).

3. D.A. Brading, *Miners and Merchants in Bourbon Mexico, 1763–1810* (Cambridge, 1971), 30.

especially the audiencias and fiscal offices, of the influence of entrenched colonial elites, replacing them with more dependable Spanish-born officials. The changes Brading identified for the Spanish empire, although somewhat overstated and only partially applicable to Cuba, have generally withstood the test of subsequent inquiry and are not questioned here.[4] The notion that the Bourbons "reconquered America," however, must itself be placed in doubt, for seen from another perspective, the Bourbon reform program entailed quite the opposite phenomenon. At the root of the colonial reorganization lay the risky decision to arm and train Americans through the disciplined militia system. Although justified by the escalation of the British challenge to the American empire as expressed by the conquest of Havana in 1762, this step entailed the fundamental shift of political power into American hands, particularly the hands of the creole elites that came to command the newly organized regiments and battalions. The sister reforms, designed to finance ever more bloated military establishments with American monies, compensated somewhat, of course, by strengthening administrative authority, but the crucial innovation was the transfer of military capability and responsibility to native sons of the colonies.

The Cuban example of this transition reveals that the government of Charles III was fully aware of the dangers that the new colonial policy entailed and that every effort was made to structure an understanding with Havana that would work both to sustain the reorganized army and to safeguard Spain's imperial position. The crown's indulgence of Cuban interests was, however, at least partly reflective of the island's special status within the empire and may well have been unique. The degree to which the crown attempted to establish similar accommodations elsewhere and the extent of its success of failure remain subjects for future research. It is evident, nevertheless, that at least by the ministry of José de Gálvez (1776–1787) the crown came to depend to an unfortunate degree upon anti-Americanism in its colonial administration as the means to have its way, a fact suggesting that accommodation and understanding, if extended beyond Cuba, may have perished early in Charles III's reign.

The extent to which the arming of Americans actually strengthened the empire's international position remains an open question, largely because few of the reformed armies were tested by foreign invasion. The studies of Christon I. Archer and Leon G. Campbell and my own work show repeated disappointments with the quality of the disci-

---

4. See, for example, Mark A. Burkholder and D.S. Chandler, *From Impotence to Authority: The Spanish Crown and the American Audiencias, 1687–1808* (Columbia, Mo., 1977), and John Leddy Phelan, *The People and the King: The Comunero Revolution in Colombia, 1781* (Madison, 1978).

plined militia of Mexico, Peru, and New Granada, difficulties in equipping it and in sustaining enlistments, and a seemingly endless succession of new troop plans and reorganizations.[5] Cuba, where stability prevailed, provides a sharp contrast. The militia structure established during 1763–1764 remained unchanged through the reigns of Charles III and Charles IV and after. Cuban volunteers repeatedly answered the call to arms effectively. They mannned the home front during the War of the American Revolution while the regular army won victory in Florida. Later, during the ordeal of the wars of the French Revolution and Napoleon, they filled the gaps left by a withering veteran garrison. In that the Puerto Rican militia repulsed a major British invasion in 1797 and Buenos Aires did so twice during the Second British War, it seems evident that the disciplined militia system worked best in coastal areas where a greater probability of foreign invasion loomed and where the port cities stood to gain from military spending. Significantly, despite poor initial planning, the militia of Cartagena de Indias, the port and strongpoint that probably most resembled Havana, generally functioned well despite frequent failures in other jurisdictions of the Viceroyalty of New Granada.

The impact of the *fuero militar* upon colonial society and politics also varied from colony to colony. Lyle N. McAlister showed that in New Spain military privilege as extended to the disciplined militia was the source of repeated jurisdictional conflicts motivated by corporate pride and jealousy, confusing the cause of justice and clogging the royal administration with interminable litigation; but Campbell found little of this phenomenon in Peru.[6] New Granada followed a pattern similar to that of New Spain although with distinct overtones. Corporate pretense was undoubtedly a factor behind many jurisdictional disputes, but the deeper source was creole resistance to unwelcome reform initiatives imposed by Madrid and backed by Spanish officers in command of militiamen who were recruited from the lower orders and whose privileges they supported in return for political loyalty. The situation was different in Cuba. There, the *fuero militar* was unquestionably taken as a major privilege, particularly by the planter officers whose vanity and martial image it sustained. Yet jurisdictional strife did not emerge until relatively late in the reform period, for in Cuba, unlike New Granada, cooperation between patrician and royal bureaucrat prevailed and the interlocking nature of the several Cuban

5. Christon I. Archer, *The Army in Bourbon Mexico, 1760–1810* (Albuquerque, 1977); Leon G. Campbell, *The Military and Society in Colonial Peru, 1750–1810* (Philadelphia, 1978); Allan J. Kuethe, *Military Reform and Society in New Granada, 1773–1808* (Gainesville, 1978).

6. Lyle N. McAlister, *The "Fuero Militar" in New Spain, 1764–1800* (Gainesville, 1957); Campbell, *The Military and Society*.

directories minimized internal division. Only when the elite of Havana society divided over its vision of the future did jurisdictional conflict rage and then with important implications for the political future of the island.

The military corporation tended to reinforce rather than to modify the existing social order. In New Granada, where, in areas such as Guayaquil, Santa Marta, and provincial Cartagena, extensive racial miscegenation and fluid social structures existed, militia office became a source of upward mobility, even to the point where individuals of obscure social origin managed to establish status in the white estate. And backed by Spanish officers, volunteers of humble background escaped the jurisdiction of local elites, answering juridically to their military superiors who often sympathized little with creole pretensions. In Cuba, except for Cuatro Villas, Guanabacoa, and Matanzas, where bona fide elites emerged relatively late, the military reform found already in place a high degree of stratification that hardened with the advance of the sugar revolution. Given the level of cooperation between the crown and the colonial patriciate, militia office confirmed already established social rank, and although the uniform was an unquestionable asset in the acquisition of habits in crusading orders or of supremely prestigious titles of Castile, it did not alter the overall composition of the elite. Within the colored estate, military decorations, uniforms, and privileges provided a measure of distinction, but neither Cuban nor Spanish authorities were prepared to indulge the pretenses of blacks or mulattoes beyond their assigned condition, despite what proved to be imaginative pressures from below.

This study focuses upon the elites, the primary beneficiaries of the military reform, and on their relationship to the court where they converted their military services into an ongoing series of special concessions to the advantage of their estate. It also focuses primarily upon Havana and, to a lesser degree, on its satellite Matanzas not only because those districts possessed well over half of the Cuban army but because Havana was the political center of the island and *habaneros* were the primary actors in the dialogue with the court that made the Cuban military reform work. Moreover, their achievements, especially in the area of commercial concessions, bore major implications for the rest of the empire.

Finally, the question of Cuban fidelity during the Wars for Independence is addressed anew. Historians have universally understood that the fear of a slave rebellion enforced a moderating effect upon Cuban political aspirations during the crisis that gripped the empire following the French invasion of Spain. Although the present study has produced no evidence to challenge the validity of that interpretation in a general sense, other factors most certainly emerge.

It has also been argued that Cubans were unable to join their fellow Americans in a revolt against Spain because of the overwhelming Spanish military presence that dominated the garrison island.[7] Nothing could be further from the truth. By 1808, after having suffered the debilitating effects of the wars of the French Revolution and Napoleon, the regular army was anything but an impressive combat force; moreover, it was essentially an American army. Creoles not Spaniards dominated the officer corps, and consequently Cubans controlled their own destiny. In this respect, Cuba was typical, for Charles III not only armed Americans through the disciplined militia but, owing to financial and personnel difficulties, tolerated the gradual nativization of the officer corps of the regular army across the empire.

Recently, Jorge I. Domínguez, while acknowledging that the fear of a slave uprising posed a serious restraint on political alternatives, has argued that Havana's unique, satisfying relationship with the royal administration on both sides of the water was also a determining factor in holding Cuba in the empire. Recognizing the island's strategic importance, the crown and its colonial officials had worked effectively to co-opt the Cuban elite into a stable political relationship with Spain. In effect, the creole elite was able to "nationalize decision making" within the existing imperial structure.[8] The research to be presented here sustains that interpretation, although I would broaden the concept of royal co-optation to one of mutual co-optation in that *habaneros* were adept at seduction on their own level. Furthermore, because he was conducting a comparative analysis with Chile, Venezuela, and Mexico, Domínguez did not attempt to explore the historical basis for the Havana-Madrid political relationship in depth. That subject is addressed here.

Despite these considerations, Havana was more divided in 1808 than is generally supposed and in fact came close to revolutionary action. During that confused time, *habaneros*, like the creoles of the other colonies, confronted complex issues and were divided by personalist factions. A full analysis of those murky waters is beyond the scope of this book, but the history of the Cuban army and its behavior in 1808 offers new insights into Havana's decision to make Cuba Spain's "ever faithful isle."

7. Philip S. Foner, *A History of Cuba and Its Relations with the United States* (New York, 1962), I, 81–82.
8. Jorge I. Domínquez, *Insurrection or Loyalty: The Breakdown of the Spanish American Empire* (Cambridge, Mass., 1980), 103–6, 125–26, 142, 160–63.

Acknowledgments

Those who have contributed toward the making of this book have my deepest gratitude. G. Douglas Inglis shared materials, rendered thoughtful, constructive criticism of the manuscript as it developed, and through IberSoftware gave unselfishly of his time and equipment to advance the preparation of the final typescript. Franklin Knight, Bibiano Torres Ramírez, and Pablo Tornero shared their ideas about eighteenth-century Cuba, and Jacques Barbier, Mark Burkholder, Sam Chandler, and James Lewis about its place in the larger imperial setting. To Christon I. Archer, Leon Campbell, Juan Marchena Fernández, Lyle N. McAlister, and Santiago Gerardo Suárez, I am indebted for the insights they provided into the nature of the colonial military. The staffs of the Archivo General de Indias, the Archivo General de Simancas, the Archivo Histórico Nacional, the Servicio Histórico Militar, and the Museo Naval extended every courtesy despite the innumerable demands that I placed upon them. I also wish to thank Joaquín Vaquero and his son, Joaquín Vaquero Turcios, for the assistance rendered me during my work in the Archivo General Militar de Segovia. Without the financial assistance repeatedly provided by the American Philosophical Society and the Texas Tech Institute for University Research, this work would have been impossible. I am also grateful to Gary Elbow who generously prepared the maps. Finally, a special word of thanks to my wife, Lourdes, and my children, John, Jennifer, Allan Ray, and Christian, who endured.

CUBA, 1753–1815

Crown, Military, and Society

1. Humiliation

When the British marched into Havana on August 14, 1762, the vulnerability of Spain's vast colonial empire lay exposed to the world. Of all the American strongpoints, Havana had been the most heavily defended, but the highly tuned British war machine, fresh from sensational victories in Canada and the French West Indies, pounded the Spanish army into submission during a siege of over two months. Although the Spanish regulars fought well, in the long run they simply did not have the manpower to prevail. The conclusions that the government of Charles III drew from these events worked to reshape his Cuban colony in the profoundest way and, indeed, led to major changes in the rest of his American empire as well.

Spain was humiliated at Havana primarily because the crown had failed to adjust its colonial defenses to the changing military realities in America following the War of Jenkins' Ear. Ferdinand VI (1746–1759) had inherited from his father, Philip V (1700–1746), a promising defense system that had to its credit a dramatic victory over the British at Cartagena in 1741. But misplaced confidence arising from that very triumph, as well as new hopes for long-term peace that the temporary successes of a neutral foreign policy inspired, lulled Ferdinand into an unimaginative perpetuation of his father's system despite the ever-growing power of Great Britain in Europe and America.

The central problem in 1762 arose from the limited contribution of native Americans to defense. Under the early Bourbons, the small regular army had been largely the province of the European Spaniard; Americans had performed a secondary, almost peripheral role. The larger militia, although an American force, was assigned small importance and was so poorly structured that it could contribute little. Consequently, when Spain entered the Seven Years' War, the American army, including the Havana garrison, lacked the strength requisite to marshal effective resistance. The British invasion of Havana made this lesson painfully clear.

When Philip V succeeded to the Spanish throne in 1700, he had established the rebuilding of the armed forces as a major priority. Both the fleet and the army, if they deserved those names at all, were in shambles, and smugglers so dominated the American trade that Spain's mercentilistic pretenses amounted to an empty hope. Guided by able ministers such as José Patiño, the Marqués de la Ensenada, and José del Campillo y Cossío, Philip's administration launched an ambitious program to revitalize Spain's military and commercial position. The construction of a competitive fleet was essential both to enhance Spain's grandeur and to recapture and protect the American trade, thus generating the revenue to finance a resurgence of Spanish power.[1] Essential too was the expansion and modernization of the army. The regiment replaced the *tercio* as the basic tactical unit while a new system of command, including brigadiers, colonels, and lieutenants, displaced and refined Hapsburg offices.[2] Equally important, the crown centralized promotions into its own hands.[3]

In America, Philip's government reorganized the garrisons of the strategic fortified ports into a series of fixed (*fijo*) battalions. Financial exigency, however, severely limited the scope of this action. The War of the Spanish Succession had left a huge debt, and the long series of Italian wars inspired by the dynastic designs of the queen, Isabel Farnese, consumed much of the incoming revenue. So desperate for income was the monarchy at this time that it periodically resorted to the unthinkable but lucrative practice of selling audiencia offices in America and with them dispensations from various restrictions upon the conduct of their occupants.[4] Under these circumstances, the crown ordinarily limited individual defense bases to single battalions and established them only gradually. Cartagena got its fixed battalion in 1736, Santo Domingo in 1738, Veracruz in 1740, and Panama and San

1. Jacques A. Barbier, "The Culmination of the Bourbon Reforms, 1787–1792," *HAHR* 57 (Feb. 1977), 54; Vicente Rodríquez Casado, "La política del reformismo de los primeros Borbones en la marina de guerra española," *AEA* 25 (1968), 601–15; Cesáreo Fernández Duro, *La armada española desde la unión de los Reinos de Castilla y Aragón* (Madrid, 1973), VI, 209–21; José Martínez Cardós, "Don José del Campillo y Cossío," *Revista de Indias,* nos. 119–22 (1970), 525–42.

2. Juan Marchena Fernández, *Oficiales y soldados en el ejército de América* (Seville, 1983), 42–43.

3. Previously, local officials had appointive power below the rank of colonel or *maestre de campo.* George Earl Sanders, "The Spanish Defense of America, 1700–1763" (Ph.D. dissertation, University of Southern California, 1973), 137.

4. Burkholder and Chandler, *From Impotence to Authority,* 16–80.

Juan in 1741, for example.[5] Spanish battalions would reinforce the permanent garrisons during wartime. It was hoped that these small forces, placed behind fixed fortifications, could hold at bay superior armies, which would be able to bring only part of their strength to bear effectively, while the ravages of the tropical climate depleted their ranks. Spanish military thinking was necessarily defensive in the extreme.[6]

The crown established the first of the American fixed battalions in 1719 in Havana, the most important strongpoint in America. Given its location, the city dominated the exit routes from the Caribbean, was the gateway to Mexico and served as the point of entry or departure for much of the American trade. Its magnificent bay was, therefore, heavily fortified, and the city was in 1719, as it would be in 1763, the first to benefit from the latest thinking in Bourbon military strategy.

Havana's fixed battalion was forged out of seven 100-man companies that had previously functioned individually. The new organization represented an attempt to upgrade and modernize unit operations. To tighten coordination, the crown placed at the head of the battalion a command and staff group led by a company captain. And in accord with contemporary developments in Europe, it increased the number of company officers from three to four and of sergeants from one to two, centralized promotions, and converted one of the infantry companies from fusiliers to grenadiers. As before, a hundred artillerymen and a company of cavalry complemented the infantry.[7] In later years, the authorities strengthened the garrison by adding five separate infantry companies and by replacing the cavalry company with three companies of dragoons.[8]

A conspicuous feature of the new system, codified into a regulation and promulgated in 1719, was the stipulation that the army should be predominantly European. Only 20 percent of the enlisted men might be American-born Spaniards, and that figure was allowed only because of anticipated recruitment difficulties and costs in the peninsula. Another expression of official preference for European recruits was the stipulation that, although Spaniards were eligible for enlistment at

5. *Estado militar de España* (Madrid, 1799); Allan J. Kuethe, "La batalla de Cartagena de 1741: Nuevas perspectivas," *Historiografía y bibliografía americanistas* 18 (1974), 23.

6. Marchena, *Oficiales y soldados,* 167–76.

7. File on the military regulations for Havana, including the *Reglamento para la guarnición de La Habana . . . 1719,* (Madrid, 1719), AGI, SD, leg. 2104-A. See also, Sanders, "Spanish Defense," 265.

8. Royal order, Dec. 29, 1731, Governor Juan Francisco Güemes de Horcasitas to José Patiño, Havana, May 2, 1732, troop cost report, Havana, Dec. 10, 1736, all in AGI, SD, leg. 2104-B.

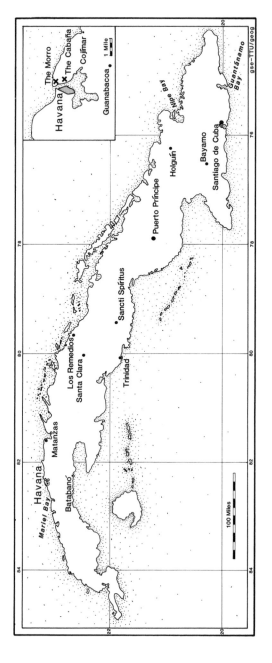

The Captaincy General of Cuba

sixteen years of age, Americans had to be at least twenty.[9] The regulation for the garrison of Cartagena de Indias in New Granada also limited creole enlistments to 20 percent, those for Santo Domingo and Puerto Rico to 50 percent; but the practice does not appear to have been applied elsewhere, probably owing to the difficulty of securing enough European recruits and transporting them to America.[10] The 1719 regulation said nothing about quotas for officers, but surely creoles were not expected to exceed the percentage defined for enlisted men. The first set of service records for the Havana garrison, completed in 1749, shows that creoles held only 17 percent of the offices.[11]

The preference for Europeans was simply a continuation of earlier practices that had assigned primary defense responsibility to the Spanish army. Part of the reason for this policy was the widespread belief that Americans were inferior to Spaniards as fighting men, but the deeper cause lay in the crown's fear that arming the colonials might compromise royal political control, a concern that certainly could not be taken lightly.[12] The great disadvantage of this strategy was that it restricted the military role of those who had the greatest stake in local defense.

The only other city in the colony that rated a permanent garrison was Cuba's second port, Santiago de Cuba on the eastern tip of the island. It possessed a contingent of five infantry companies totaling three hundred men and a small artillery detachment. Santiago's governors uniformly viewed this force as inadequate to man the bay's fortifications satisfactorily and to discharge its other obligations. Petitions for an expansion of the garrison to a full battalion accumulated in the Ministry of the Indies, but no permanent action was taken until much later.[13]

9. *Reglamento para . . . La Habana,* 1719, arts. 12, 16, 29.

10. *Reglamento para la guarnición de la Plaza de Cartagena de Indias, castillos y fuertes de su jurisdicción* (Madrid, 1736), art. 13; *Reglamento para la guarnición de la Plaza de Santo Domingo, en la Isla Española, castillos y fuertes de su jurisdicción* (Madrid, 1738), art. 14; *Reglamento para la guarnición de la Plaza de Puerto Rico, castillos, y fuertes de su jurisdicción* (Madrid, 1741), art. 12. The regulations for Chile and Yucatán contain no such provisions. *Reglamento para la guarnición de las plazas, y fuertes de la frontera de la Concepción, Valparaíso, y Chiloe del Reyno de Chile . . .* (Lima, 1753); *Reglamento para la guarnición de la Plaza de Valdivia y castillos de su jurisdi[c]ción* (Lima, 1753); *Reglamento para la guarnición de la Provincia de Yucatán, castillos, y fuerte de su jurisdicción* (México, 1754).

11. Service records, Havana garrison, 1749, AGI, SD, leg. 2108.

12. For an analysis of the prejudice against American soldiering ability, see Sanders, "Spanish Defense," 152–53.

13. Governor Pedro Ignacio Jiménez to [Ministry of the Indies], Santiago, May 21, 1730, Governor Francisco Cagigal de la Vega to [Ministry of the Indies], Santiago, Nov. 2, 1739, Oct. 30, 1741, all in AGI, SD, legs. 2104-A, 2105–6. In 1735 the crown actually authorized the formation of a fixed battalion of five 100-man companies for Santiago, but Jiménez was

A large militia supplemented the regular army. In 1737 a count of the island's volunteer units found 112 companies totaling some 9,068 men and officers, which were divided between Havana and its district; Trinidad, Sancti Spíritus, San Juan de los Remedios, and Santa Clara in the south and central part of the island; Puerto Príncipe farther east; and Holguín, Bayamo, and Santiago in the extreme east. These units, however, lacked standardized tables of organization and the guidance of veteran officers. They drilled infrequently, if at all, and possessed no regular complement of weapons.[14] That they would count for much under combat conditions was most doubtful.

The critical test of Philip's defense system came at Cartagena de Indias in the Viceroyalty of New Granada during the War of Jenkins' Ear (1739–1748). This conflict was the result of hostilities arising from the renewed Spanish assertion of monopolistic mercantile prerogatives in its colonies while the British stubbornly sought to sustain and expand the lucrative inroads that they had long enjoyed. As war drew near, Philip's government acted to strengthen its position in New Granada. In 1736 it created a fixed battalion in Cartagena and in 1739 elevated New Granada to the status of a viceroyalty under the command of Lieutenant General Sebastián de Eslava. Moreover, according to plan, Spain sent two battalions from the Regiments of Spain and Aragón to reinforce the port when war broke out.[15] During this same period, two dragoon regiments and elements from the Infantry Regiments of Granada, Milan, Victoria, and Portugal were deployed in Cuba.[16]

The British siege of Cartagena began in March 1741. The attack force, led by Admiral Edward Vernon, possessed awesome power. The fleet itself numbered at least 140 warships and transports and carried an army of some 11,000 to 12,000 troops, including 3,600 from the North American colonies. To meet the invasion, Viceroy Eslava, who was aided by Lieutenant General Blas de Lezo of the royal navy, had only three veteran battalions, five hundred untrained militiamen, six hundred Indian bowmen, and six ships with a thousand marines. Worse, death and desertion had reduced the effective strength of the veteran force to some eleven hundred men. Even considering the impressive advantage that the massive fortifications of Cartagena afforded, the battle appeared a mismatch.

---

unable to execute the order for want of personnel. File on Santiago garrison, 1735–36, AGI, SD, leg. 2104-B.

14. Militia report, May 8, 1737, AGI, SD, leg. 2104-B.

15. Kuethe, "La batalla de Cartagena," 21, 25.

16. Royal orders, Mar. 28, 1740, May 20, 1741, Mar. 5, 1742, Cagigal to Don José del Campillo y Cossío, Santiago, Sept. 27, 1742, troop review, Havana, Dec. 29, 1742, all in AGI, SD, legs. 2102, 2105–6.

Despite the overwhelming superiority of the British forces and some early successes on their part, the defenders managed a spectacular victory. After a lengthy and difficult siege, the British smashed through the powerful defenses at the mouth of the bay; they advanced slowly against bitter resistance by land and sea to the outskirts of the city; but they failed to breach the castle of San Felipe de Barajas, the final barrier to victory, which guarded the immediate land approaches to Cartagena. Made desperate by the withering effect of disease on their forces, the British futilely hurled wave after wave of infantrymen against San Felipe's massive walls before withdrawing in frustration and conceding to the Spanish military one of its most glorious victories.

The Spanish triumph can be attributed to a combination of factors, including the leadership of Blas de Lezo, who died of wounds suffered in the battle, and to a lesser degree that of Eslava; the excellent fortifications; the incredibly heroic, tenacious performance of the Spanish marines and infantry battalions; and the devastating effect of disease on the invading army. Finally, the British, who on any number of occasions were slow to exploit their opportunities, did as much to lose the battle as the Spanish did to win it.[17] Even in defeat, however, Great Britain had displayed impressive power.

During the War of Jenkins' Ear, the British also menaced Cuba. In mid-1740, they blockaded and harassed Havana for two months.[18] A year later, they landed three thousand soldiers, supported by a thousand slaves, at Guantánamo on the eastern end of the island and effected a limited probe toward Santiago, which was being used as a base by privateers operating against Jamaican shipping. In anticipation of the attack, Captain General Juan Francisco Güemes de Horcasitas had sent reinforcements from Havana. These included detachments from the Regiment of Dragoons of Itálica and the Infantry Regiments of Milan and Portugal. Seventy-four men from the Regiment of Victoria, having shipwrecked near Santiago, were already on hand. Under the leadership of Governor Francisco Cagigal de la Vega, these reinforcements and the fixed garrison, assisted by militiamen, disease, and the difficult terrain, employed guerrilla tactics to discourage any serious attempt to seize Santiago, and the invaders eventually withdrew.[19] The

17. For a variety of interpretations of the battle, see Charles E. Nowell, "The Defense of Cartagena," *HAHR* 42 (Nov. 1962), 477–501; Carlos Restrepo Canal, "El sitio de Cartagena por el Almirante Vernon," *Boletín de historia y antigüedades* 28 (1941), 447–67; and Juan Manuel Zapatero, "La heroica defensa de Cartagena de Indias ante el almirante inglés Vernon en 1741," *Revista de historia militar* 1 (1957), 115–52.

18. Ramiro Guerra, *Manual de historia de Cuba desde su descubrimiento hasta 1868*, 2nd ed. (Madrid, 1975), 155–56.

19. Ibid.; Juan Pérez de la Riva, "Inglaterra y Cuba en la primera mitad del Siglo XVII [*sic*]: Expedición de Vernon contra Santiago de Cuba en 1741," *Revista bimestre cubana* 36

British returned to Santiago in 1748, but the port's shore batteries repulsed an attempt to penetrate the bay.[20] Although none of these actions approached the significance of the events in Cartagena, they revealed a keen British interest in Cuba and further demonstrated the British capacity to apply military pressure at will.

The 1741 victory at Cartagena quite naturally occasioned great rejoicing both in Spain and in the colonies, but the battle should also have caused grave concern. Although Philip's defense system had passed its first test, it had done so by the narrowest of margins. The slightest change of fortune at any number of points during the siege could easily have meant defeat. Especially ominous were the implications of the massive striking power the British had demonstrated in mounting the invasion. Backed by a rapidly expanding economic and demographic base in America and able to select their point of attack, the British almost certainly would enjoy overwhelming numerical superiority in any future engagement. For their part, the Spanish were at a decided disadvantage. Their forces had to be divided among the numerous fortified ports of the empire, and there was no guarantee that European troops could be deployed in time or in sufficient strength. Portobelo, for example, had fallen almost without resistance to a surprise attack at the beginning of the war before reinforcements had arrived.

The American militia might have offered some hope of improving the odds, but its chronically poor state of preparation permitted it to contribute only marginally. During the siege of Cartagena, the militia had mainly performed support functions, although it did fight well on several occasions. The marines and the two Spanish battalions shouldered most of the difficult combat. Even the fixed battalion, which largely consisted of raw recruits, had performed erratically and during at least one key engagement had to be wedged between the Spanish forces, with saber-wielding officers deployed to the rear to hold it in position.[21] A careful analysis of the events of 1741 would have indicated

---

(July–Oct. 1935), 61–65; royal order, May 20, 1741, Cagigal to [Ministry of the Indies], Santiago, Oct. 30, 1741, both in AGI, SD, leg. 2106. Santiago was later reinforced by six companies from the Regiment of Portugal, which also shipwrecked on Cuba, and by the Regiment of Dragoons of Almanza, which replaced the detachments from the Regiment of Itálica. Cagigal to Campillo, Santiago, Sept. 27, 1742, AGI, SD, leg. 2106. Published documents concerning this action can be found in Leví Marrero, *Cuba: Economía y sociedad* (Madrid, 1978), VI, 89–109. See also John Robert McNeill, "Theory and Practice in the Bourbon Empires of the Atlantic: The Roles of Louisbourg and Havana, 1713–1763" (Ph.D. dissertation, Duke University, 1981), 112, 127–28.

20. Fernández, *La armada española*, VI, 342; Governor Alonso de Arcos Moreno to Minister of the Indies Marqués de la Ensenada, Santiago, Apr. 12, 1748, AGI, SD, leg. 2108.

21. Kuethe, "La batalla de Cartagena," 4–11, 18.

that basic adjustments in Spanish defense strategy were in order, but in the euphoria that reigned at court these hard lessons were lost.

Apart from the misreading of the events at Cartagena, other factors help explain the lack of innovation in military planning following the War of Jenkins' Ear. The death of Philip V in 1746 and the succession of his son, Ferdinand, brought a fundamental shift in Spanish foreign policy that became evident after the Peace of Aix-la-Chapelle. Stung during the war by the duplicity of France, Spain's ally under the Second Family Compact, and hopeful that his empire could advance its interests by steering a neutral course in the rivalry between France and Britain, the new monarch stubbornly committed his reign to the pursuit of peace. Indeed, the two men whom he named as his ministers of state, first José de Carvajal y Lancaster and then Ricardo Wall, both favored the British over the French. Areas of friction between the two powers remained, naturally, but the relations between them were tolerably cordial during most of Ferdinand's reign.[22] The improvement of relations with Spain's ancient rival did not necessarily preclude rigorous military preparations, but it certainly relieved any immediate pressure for ambitious innovations.

The immediate result of the new diplomatic orientation was the recall to Europe of all peninsular units that had been deployed in America during the war. The crown also ordered the fixed garrisons to revert to their prewar strengths, although it permitted them to complete their complements by recruiting men and officers from the departing units.[23] These measures had a particularly harsh effect on Santiago, which during the war had won authorization to organize a fixed battalion of seven 100-man companies as well as a separate company of artillery.[24] Its garrison now returned to its formerly deficient condition.

Normalization of relations with Britain and the accompanying opportunity to contain military expenditures enabled Ferdinand to increase the remission of colonial revenues to Spain.[25] Indies income, including monies patriated from America, peninsular taxes on the colonial trade, and various fees and fines collected in Spain, had grown remarkably since Philip had first inherited an empty treasury, reaching levels during the 1750s that would not again be equaled until the late 1780s. By his death in 1759, Ferdinand had accumulated the handsome

22. Richard Pares, *War and Trade in the West Indies, 1739–1763,* 2nd ed. (London, 1963), 517–59; Lucio Mijares Pérez, "Programa político para América del Marqués de la Ensenada," *Revista de historia de América,* no. 81 (Jan.–June 1976), 85–93, 101–109.

23. Royal order, Jan. 25, 1749, Cagigal to Ensenada, Havana, Nov. 6, 1749, both in AGI, SD, legs. 2108, 2109.

24. Cagigal to Campillo, Santiago, Sept. 27, 1742, Arcos to Ensenada Santiago, Mar. 18, 1749, both in AGI, SD, legs. 2106, 2108.

25. Sanders, "Spanish Defense," 274.

sum of 123,853,177 *reales de vellón* in the Depositaria de Indias in Cádiz, money that Charles III would quickly transfer to Madrid and use to help finance the first of his wars.[26] The solvency of the royal treasury increased the political options available to the crown. The Ministry of the Indies, for example, put a stop to the sale of audiencia offices in 1751 and initiated the long, painful struggle to regain control of the colonial courts from the hands of local investors.[27] All in all, during the reign of Ferdinand financial exigency no longer served as an explanation for the inadequacy of the American army. His government perpetuated the status quo in defense strategy because it saw no reason to do otherwise.

Another factor that contributed to the absence of original military thinking under Ferdinand was the promotion of men who had won reputations in the War of Jenkins' Ear to positions of high administrative influence. Sebastián de Eslava, the victor at Cartagena, in 1749 became captain general of Andalusia; Juan Francisco Güemes de Horcasitas, now the Conde de Revillagigedo, advanced in 1746 from captain general of Cuba to viceroy of New Spain; and Francisco Cagigal de la Vega, became captain general of Cuba. Eslava quickly became the confidant of the Marqués de la Ensenada, who had risen to power under Philip V following the death of Campillo in 1743. Acting simultaneously as minister of war, finance, navy, and the Indies, Ensenada shaped American policy through a series of ad hoc juntas comprising men such as Julián de Arriaga, Francisco Fernández de Molinillo, Manuel Pablo de Salcedo, and of course, Eslava. The latter dominated military proceedings for the Indies, and it is evident that his attachment to the system that had advanced his career did much to prevent imaginative defense planning.[28] Ensenada, who personally favored French over British interests and who acted as a counterbalance to Carvajal, advocated a vigilant neutrality in America. For land defenses, however, Ensenada, as counseled by Eslava, emphasized the repair and construction of fixed fortifications of the kind that worked at Cartagena rather than attempting any basic reorganization of the defense system.[29] The small colonial army thus commanded relatively little attention and experienced few significant innovations.

The continuity in defense strategy between the regimes of Philip V and Ferdinand VI is well illustrated by the reorganization that Ensenada and Revillagigedo effected in 1753 for the army of Cuba. Revillagigedo, acting under a 1748 order from Ensenada, formulated a system

26. Jacques A. Barbier, "Towards a New Chronology for Bourbon Colonialism: The *Depositaria de Indias* of Cádiz, 1722–1789," *Ibero-Amerikanisches Archiv* 6 (1980), 335–53.

27. Burkholder and Chandler, *From Impotence to Authority*, 83–97.

28. Mijares, "Programa político," 82–103.

29. Ibid., 86, 93–105.

to coordinate defense planning and troop deployments for Havana and the outlying provinces of Santiago de Cuba and St. Augustine in Florida.[30] This plan, which was codified into a special regulation, simply reaffirmed the established policy of depending primarily upon fixed garrisons for immediate defense with the expectation that Spanish troops could adequately meet the remaining wartime needs. The new regulation increased the infantry from one battalion and five separate companies, totaling 1,200 men, to a regiment of four battalions with six companies each, totaling 2,080.[31] Individual battalions were, as before, placed under the command of the highest ranking company captain, but the plan attempted to upgrade the fixed garrison's leadership by adding a colonel, a lieutenant colonel, and a *sargento mayor* (plans and training officer) to head the regiment's command and staff group. The artillery company that continued to complement the infantry was expanded from 100 to 172 men and later subdivided into two companies. The dragoons were increased from three 70-man companies to four with 65 men each. Under the new plan, Havana became responsible for providing troops for both Santiago and St. Augustine. Santiago received 440 infantrymen and 30 artillerymen, improving its defenses somewhat; and 310 infantrymen, 40 artillerymen, and 50 dragoons went to St. Augustine.

These changes, although they slightly strengthened the Havana garrison, in a deeper and more important sense amounted simply to a refinement of traditional policy. Spain, continuing to think defensively, would concede numerical superiority although fighting on home soil and would depend upon the climate to destroy the enemy.

Recruitment regulations also sustained continuity between the practices of Philip and Ferdinand. As in 1719, the new regulation placed strict limitations on creole enlistments. Although the permissible ratio of creoles to Spaniards varied somewhat in the different branches of the defense force, the composite average actually dropped to slightly over 19 percent. To procure Spaniards, the infantry regiment was to maintain a recruitment party in the Canary Islands, and if that measure proved inadequate, another party was to operate in Mexico City and Puebla to enlist vagrant Spanish immigrants.[32] Traditional inhibitions about arming Americans remained very much alive.

30. Conde de Revillagigedo to Ensenada, México, Feb. 10, 1749, royal order, May 16, 1751, both in AGI, SD, leg. 2109.

31. Each company of fusiliers possessed ninety-four men; each grenadier company, fifty.

32. Revillagigedo to Ensenada, México, Oct. 23, 1753, AGI, SD, leg. 2110; *Reglamento para la guarnición de La Habana, castillos, y fuertes de su jurisdicción, Santiago de Cuba, San Agustín de la Florida; y su annexo San Marcos de Apalache* (México, 1753); *Suplemento de algunos particulares que quedaron omisos, y sin comprehenderse en el Reglamento para*

The regulation contained no specific limitations on creole officers, although Spaniards were obviously much preferred. In practice, nevertheless, Cubans were beginning to penetrate the officer corps. Wellborn creoles were eligible for enlistment in the regular army as cadets, and during the 1740s and 1750s many parents availed themselves of the opportunity to begin military careers for their sons. The expansion of the officer corps in 1753 without a corresponding injection of European officers enabled a goodly number of these cadets to acquire positions as ensigns or second lieutenants. Consequently, creoles held 41 percent of the garrison's offices by 1758 as compared to only 17 percent in 1749. At the rank of captain and above, naturally, Spaniards predominated overwhelmingly.[33]

The most important omission in the new regulation was its failure to incorporate the civilian population of Cuba directly into the defense structure. In Spain the government of Philip V, working largely through the Conde de Montemar, had devised what it called a disciplined militia in 1734 during the War of the Polish Succession. Established in the thirty-four provinces of Castile, this militia enjoyed a standardized table of organization, received uniforms and equipment, and drilled regularly under the supervision of veteran officers and enlisted men. To enhance its sense of corporate identity and pride, the crown also conceded to the disciplined militia extensive military privileges in the manner of the regular army.[34] This system, at a relatively low cost, introduced thousands of inhabitants to the rudiments of military training, enabling them to function as a reserve and to share in the peninsular defense burden. Neither Philip nor Ferdinand, however, seriously considered extending the disciplined militia program to America. Consequently, during the 1750s, the Cuban militia continued to languish without formalized organization or systematic training.

In 1754 Ferdinand learned that the Marqués de la Ensenada, disturbed by the course of negotiations over the Portuguese colony of Sacramento in the Río de la Plata region, had exceeded his authority by secretly opening negotiations for a French alliance.[35] Ferdinand had no

---

la Plaza de La Habana . . . (México, 1754). Half of the detachments for Santiago and St. Augustine were to be relieved each year. For the impact of this regulation in Florida, see John Jay TePaske, The Governorship of Spanish Florida, 1700–1763 (Durham, 1964), 156–57.

33. The last service records compiled before the war, those for 1758, are unfortunately incomplete. The records for the third battalion of infantry and the artillery are missing. For the latter, however, records exist for 1756, and as late as 1760 only one position had changed hands. AGI, SD, legs. 2111–13.

34. Johann Hellwege, Die spanischen Provinzialmilizen im 18. Jahrhundert (Boppard am Rhein, 1969) chs. 1–2; Félix Colón y Larriátegui Ximénez de Embún, Juzqados militares de España y sus Indias . . . , 2nd ed. (Madrid, 1788), II, 469, 562.

35. See John D. Bergamini, The Spanish Bourbons: The History of a Tenacious Dynasty (New York, 1974), 82.

choice but to dismiss him, but Ensenada's fall did little to alter the nature of Spanish military strategy in America. Baylio Frey Julián de Arriaga, one of Ensenada's disciples, replaced him as minister of the Indies. Arriaga had firsthand American experience, having served as governor of Caracas from 1749 to 1751, where he was instrumental in effecting a prudent pacification of the León revolt against the policies of the Caracas Company. Although a distinguished, venerable personage, Arriaga became very much subordinated in court politics to Ricardo Wall, the pro-British minister who had succeeded Carvajal upon the latter's death in 1754.[36] Moreover, Ferdinand named Sebastián Eslava to assume Ensenada's duties as minister of war, an appointment that ensured continuity in military thinking.[37] And in June 1759, when Eslava died, Wall added that portfolio to his other duties.[38] Consequently, the policies charted for Cuba in 1753 remained in place as Spain approached its fateful confrontation with Great Britain.[39]

The Seven Years' War had been underway for three years in August 1759 when Charles III abandoned his rule in Naples to succeed his half brother as king of Spain. Having conquered Louisbourg during the previous year, the British were well on their way toward driving the French from Canada. In September, James Wolfe scored his brilliant victory at Quebec, and in the following year the United Kingdom completed its Canadian conquests. Moreover, British forces had seized Guadeloupe and threatened further gains in the French islands. Charles initially hoped that he, like Ferdinand, might maintain neutrality, but the magnitude of the British successes made such a course difficult. Fearful that Spain might be left to face Britain alone in the future and hopeful of restoring the balance of power in America, Charles signed the Third Family Compact with France in August 1761, thereby abandoning the strategy of neutrality so carefully nurtured by his predecessor. The British declared war on January 4, 1762. Within six months they were poised to strike at Havana.

36. Modesto Lafuente, *Historia general de España desde los tiempos primitivos hasta la muerte de Fernando VII* (Barcelona, 1889), XIV, 19–20, 30–31; Roland Dennis Hussey, *The Caracas Company, 1728–1784: A Study in the History of Spanish Monopolistic Trade* (Cambridge, Mass., 1934), ch. 5.

37. Lafuente, *Historia general,* XIV, 31.

38. Ricardo Wall to Captain General Juan de Prado, Villaviciosa, June 25, 1759, royal order, Aug. 5, 1759, both in AGI, SD, leg. 1586.

39. It should be noted that the practice of periodically rotating troops from Havana to St. Augustine and Santiago as prescribed by the 1753 regulation proved difficult and costly and caused hardships for the families of the troops. In 1761 Prado proposed that the detachments for Santiago and St. Augustine be placed on a separate fixed footing. Accordingly, Havana's infantry would be reduced to three battalions, its dragoons to three companies, and its artillery to one company. Prado's argument persuaded the crown, but the final implementation of the reorganization was interrupted by the British invasion. Prado to Julián de Arriaga, Havana, Apr. 15, 1761, Feb. 1, 1762, royal orders, July 14, 1761, Oct. 8, 1762, all in AGI, SD, legs. 2114–15, 2155.

Except for the outcome, the events at Havana during the summer of 1762 closely resembled the Battle of Cartagena. As in 1741, the British enjoyed overwhelming superiority. The attack fleet, which numbered over two hundred warships and transports, carried an invasion force of fourteen thousand or more men, plus thousands of marines under the command of George Keppel, Earl of Albemarle.[40] To counter this force, Havana could muster only a small army composed of Spanish regulars, the fixed garrison, and an untrained militia and supported by a fleet of eighteen warships, four of them temporarily out of commission. According to plan, Spain had managed to reinforce Havana with thirteen companies of Spanish regulars from the second battalions of the Regiments of Spain and Aragón, the same units that had prevailed at Cartagena; and just before the invasion 150 dragoons from the Regiment of Edimbourg arrived.[41] Nevertheless, the veteran units were caught seriously shorthanded. Since the reorganization of 1753, the infantry regiment had never found enough recruits to fill its complement, and an epidemic of yellow fever in 1761 had ravaged both the permanent garrison and the Spanish reinforcements.[42] Subtracting the detachments for St. Augustine, Santiago, and elsewhere in Cuba, Havana could count on only 2,330 regulars as of May 18, and many of them were sick. The militia of the Havana region numbered 4,753 volunteers, but the quality of their training had not prepared them for battle.[43] Only another miracle could have saved Havana.

Juan de Prado y Portocarrero Malleza, who had become captain general in early 1761, led the defense. A veteran of the Italian wars and a former subinspector of infantry in Aragón, Prado had been promoted to the rank of field marshal following his assignment to Cuba. Assisting Prado were Lieutenant General Conde de Superunda, the former viceroy of Peru, and Field Marshal Diego de Tabares, the retiring governor

40. Estimates of the size of the invasion force vary. Guerra, *Manual de historia de Cuba,* 162, estimates the landing army at 12,041, the support force at 2,000, and the marines available for shore duty at 8,226. Juan Manuel Zapatero, "Las batallas por la Isla de Cuba, 'llave del nuevo mundo y antemural de las Yndias Occidentales,'" *Revista de historia militar,* 8 (1961), 56, accepts the total of these figures. C. Martínez-Valverde, "Operaciones de ataque y defensa de La Habana en 1762," *Revista general de marina,* 164 (Apr. 1963), 490, generally agrees, although numbering the army at 12,100. Jaime Delgado, "El Conde de Ricla," 67, states that the assault troops alone numbered 18,000, not including the artillery corps, with a support force of 2,000.

41. Prado to Arriaga, Havana, July 2, 8, 1761, Colonel Carlos Caro to Prado (copy), Havana, Aug. 25, 1762, Prado to Arriaga, Havana, May 18, 1762, all in AGI, SD, legs. 2114, 1581, 1584. The two Spanish battalions had nine companies each, but three companies were assigned to Santiago and two to San Juan.

42. Troop reviews, Fixed Infantry Regiment of Cartagena, Apr. 30, Sept. 30, 1760, June 30, 1761, Feb. 28, 1762, Prado to Arriaga, Havana, May 20, 1761, defense report, Engineer Baltasar Ricaud, Havana, Aug. 1, 1762, all in AGI, SD, legs. 1213–14, 1581, 1584.

43. Militia review, Havana and Guanabacoa, June 6, 1762, AGI, SD, leg. 1578.

Table 1.	**Troop Strengths at Havana, May 18, 1762**	
	Unit	*Number of men* *
	Fixed Infantry Regiment	1,156
	Battalion of Spain	506
	Battalion of Aragon	303
	Artillery companies	105
	Dragoon corps	110
	Dragoon Regiment of Edimbourg	150†
	Total	2,330

SOURCE: Troop review, Havana, May 18, 1762, Caro to Prado (copy), Havana, Aug. 25, 1762, both in AGI, SD, 1581, 1584.

*These figures do not include officers.

†Prado expected 206 men, but only 150 appeared.

of Cartagena, both of whom were returning to Spain; and the Marqués del Real Transporte, a rear admiral of the royal navy, who had conveyed the peninsular reinforcements to Havana in 1761. These men, along with a number of lesser officers, formed the Junta de Guerra to direct the resistance.[44]

On June 7, the British began landing their forces at Cojímar, a beach some six miles east of Havana. They quickly advanced westward, seizing Guanabacoa, a town situated on the highway that connected the capital to eastern Cuba. More important, they also occupied a strategic hill called the Cabaña. The Cabaña overlooked the Morro Castle, the key strongpoint in Havana's defense complex, which from the east guarded the entrance to the port. Once situated on the Cabaña, the British were free to position their artillery within close range to do battle with the Morro.

To prevent the British navy from penetrating the bay, the Junta de Guerra quickly ordered three ships scuttled at the entrance. This tactic, reminiscent of the strategy employed at Cartagena, did indeed safeguard the naval approaches to the city, but it also sealed in the remaining warships and thus conceded to the enemy freedom of maneuver at sea. Consequently, the British were able to introduce reinforcements and supplies from Jamaica and the northern colonies without interference when shortages and disease began to weaken their army. Moreover, they were able to split their forces and effect a second landing to the west of the city. The operation in the west, largely diversionary, eventually severed Havana's highway connection to the south and, near the end of the battle, diverted its fresh water supply into the bay.

44. Delgado, "El Conde de Ricla," 54; Hugh Thomas, *Cuba: The Pursuit of Freedom* (New York, 1971), 6–7.

The British thus systematically and relentlessly squeezed Havana and its defenders. The final tragedy was the fall of the Morro Castle on July 31 and with it any hope of defending Havana, which could now be bombarded effortlessly from all sides. On August 11, the Junta de Guerra asked for surrender terms and officially capitulated two days later.[45]

Most historians agree that the loss of the Cabaña heights was a decisive factor in the outcome of the battle.[46] During his administration, Governor Cagigal had alerted the crown to the problem posed by the exposed hill, but Ferdinand VI did nothing substantive to improve its defenses.[47] In August 1760, shortly after Prado was named captain general, Arriaga specifically instructed him to fortify the Cabaña, and in a second order, February 1761, reemphasized the importance of the project.[48] Owing to a labor shortage; to the effects of the epidemic, including the death of Francisco Ricaud, the head engineer; and also to a degree of personal negligence, however, Prado had accomplished little by the time of the invasion.[49] In any case, even under more favorable conditions, he would have had little time to execute his instructions.

Albemarle may well have blundered by attacking from the east. Located on the western side of the bay, Havana itself was weakly defended. Its walls were in a grievous state of disrepair, some portions

---

45. There are no exhaustive accounts of the battle. The most perceptive treatment is the study of Martínez-Valverde, "Operaciones de ataque," 487–503, continued in 164 (May 1963), 706–27. Two brief but somewhat flawed monographs are Pedro J. Guiteras, *Historia de la conquista de La Habana por los ingleses seguida de Cuba y su gobierno* (Havana, 1932); and Francis Russell Hart, *The Siege of Havana, 1762* (London, 1931). Two accounts that have been extracted from larger histories and published as separate volumes with introductions by Emilio Roig de Leuchsenring are *Cómo vio Antonio de Valdés la toma de La Habana por los ingleses* (Havana, 1962); and *Cómo vio Jacobo de la Pezuela la toma de La Habana por los ingleses* (Havana, 1962). Useful summaries can be found in Delgado, "El Conde de Ricla"; Guerra, *Manual de historia de Cuba*; and Zapatero, "Las batallas." For firsthand accounts, see Amalia A. Rodríguez, ed., *Cinco diarios del sitio de La Habana* (Havana, 1963). Four additional volumes of documents exist: Guillermo de Blanck, Introduction to *Papeles sobre la toma de La Habana por los ingleses en 1762* (Havana, 1948); Rafael Nieto y Cortadellas, ed., *Nuevos papeles sobre la toma de La Habana por los ingleses en 1762* (Havana, 1951); Juan Pérez de la Riva, ed., *Documentos inéditos sobre la toma de La Habana por los ingleses en 1762* (Havana, 1963); and David Syrett, ed., *The Siege and Capture of Havana, 1762* (London, 1970). Manuscript accounts of the battle can be found in AGI, SD, leg. 1586.

46. For example, see Martinez-Valverde, "Operaciones de ataque," 708, 723–25; Guiterras, *Historia de la conquista,* 69–84; Delgado, "El Conde de Ricla," 51–68; Guerra, *Manual de historia de Cuba,* 169–75; and Zapatero, "Las batallas," 59–61.

47. Arriaga to Prado, Madrid, Aug. 23, 1760, AGI, SD, leg. 1581.

48. Ibid.; report of Fiscal Manuel de Craywinkel, Madrid, Dec. 30, 1764, AGI, SD, leg. 1579.

49. Guerra, *Manual de historia de Cuba,* 163; Rodríguez, ed., *Cinco diarios,* 12; Delgado, "El Conde de Ricla," 54, 62–63.

having collapsed after years of neglect, and the army was plainly too small to have offered much resistance to a major force without the help of strong fortifications.[50] The eastern approach forced the British to contend with the massive Morro Castle. A strong Spanish position on the Cabaña could have seriously obstructed the advance to that strong-point and perhaps have turned the battle. The defenders had so little confidence in their ability to hold those strategic heights, however, that they panicked when the British approached and abandoned them without a fight. In the subsequent investigation, Prado's failure to fortify the Cabaña and his premature decision to abandon it were causes for major charges against him.

In a deeper sense, nevertheless, the Spanish simply lacked the trained soldiery to repulse the British invasion. Since early in the century, Bourbon strategists had recognized that the ideal way to conduct siege defense was to meet the enemy at his landing point and to obstruct his every step toward the fortified strongpoints.[51] Such a strategy required trained manpower; it was unworkable in 1762 because the economizing policies of the early Bourbons had provided the Havana garrison with too few soldiers. Indeed, one consideration in the Junta de Guerra's decision to withdraw the fleet into the bay was the need to compensate for deficiencies in the garrison by transferring the marines to land duty. The manpower shortage also prevented the Spanish from counterattacking effectively. Prado made only two feeble attempts to dislodge the British from the Cabaña and their positions outside the Morro, and both failed miserably. Indeed, throughout most of the engagement, the British were free to execute their battle plan at their leisure, without serious harassment.

The Spanish regulars generally fought well, occasionally with in-credible heroism. Certainly the contingent of infantrymen, artillery-men, and marines that defended the Morro could not be faulted. Naval Captain Luis Vicente Velasco, who led the defense of the castle and died of wounds suffered there, has taken his place as one of the foremost heroes of Spanish military history.[52] Moreover, the Spanish army, de-spite heavy casualties, resisted for over two months, longer than the entire Battle of Cartagena. When Governor Prado and the Junta de Guerra surrendered, only 631 veteran troops remained.[53]

The militia, by contrast, contributed very little. Many volunteers failed to answer the call to arms, and those who appeared were poorly equipped, confused, and frightened. If they fought at all, they fought

50. For a detailed analysis of the condition of Havana's fortifications, see Delgado, "El Conde de Ricla," 51–64.

51. Marchena, *Oficiales y soldados,* 171.

52. Zapatero, "Las batallas," 62–63.

53. Troop review, Havana, Aug. 11, 1762, AGI, SD, leg. 1581.

timidly.[54] In an important early action, Prado dispatched a corps of volunteer lancers from the countryside in the company of several militia infantry detachments and the Dragoons of Edimbourg to obstruct the British advance from Cojímar to Guanabacoa. The maneuver failed completely when, upon hearing the unfamiliar sound of gunfire, the militia panicked and fled, leaving the veteran dragoons so badly outnumbered that they were forced to withdraw. Thereafter, the Junta de Guerra had little choice but to operate from behind fortified positions. Some 3,350 militiamen subsequently arrived from outlying districts, but their contribution did not vary significantly from that of their Havana counterparts.[55] Without an effective militia to support it, the army of Cuba simply lacked the personnel to cope with the invasion.

After regaining Havana in the Treaty of Paris, February 10, 1763, in exchange for Florida, Charles III summoned Governor Prado, the Marqués del Real Transporte, the Conde de Superunda, Diego Tabares, and seven other officials to Madrid to face a court of inquiry. Headed by the Conde de Aranda, this tribunal possessed the authority to conduct court-martial proceedings if, as anticipated, they were warranted. Aranda, who held the office of captain general and who had just won laurels for personal valor in the Portuguese campaign, was one of the enlightened luminaries of his time and an ambitious politician. The other officials included Lieutenants General Marqués de Cevallos, Conde de Vega Florida, and Duque de Granada de Ega; Field Marshals Marqués de Sipli and Diego Manrique; and the famous Jorge Juan. Captain Manuel Craywinkel of the Walloon Guards acted as prosecutor. After a preliminary investigation that produced volumes of documentation, the court levied charges against all of the officers, the most serious those against Prado. Through formal judicial proceedings, Charles III hoped to placate public opinion and to save face for the humiliated royal administration, but the whole affair had the unfortunate appearance of a show trial. As will be seen in the next chapter, Charles and those around him had already determined that the causes for the loss of the battle went well beyond the limits of Havana's leadership. Aranda's cousin, the Conde de Ricla, had already left for Cuba to reorganize the army.

---

54. There were, of course, isolated exceptions to this pattern of behavior, of which the mid-nineteenth-century Cuban nationalist Guiteras made much in his *Historia de la conquista*, 103–6.

55. Prado to Arriaga, Havana, June 8, 1762, file on militia record during the battle of Havana, reports of Ricaud, Havana, Aug. 1, 1762, and Junta de Guerra, Aug. 1, 1762, all in AGI, SD, legs. 2115, 1581, 1584. The lancers should have numbered 962 men, although the authorities did not specify how many actually appeared for duty. Militia review, Havana and Guanabacoa, June 6, 1762, AGI, SD, leg. 1578.

The court charged Governor Prado with manifest disobedience and negligence for failing to take proper measures to fortify the Cabaña heights both before and after the declaration of war; with incompetence for demobilizing the fleet by scuttling the three ships in the entrance to the bay and for abandoning the Cabaña without a fight; and with malfeasance for neglecting to counterattack. The court also charged Prado with failing to conduct a proper evacuation of the city, alleging that he should have destroyed the remaining fortifications, scuttled the rest of the fleet, and withdrawn his forces to prepare for the reconquest of the city. Finally, he failed to save over 600,000 pesos of the royal treasury, as well as additional merchant funds, all of which enriched Lord Albemarle and his lieutenants. The other officers were charged with varying degrees of complicity in Prado's actions.[56]

That the hapless Juan de Prado was a less than able commander is indisputable; he consistently showed flawed judgment in his conduct of the defense, especially during the panic that enveloped Havana following the fall of the Morro Castle. But it is not at all clear that he was criminally negligent except possibly in his failure to destroy the fleet and to save the king's money. The deeper causes for the loss of Havana lay in the mistaken policies of the previous administration for which Prado shared no blame at all. In his own defense, the unhappy governor persuasively argued that the poverty of available military resources denied him the means to prepare the city properly for battle and, later, to conduct an effective resistance. Significantly, the actions of Charles's government in America during the course of the trial showed that it had reached the same conclusion. Less convincingly, Prado excused his failures at the end of the siege by citing the lack of supplies and fighting men and the need to procure favorable surrender terms for the city. Finally, he claimed that the British control of the communication routes out of Havana prevented the rescue of the royal treasury.[57]

After two years, the court concluded its deliberations, but the final decision was sharply divided. During the proceedings, Prosecutor Craywinkel had become skeptical himself about the extent of Prado's culpability, and in making his summation he softened his statement to an extent that angered Aranda. The Marqués de Cevallos voted for outright acquittal, arguing that the fundamental cause for the loss of Havana was poor long-range defense planning. His attempts to explain

56. A summary of the inquiry and of the trial that followed can be found in Delgado, "El Conde de Ricla," 69–75. The documents of the proceedings are in AGI, SD, legs. 1578–88.

57. "Satisfacción del Mariscal de Campo D. Juan de Prado . . . a los cargos, que se le han formado en la causa pendiente en la Junta de Generales," May 20, 1764, AGI, SD, leg. 1582. Prado did not accept responsibility for the fate of the merchant funds, asserting that responsibility for those funds resided in private hands.

away Prado's various personal blunders were, however, less than satisfactory. The Conde de Vega Florida leaned toward Cevallos' position
but recommended the confiscation of Prado's property to compensate
the king for the losses the royal treasury had sustained. He deferred to
the king on the matter of merchant compensation, and although he
thought a suspension from military employment appropriate, he suggested that the hardships already endured might satisfy justice. The
degree to which court politics may have influenced the thinking of
these men is unclear, but the governor was not without his supporters.
He owed his assignment to Cuba to the connections of his brother, the
Marqués de Villel, and he presumably still had important friends.

The other five judges favored harsh penalties. Three, including
Aranda, found Prado guilty of criminal negligence and malfeasance and
demanded death. Juan and the Duque de Granada de Ega, although
finding Prado guilty of misconduct, did not think his offenses serious
enough to justify execution. They took a more moderate position by
asking for his suspension from military office, his exile from court, and
the confiscation of his property.[58] Aranda, who had attempted to
orchestrate the trial from the start and who had lobbied the members of
the court intensely, was plainly distressed at his failure to produce a
unanimous decision. In a private letter to the Marqués de Grimaldi,
who had replaced Wall as minister of state, he expressed his anger: "If I
were the King, I would pardon the most culpable of the prisoners; but
for Cevallos, Vega Florida, and Craywinkel, I would put them where
they could never get out."[59] Aranda's frustration should not lead to the
conclusion that he lacked political skill, for he became president of the
Council of Castile a year after the trial's end. He simply had to make do
with a poor case.

Charles III, who from the start had intended to intervene be-
nevolently to show mercy if Aranda succeeded in producing a death
verdict, pronounced sentences on March 4, 1765. He moved between
the extreme positions by accepting the judgments of Juan and Granada
de Ega. In so doing, he ordered Juan de Prado and the Marqués del Real
Transporte perpetually deprived of further military commissions, ex-
iled them to a distance of forty leagues from court for a period of ten
years, and confiscated their property to help defray the losses of the
royal treasury and the merchants. He administered the same sentence
to the Conde de Superunda and Diego Tabares, except that their banishment from military service was limited to ten years.[60] These sentences,

58. Delgado, "El Conde de Ricla," 73–74. The individual votes and the supporting
justifications can be found in AGI, SD, leg. 1579, and in the "Diario de la Junta . . . ,"
Madrid, 1763–65, AGI, SD, leg. 1578.

59. Quoted in Delgado, "El Conde de Ricla," 74.

60. Ibid., 74–75. Copies of the royal sentence can be found in AGI, SD, legs. 1578, 1580.

although harsh, in the final analysis displayed a sense of justice. The crown could hardly be blamed for refusing Prado and Real Transporte further military positions or for trying to recoup as much as possible of the royal purse that they had so blunderingly lost. Perhaps the meanest part of the sentence was Charles's refusal to permit the convicted men to come to court to beg for favors as was the custom of their class. As for the rest of the officials, they received relatively light punishments. Meanwhile, farsighted men had taken a more realistic look at the implications of the defeat and were already laying the groundwork for an ambitious reorganization of imperial defense strategy and the Spanish empire.

2. Reform

While military justice was making Juan de Prado a scapegoat for contemporary Spain and posterity, critically important events were unfolding both at court and in Cuba. On one level, the government of Charles III labored to shape a defense strategy capable of averting a repetition of 1762. To that end the momentous decision was made to involve Cuban subjects directly in their own defense by introducing the Spanish disciplined militia system into the island. On another level, the crown began to chart the fiscal, economic, and political adjustments required to support an expanded military establishment. Together, these reforms laid the foundation for a profound transformation of Cuba during the closing decades of the eighteenth century and after and established a model that Charles would extend to the rest of his empire.

In the wake of the British victory, it was abundantly clear that the fatal defects in Havana's defenses went well beyond the question of fortifications or the leadership qualities of Governor Prado. As early as 1760, Arriaga had informed Wall that he believed the American army too small to carry out its assignment.[1] Moreover, the pitiful failure of the Cuban volunteers to fulfill their mission as a reserve was far from unique; leaders in colony after colony found their militia without arms, organization, or training.[2] The time had plainly arrived for new ideas and new leadership.

---

1. Arriaga to Wall, Apr. 2, 1760, reproduced in Vicente Rodríguez Casado, *La política y los políticos en el reinado de Carlos III* (Madrid, 1962), 105–8.
2. Archer, *The Army in Bourbon Mexico*, 9; Campbell, *The Military and Society*, 34; Juan Marchena Fernández, *La institución militar en Cartagena de Indias, 1700–1810* (Seville, 1982), 417–18.

The man who answered these needs was Ambrosio Funes de Villalpando, the Conde de Ricla. Ricla was a man of proven administrative
skill and broad military experience, and equally important, he enjoyed
extensive personal influence at court. He was born in Zaragoza in 1720,
the second son of the Conde de Atarés and, significantly, the cousin of
the Conde de Aranda. Funes de Villalpando entered the army at an early
age and advanced rapidly in rank, presumably owing in part to his
family connections. He made captain at age seventeen, brigadier at
only twenty-four, and field marshal at twenty-six. Although he fought
in the Italian theater during the War of Jenkins' Ear, the step that
capped his meteoric ascent seems to have been his marriage to his
cousin, Doña Leonor Gómez de los Cobos Luna Zúñiga y Sarmiento,
Condesa de Ricla and Marquesa de Camarasa, who, incidentally, was
twenty years his senior. Shortly thereafter, Funes was named gentleman of His Majesty's Bedchamber with entrance. During the 1750s, he
acquired administrative experience through various political assignments in the Spanish provinces, including the governorship of Cartagena de Levante. He obtained the Encomienda de Reina in the Order
of Santiago in 1760, was promoted to lieutenant general the following
year, and during the Seven Years' War commanded one of the divisions
that invaded Portugal.[3]

By the time the war had ended, Ricla had already opened the way to
leave his stamp on the history of Cuba and America. On January 20,
1763, he proposed through the Ministry of the Indies a radical reorientation of Cuban—and by implication American—defense
strategy.[4] He argued that an effective resistance to the kind of invasion
that Havana had experienced depended not only on strong fortifications and solid veteran forces but on the participation of the native
population. Citing its proven value in Spain, he went on to propose the
introduction of the disciplined militia system into Cuba. To maintain
in Cuba a regular army of sufficient size to meet the kind of power that
the British possessed was impossible for both financial and demographic reasons, according to Ricla, while the tactic of shuttling Spanish units to the island during times of crisis was excessively risky. He
saw, therefore, little alternative but to develop a workable militia
system.

Admitting to a lack of specific knowledge about conditions in Cuba,
Ricla advanced a tentative defense plan that called for three militia
regiments with three batallions each, one for Havana, one for Trinidad
in the south-central section of the island, and one for Santiago. He also

3. Delgado, "El Conde de Ricla," 82–83. Delgado believes that Ricla's assignment to
the provinces resulted from differences with Ensenada.
4. Ricla, general discourse, Jan. 20, 1763, AGI, SD, leg. 2116.

proposed arming Negroes but did not suggest troop levels. Finally, he recommended raising some fifteen hundred cavalrymen and dragoons. To train these forces, he advocated the integration of regular army personnel into the units, and to arm them, he urged sending some twelve to sixteen thousand muskets from Spain. For the veteran garrison, Ricla proposed six Spanish battalions, which would be sustained by replacements from Spain. Part of this force would be employed as veteran cadres to train the militia. Finally, Ricla cited the need for a separate commandant general to act as troop inspector for the island.

Ricla recognized the risks implicit in educating Americans in the use of arms, but he saw no realistic alternative. He took comfort from his conviction that in the event of political difficulty the six Spanish battalions would dominate the militia. To that end, he stipulated that replacements for the veteran units should come from Spain, not the militia. And for additional insurance, he specified that the militia arsenal should be placed in the custody of the regular army.[5] As he predicted, events would prove specific aspects of his proposal unworkable. The size of the proposed units, for example, was excessive even for Havana. But the plan established the general shape of the Cuban military organization for the remainder of the eighteenth century and beyond.

Ricla's ideas found ready acceptance at court, where defeat in war had created a fluid political situation whose full implications were still unclear. As king of the Two Sicilies, Charles had repeatedly shown himself reluctant to dismiss those in his government abruptly, a pattern of behavior that he continued on the Spanish throne; but changes in his discredited administration were plainly in order. When he became king in 1759, he had retained all of Ferdinand's ministers except the Conde de Valparaíso at Finance, whom he replaced with Leopoldo di Grigorio, Marqués de Esquilache, a Sicilian who had served him as minister of finance, war, and the navy in Italy.[6] The portfolio for War, vacant since the death of Eslava in June, Charles added to Wall's responsibilities at the Ministry of State. Even before Ferdinand had died, Wall, encouraged by the aging queen mother, Isabel Farnese, had labored to pave the way for Charles's succession to the Spanish throne, and for the moment he had enjoyed Charles's full confidence. Now, as a minister whose policies were identifiable with the old order and defeat, Wall saw his influence with the king decline sharply. As minister of the Indies and the navy, Julián de Arriaga shared the responsibility for Spain's humiliation, and he also lost status. Esquilache's influence

5. Ibid.
6. His name was Squilache in Italian, but the Spanish insisted upon adding the vowel.

grew as Wall's and Arriaga's waned. The Italian would be the dominant force in Charles's government for the next three years.[7]

Charles's mother was another force in the inner circle at court. Isabel had exercised extensive influence in the government of her husband, Philip, but following his death in 1746 her position had collapsed. Ferdinand, Philip's son by his first marriage, had rid himself of the troublesome old woman by in effect exiling her to La Granja de San Ildefonso in the north and her nearby estate at Río Frío. During her years of frustration, she had faithfully corresponded with her beloved Charles, and when the opportunity developed she worked for his succession to the Spanish throne. Her return to court brought a strong attachment to things Italian. She quickly became an avid supporter of the ambitious Esquilache.

Wall's resignation came in August, ostensibly for reasons of age. This explanation, given his years, appeared logical and provided him a graceful exit much in keeping with Charles's style in handling such affairs. Esquilache added the portfolio for war to his powers, and the Marqués de Grimaldi, architect of the Third Family Compact, returned from his ambassadorship at Versailles to become minister of state. An Italian by birth, Grimaldi had served under Philip and Ferdinand as well. Esquilache had strongly supported him for the ministry against Agustín de Llanos, the candidate of a nativist faction. Significantly, Charles also consulted at length with his mother before naming Grimaldi. Key positions of power—War, Finance, and State—were thus concentrated in the hands of Italians.

The ministerial reorganization reached its climax following Grimaldi's return from France in October when Charles established the Junta de Ministros. Charged with the development of colonial policy and scheduled to meet every Thursday, the junta provided Esquilache with the institutional means to involve himself officially in the affairs of the Indies. With Grimaldi's support, he quickly established dominance over Arriaga, as Charles fully expected. Arriaga suffered from poor health, including failing eyesight; carried the stigma of 1762; and found himself increasingly isolated from the affairs of court. Charles often ignored him, even to the point of naming officials to his ministry without consulting him.[8] To his credit, nevertheless, Frey Arriaga was

7. The ministerial reorganization is treated in greater depth in Allan J. Kuethe and Lowell Blaisdell, "The Esquilache Government and the Reforms of Charles III in Cuba," *Jahrbuch für Geschichte von Staat, Wirtschaft und Gesellschaft Lateinamerikas* 19 (Cologne, 1982), 120–29.

8. The French diplomatic correspondence of this period is replete with descriptions of Arriaga's fallen influence. See, for example, Ambassador Count d'Ossun to Duc de Choiseul, Madrid, Mar. 8, 1764, AAE, CE, vol. 539, fols. 182–86. Arriaga described his

a magistrate of unquestioned integrity and a reasonably efficient administrator, who provided a native presence in the royal cabinet and a conservative balance to the Italians that, in the event of a change of political climate, might serve the king well. Unlike Esquilache and Grimaldi, Arriaga would serve until his death, which came in January 1776.

Charles's acceptance of Ricla's plan to arm his Cuban subjects was a step of enormous moment. The greatest of all the Bourbon monarchs, Charles brought to the throne a freshness of mind that enabled him to experiment boldly and, when necessary, to challenge ancient customs and entrenched privileges in the search for modern alternatives. The enlightened tone of his administration was unmistakable, but his ambitious reforms, structured in the face of relentless international pressure, were less a response to the lofty, liberating ideals of the Philosophes than a pragmatic design to make Spain a power of the first order and to provide him with the means to wage war effectively.

Charles's alternatives in 1763 were at once simple and incredibly complex. If Havana could be taken, so too could other strongpoints of the empire unless profound changes were effected. The thought of losing pieces of an imperial domain would be disagreeable to any monarch and especially to Charles. Humiliated by the British while he was king of the Two Sicilies and now once again, he could not ignore the challenge. The disciplined militia system provided the means to create at a reasonable cost a large trained reserve that would even the numerical odds in the event of invasion or, if the opportunity developed, man the home front while the regular army assumed the offensive. Charles's confidence in the disciplined militia arose not only from its record in Spain but also from his faith in its founder, the Conde de Montemar. It was Montemar who, with the king at his side, led a combined Spanish and Italian army to victory over the Austrians, securing for Charles his throne in the Two Sicilies.[9]

The risks, however, of shifting the responsibility for defense to Americans were enormous. Even if victory over the hated British ensued—something that was not at all a certain prospect—effective control over the Indies would be compromised as never before. To place muskets in the hands of Americans and to train them in their use according to the latest practices in Europe, no matter what the rationalization, amounted to a basic shift of political power into colonial hands. The Ricla proposal fully recognized this reality and tried, albeit

---

physical problems and isolation from court in a private letter to the Conde de Ricla, San Lorenzo, Nov. 16, 1764, AGI, IG, leg. 1630.

9. Anthony H. Hull, *Charles III and the Revival of Spain* (Washington, D.C., 1981), 28–33; Hellwege, *Die spanischen Provinzialmilizen*, ch. 2.

feebly, to provide safeguards. In fact, the precautions Ricla envisioned would prove unworkable in practice and would never be implemented.

On another level, Charles and Esquilache understood that far-reaching commercial and fiscal changes would be imperative to finance a militarization of the colonies. Such adjustments implied that creoles would not only bear the arms to defend America but finance them as well, often, probably, directly. A counterbalance might be achieved through a tightening of administrative authority, a process begun by the early Bourbons, but even so, the creation of American armies implied very real limitations upon royal authority. The choices were thus difficult in the extreme. If he continued the policies of his predecessors, Charles would most certainly lose additional portions of his empire. If he armed the Americans, he stood a reasonably good chance of preserving his domain and perhaps even exacting sweet revenge upon the British, but he risked losing everything in the long run by shifting too much power away from the metropolis. Not surprisingly, Charles elected to counter the more immediate danger posed by British imperialism, while hoping to construct a new relationship with the colonists that might minimize his political risks.

On March 16, Arriaga formally notified Ricla that the king had accepted his plan and had named him governor and captain general of Cuba to implement the reorganization personally.[10] The need to build a competitive army had acquired a sense of urgency. Differences that had developed between Spain and France during the peace negotiations had been resolved for the moment, and the partners under the Family Compact emerged united in the search for an opportunity to renew the conflict with their British tormentor on favorable terms. Indeed, all concerned understood that the Treaty of Paris amounted to little more than a truce, and the Bourbon cousins spoke of reopening hostilities as early as 1768.[11] Under these circumstances, the royal authorities moved with unaccustomed haste to construct and outfit a reform commission for Cuba.

On March 29, Arriaga in a secret memorial gave Ricla his official instructions. These orders, which dealt solely with his diplomatic responsibilities in taking possession of Havana and his urgent military duties, were a clear reflection of the administration's priorities. Once in command of the island, Ricla's first obligation was to act with all haste to repair the destroyed fortifications and to conduct the reorganization of the Cuban army. To advance the former objective, the

10. Royal order, Buen Retiro, Mar. 16, 1763, cedula of appointment, Mar. 25, 1763, both in AGI, SD, 1211. As early as Feb. 24, Arriaga informed the governor of Santiago, Lorenzo Madariaga, of Ricla's assignment.

11. Choiseul to d'Ossun, Versailles, Nov. 13, 1763, AAE, CE, vol. 539, fols. 318–19.

crown provided for emergency supplies of money and laborers as well
as a staff of engineers and technicians. For the latter, Ricla received
most of what he originally proposed. To advise the new disciplined
militia, he was provided a separate cadre of 50 officers and 550
sergeants, corporals, and soldiers—nearly a full battalion. For the regular forces, the crown assigned to Havana the Regiment of Córdoba at
the strength of two battalions, which was to be relieved after three
years. The Fixed Infantry Regiment of Havana, known simply as the
Fijo, would be reestablished at two battalions of 679 men each. Ricla
was to forge the unit out of worthy remnants of its predecessor and the
companies of the Regiment of Aragón and to complete it with personnel from the Spanish battalions of Murcia and Granada, which were
destined for Cuba following other assignments in America. Cuba's
dragoons were to be expanded to a regiment with eight companies of
forty men each by combining reinforcements from Spain with the men
remaining from the Regiment of Edimbourg and the four companies of
Havana. A full company of artillerymen would be added to the surviv-
ing Havana forces, thus reestablishing a corps of two companies. Politically, the king vested Ricla with broad powers that rendered him
independent of possible jurisdictional rivalries.[12] In a second communication, he also empowered Ricla to conduct an investigation into
the behavior of the city during the occupation and to take appropriate
steps to eradicate any internal disloyalty or division that the British
occupation might have nurtured.[13]

Upon Ricla's request, the crown assigned to the reform commission
Field Marshal Alejandro O'Reilly as subinspector general of the militia
and the regular army. O'Reilly was a fast-rising officer with a brilliant
service record. Born of Irish nobility in 1725, he emigrated with his
parents to Spain during his childhood. He began his military career as a
cadet in the Infantry Regiment of Hibernia. Owing to his outstanding
talent and his battlefield heroics, he had advanced rapidly in rank. He
saw action in the Italian theater of the War of Jenkins' Ear, where he
was severely wounded, retaining a limp for the remainder of his life.
Following the war, the army assigned him to the Austrian army to
study the tactics recently developed in Prussia. During the early phases
of the Seven Years' War, he served in more than twenty engagements
with the Austrian army and was then sent to observe the French
military during 1759 and 1760. On the strength of the recommendation
of King Louis XV and his foreign minister, the Duc de Choiseul,
Charles promoted him to colonel. Upon his return home on the eve of
Spain's entrance into the war, the Consejo Supremo de Guerra ordered

12. Secret instructions for Ricla, Buen Retiro, Mar. 29, 1763, AGI, SD, leg. 1211.
13. Royal order, Madrid, Apr. 16, 1763, AGI, SD, leg. 1211.

Field Marshal Alejandro O'Reilly. Courtesy of Bibiano Torres Ramírez.

him to teach Prussian tactics to various units of the Spanish army, a commission that earned him promotion to brigadier. During the war, he served in a subordinate capacity in Portugal but nevertheless advanced in rank to field marshal.[14]

O'Reilly brought ideal qualifications to the reform commission. He was a close personal friend of Ricla, a relationship that would serve them both well in Cuba. Because the French had confidence in O'Reilly, his mission to Cuba reassured them as the two countries prepared for the next phase of their conflict with England. Moreover, O'Reilly's stature as a tough, uncompromising officer seemed exactly what Cuba required for its defeated and demoralized army. Finally, he could speak English, a significant skill given the diplomatic responsibilities awaiting Ricla in effecting the exchange of Florida for Havana.[15]

O'Reilly also brought liabilities to the reform commission. He was a big talker with a strong tendency to overestimate his own abilities as, for example, in 1761 when he boasted that he could defend America with a mere twelve battalions.[16] He was also something of an opportunist. Both he and Ricla were, after all, more than simple soldiers. They were politicians advancing a new idea in a momentarily fluid bureaucratic structure, and they clearly intended to make the most of their opportunities. O'Reilly, unfortunately, sometimes overplayed his role despite his great natural talents. Perhaps this tendency related to his trials as an Irishman trying to rise to the top of the Spanish political system, a system generally hostile to outsiders, despite the momentary successes of Esquilache and Grimaldi.

The formation of the expedition proceeded quickly. Drawing upon his extensive knowledge of the Spanish army, O'Reilly took a direct hand in selecting the personnel for the venture.[17] By April 26, all components had gathered in Cádiz for final inspection.[18] The fleet departed the following day, but for reasons not entirely clear—presum-

---

14. O'Reilly was left for dead on the battlefield of Camposanto. He saved his life by convincing an enemy soldier who was about to administer the *golpe de gracia* that he was the son of the Duque de Arcos, a grandee of Spain. This pretended distinction won him medical care and a return to the Spanish forces. After recovering from his wounds, he resumed active duty. Valuable accounts of O'Reilly's background can be found in Torres Ramírez, *Alejandro O'Reilly,* 5–8, 17; Delgado, "El Conde de Ricla," 83–85. For his connections with the French, see A.S. Aiton, "Spanish Colonial Reorganization under the Family Compact," *HAHR* 12 (Aug. 1932), 276–79. See also Eric Beerman, "Un bosquejo biográfico y genealógico del general Alejandro O'Reilly," *Hidalguía: La revista de genealogía, nobleza, y armas* 24 (Mar.–Apr. 1981), 225–44.

15. Ricla to Marqués de Esquilache, Havana, July 22, 1763, AGS, Hac, leg. 2342.

16. Aiton, "Spanish Colonial Reorganization," 277.

17. Torres Ramírez, *Alejandro O'Reilly,* 17–18.

18. Ricla to Arriaga, Cadiz, Apr. 26, 1763, AGI, SD, leg. 2116.

ably bad weather—it did not reach Havana until June 30. Following a week of diplomatic formalities, Havana was again in Spanish hands.[19]

At this point, Esquilache's institutional authority had not yet been defined, but Ricla pragmatically conducted a dual correspondence with both the Italian and Frey Arriaga. Having received oral instructions from Esquilache on financial reform, and probably much more, before he left, the captain general understood where real power resided. Along with the first mail sent to court in 1763, revealingly, he sent a generous quantity of Cuban tobacco to the marqués, who was a heavy smoker, and he continued this practice during his tenure in Havana.[20] Dominating the Junta de Ministros from its establishment in October, Esquilache did not formalize his authority over the army of America until late 1764 or early 1765. At that time, the Ministry of War displaced the Ministry of the Indies in the administration and financing of all veteran units in America, both permanent and Spanish.[21]

The Conde de Ricla, burdened by his obligation to restore orderly administration to the island, to supervise the vast task of rebuilding and reshaping the fortifications of Havana, and to develop the means to finance the expanded military, permitted O'Reilly a free hand in conducting the military reorganization. The subinspector general first addressed himself to rebuilding the regular army. He quickly reestablished the Havana Fijo and the artillery companies and organized the new regiment of dragoons. An important part of O'Reilly's work was to cull the derelict, the infirm, and the aged from among the competent officers. As he proceeded, officers from the defeated army overwhelmed him with certificates and testimony attesting their honor and courage, but he was unimpressed. He remarked that ". . . it would be easier to review an army of 100,000 men than to process all the stories, examinations of officers' conduct, troop reviews, etc. There was hardly an officer or even a soldier who did not have numerous certificates and legal papers to make me read, and that said nothing of substance; they appeared more like a corps or notaries than an army.'"[22] O'Reilly indignantly dismissed over half of the Fijo's officers from service, and he denied promotion to the others because of the lack of discipline in the unit. To fill the vacancies in the officer corps and in the ranks, he drafted personnel from the Battalions of Murcia and Granada that had

19. Torres Ramírez, *Alejandro O'Reilly*, 18; Delgado, "El Conde de Ricla," 90–91.

20. Ricla's private correspondence with Esquilache can be found in AGI, IG, leg. 1629.

21. File on the responsibilities of the Ministry of War, 1764, AGI, IG, leg. 1885; Esquilache to Lieutenant General Juan de Villalba, El Pardo, Feb. 8, 1765, AGI, Mexico, leg. 1245.

22. Quoted in Torres Ramírez, *Alejandro O'Reilly*, 19.

been sent to Havana as well as from the remaining companies of the Regiment of Aragón.[23]

O'Reilly, however, was still not satisfied. Backed by Ricla, he recommended that the Havana Fijo be transferred to Spain as punishment for its performance during the siege, that its name be removed, and that there never again be a fixed regiment in Havana.[24] Moreover, he went on to propose that all fixed units in America be abolished and replaced with Spanish-based units. This measure, he argued, would ensure high morale and eliminate the kind of debilitating local attachments associated with permanent troops.[25]

O'Reilly treated the Fijo extremely callously, considering the unit's achievement in holding out for two months against overwhelming odds, but serious problems certainly existed. During their years of service in Havana, many of the enlisted men had married and fathered children. Their meager salaries as soldiers were inadequate to support a family, and many were compelled to seek additional sources of income. These men associated with their unit only irregularly and seemingly had lost their expertise and any real sense of military discipline. Others were chronically ill or permanently disabled but had remained in the unit to collect their wages. In permitting these abuses, the officers were culpably negligent or perhaps worse, and many had developed local interests themselves. Moreover, during the battle the officer corps had appropriated some sixty thousand pesos from the unit's treasury, a matter that raised suspicions. All claimed that they had acted innocently, only to protect His Majesty's monies from the British, but some may well have been disappointed to see the island returned to Spanish control. O'Reilly demanded a full restitution of the army funds, going so far as to put one officer's house up for sale to recover the money that he owed.[26]

Ricla and O'Reilly's motives for wishing to abolish the Fixed Infantry Regiment may well have been political. No one pretended that the new militia would be a complete substitute for the regular army, but the proposal to rotate all veteran troops would make the militia the one permanent pillar of the colonial defense establishment, thus magnifying its importance. Presumably, the administrative fortunes of the men most closely associated with the new militia system would improve accordingly, a possibility certainly not lost on either man. Indeed, the contempt that O'Reilly showed for the defeated Cuban army very much resembled the righteous abuse that Ricla's ambitious cousin, the

23. Alejandro O'Reilly to Wall, Havana, Dec. 6, 1763, AGI, SD, leg. 2078.
24. Ibid.; Ricla to Arriaga, Havana, Apr. 20, 1764, AGI, SD, leg. 2118.
25. O'Reilly to Arriaga, Havana, Dec. 6, 1763, AGI, SD, leg. 2078.
26. O'Reilly to Wall, Havana, Dec. 6, 1763, AGI, SD, leg. 2078.

Conde de Aranda, was concurrently inflicting upon hapless Governor Prado in Madrid, obviously for political purposes.

The limitations of the permanent garrisons notwithstanding, O'Reilly's scheme entailed problems of such magnitude that it bordered on the irresponsible. A battalion was out of service for one to two months on its way to Cuba and again on its way back to Spain. Moving troops from within Spain to Cádiz consumed more months, as did the wait for embarkation. Thus, the Spanish army lost the services of one battalion for approximately half a year every time a battalion rotated to America. Moreover, many men were lost to disease during the transatlantic crossings and the subsequent period of acclimatization.[27] It is difficult to believe that the experience of the early Bourbons in these respects could have escaped O'Reilly's attention. Finally, transportation was expensive. To rotate part of a large garrison, thus providing some fresh European troops, might be feasible, but to transfer the full complement of troops would be extremely costly. Despite the evident difficulties in the plan, however, the Junta de Ministros, which approved nearly everything that O'Reilly proposed, agreed to modify the rotation schedule for Spanish regiments from three years to two and to recall the Fijo to Spain.[28] Understandably, it never enforced the latter provision.

Despite his professed contempt for the Fixed Infantry Regiment and his misgivings about fixed units in general, O'Reilly quickly claimed great success in reforming the Havana garrison. In December 1763, just before departing from Havana to extend his mission to the rest of the island, he bragged to the crown that "there is not today in Europe a defense base where service is rendered with greater diligence and rectitude than in Havana."[29] Events during his absence soon proved that the subinspector general spoke prematurely.

In the name of economy, O'Reilly had proposed in his December report a military budget designed to lower the already meager wages of the army substantially. When rumors of this proposal reached the garrison, thirty grenadiers from the Regiment of Córdoba and some twenty veteran dragoons mutinied and took refuge in a church as an act of protest. Ricla promptly removed the men from their sanctuary, but an additional thirty soldiers from the Fijo followed suit out of anger over their selection for garrison duty in Santiago. When O'Reilly returned in April, he banished some of the grenadiers to the less prestigious fusilier companies; others, including most of those from the Fijo,

27. The problem of high death rates during troop shipments from Spain has been treated by Marchena, *Oficiales y soldados*, 212–15.

28. Royal orders, San Ildefonso, October, 1764, July 27, 1764, AGI, SD, legs. 2078, 2118.

29. O'Reilly to Wall, Havana, Dec. 6, 1763, AGI, SD, leg. 2078.

he sent off in shackles to royal labors; and one dragoon ran the gauntlet. With that, according to O'Reilly, the garrison "remained pacified and under rigorous discipline."[30]

O'Reilly's difficulties were still far from over. In desperate financial straits as a consequence of the war, the crown on April 24, 1764, responded to the O'Reilly budget proposal by ordering a reduction in the wages and support allowances of the Cuban army. Given the delicate situation in Havana, Ricla and an embarrassed O'Reilly concurred in a decision to suspend the royal order temporarily.[31] O'Reilly refused to let the matter rest there. In a remarkable display of leadership, he summoned the officers of the garrison to meet with him and at least superficially convinced them of the justice of the pay cut. He then had each captain present his company before him personally to avow its obedience to the king and its acceptance of the new regulation. So pleased was the subinspector general by the performance of the Fijo's officers in this affair that he forgave them their past failures, declaring them free from further stigma in the consideration of promotion.[32]

The incident over wages, apart from what it revealed about O'Reilly's character, reflected the enormous difficulty that confronted Spain in sustaining a competitive army in America. To reduce the wages of the military in a time of international crisis was an act of sheer financial desperation. Ricla, O'Reilly, and the officials in Spain well understood the urgency of accompanying military reforms with economic and political reforms that would in the long run permit greater latitude in shaping defense strategy. In the meantime, the effect of the order of April 24 was to cut the cost of the Cuban forces from 647,775 pesos annually to 487,453, a savings of 160,322 pesos.[33] When the crown learned of O'Reilly's apparent success in Cuba, it promptly extended the new wage regulations to the rest of the regular army in America.[34]

As O'Reilly's knowledge of Cuba grew, he readjusted the composition and deployment of the regular army to conform to local realities. The subinspector general quickly discovered that the broken, forested terrain of the island, even around Havana, did not lend itself to the use of mounted troops. Consequently, he recommended the reduction of the dragoons to a single squadron into which militia cavalrymen could be integrated during wartime to bring it up to regimental strength. The

30. O'Reilly to Arriaga, Havana, Apr. 12, 1764, AGI, SD, leg. 2118.

31. Ricla and O'Reilly to Esquilache, Havana, July 6, 1764, AGI, SD, leg. 2078.

32. Ricla to Esquilache, Havana, July 28, 1764, O'Reilly to Esquilache, Havana, July 28, 1764, both in AGI, SD, leg. 2078.

33. General cost summary, veteran garrison of Cuba, in O'Reilly to Esquilache, Havana, July 28, 1764, ibid.

34. Royal order, San Ildefonso, October, 1764, ibid.

Table 2.   **Veteran Garrison of Cuba in 1769**

Unit	Authorized Strength *
Spanish rotating regiment	1,358
Fixed Infantry Regiment of Havana	1,358
Catalonian Light Infantry (3 companies)	306
Dragoon Squadron of America	160
Artillery (2 companies)	172
Total	3,354

* These figures do not include officers or command and staff group personnel.

dragoons would serve principally to keep supplies moving, to maintain lines of communication, and to blunt advance enemy probes. In lieu of the less useful dragoons, O'Reilly asked for two light infantry companies of Catalonian mountaineers (one for Santiago, the other for Havana), who would be adept at operating in hilly, forested areas. Havana already possessed one such company. It had been withdrawn in 1763 from Florida, where nearly all the men had married and taken up farming. O'Reilly proposed to deactivate these troops and send them to colonize an appropriate site in Cuba. By dropping a squadron of dragoons, O'Reilly's proposal would save the crown 47,040 pesos, of which only 10,419 pesos would be needed to cover the net increase of one company of Catalonians for Santiago. Meanwhile, O'Reilly wanted to increase Santiago's veteran garrison to a full Spanish battalion, which would be transported directly from Europe—not through Havana—to reduce costs.[35] The Junta de Ministros approved all these proposals, but in practice Santiago would be garrisoned by the Second Battalion of the Fijo. Finally, in 1769 the crown increased the number of light infantry companies to three.[36]

If the attempt to improve the regular army provided O'Reilly with his greatest trials, his work to reform the colonial militia produced his greatest triumphs. From his arrival in Cuba until December, he worked diligently to create a viable reserve system in the Havana district, and from December until April, he extended that undertaking to the rest of the island. The result was a disciplined militia of eight infantry battalions, a regiment of cavalry, and a regiment of dragoons. In structuring this militia, he established policies that endured for nearly a century in Cuba and that were either applied directly to the other jurisdictions of America or used as general guidelines.

35. Ricla to Esquilache, Havana, July 28, 1764, O'Reilly to Esquilache, Havana, July 28, 1764, both ibid.
36. "Puntos de respuesta a Ricla y O'Reilly," ibid.

Considerations of strategy, demography, and economy determined the size and shape of the Cuban militia. In Havana, to reinforce the veteran infantry and dragoons, O'Reilly raised a white infantry regiment of two battalions, one of which he based in Guanabacoa across the bay but with companies reaching as far east as Cojímar; a *pardo* (mulatto) infantry battalion; and a cavalry regiment of whites. He also organized a *moreno* (Negro) battalion of light infantry, or skirmishers, to specialize in ambush and harassment.[37] To support the veteran battalion deployed in the Governorship of Santiago, he raised two infantry battalions, one white the other *pardo*. O'Reilly also established white infantry battalions in the district of Cuatro Villas in the south-central section of the island and in Puerto Príncipe (modern-day Camagüey) and a regiment of white dragoons in Matanzas to patrol the coastline east of Havana and to protect the city's supply routes.[38] Although the latter jurisdictions possessed no fixed garrisons to act as the front line for their defenses, Havana regularly deployed veteran detachments in Matanzas and the Cuatro Villas region, while Santiago or Havana did the same in Puerto Príncipe.

O'Reilly fixed the size of the infantry battalions at 800 men (not including officers and command and staff group personnel), the calvary regiment at 650, and the dragoons at 450, for a total of 7,500 volunteers (see Table 3 and Appendix 1). In addition, each company had provision for ten supernumeraries to fill vacancies as they developed.[39] This amounted to a sizable but not impossible portion of the population. In Havana, which had a relatively large population base, O'Reilly set enlistment age limits at sixteen to forty, and in the outlying districts, where manpower was in short supply, he modified those limits to fifteen to forty-five.[40]

The first official comprehensive census for Cuba, which was taken in 1775, found 171,628 inhabitants. Three years later, with war approaching, that figure was updated and refined for military purposes. The 1778 census provides, however, only an approximate tabulation. Not only were counting techniques primitive but the census table itself was replete with mathematical errors and inconsistencies at nearly every level, perhaps because of the attempt to graft one count

37. O'Reilly to Arriaga, Havana, Dec. 6, 1763, Ricla to Arriaga, Havana, Dec. 6, 1763, both ibid.; *Reglamento para las milicias de infantería, y caballería de la Isla de Cuba* (Madrid, 1769), *estado* 2.

38. O'Reilly to Esquilache, Havana, Apr. 12, 1764, O'Reilly to Arriaga, Havana, Apr. 13, 1764, both in AGI, SD, legs. 2078, 2118.

39. A summary of the location and strengths of the disciplined militia can be found in the *Reglamento para las milicias*, 1769, ch. 1, ch. 2, art. 46, and *estados* 1–5.

40. O'Reilly to Arriaga, Havana, Dec. 6, 1763, AGI, SD, leg. 2078; *Reglamento para las milicias*, 1769, ch. 2, art. 31.

Volunteer, White Infantry Regiment of Havana. Courtesy of Archivo General de Indias.

Table 3.   **Disciplined Militia of Cuba**

Unit	Authorized Strength *
Cavalry Regiment of Havana	650
White Infantry Regiment of Havana	1,600
Pardo Infantry Battalion of Havana	800
Moreno Infantry Battalion of Havana	800
Dragoon Regiment of Matanzas	450
White Infantry Battalion of Cuatro Villas	800
White Infantry Battalion of Puerto Príncipe	800
White Infantry Battalion of Santiago-Bayamo	800
Pardo Infantry Battalion of Santiago-Bayamo	800
Total	7,500

*These figures do not include officers or command and staff group personnel.

upon another.[41] Nevertheless, for the purposes of the present analysis it provides a useful rough estimate.

The 1778 census placed the population of Cuba at 179,484 people, but nearly 50,000 were slaves. In the age group fifteen to forty-five, it listed 28,327 white males, 3,652 free mulattoes, and 1,931 free Negroes. These figures, however, do not harmonize with the population totals listed for the eighteen separate jurisdictions of the island. The latter show 25,997 whites, 4,143 free mulattoes, and 2,332 free Negroes in the military age group. Presumably the latter is the more accurate count. Havana and its immediately dependent surrounding districts showed a population of 82,143 people, which amounted to just under one-half of the total for the island. That figure was somewhat inflated, however, because the census counted veteran troops.

The small number of free men of military age in the outer districts of the island compelled O'Reilly to combine widely separated municipalities for the purposes of sustaining battalions. In the south-central section of the island, no single municipality possessed enough able-bodied whites to form a complete battalion. O'Reilly therefore linked Trinidad with Sancti Spíritus, Santa Clara, and San Juan de los Remedios to support what he called the Volunteer Infantry Battalion of Cuatro Villas. In 1778 these municipalities would have 886, 569, 936, and 716 men of service age, and they presumably had about the same number in 1764. Santiago and its surrounding villages, which possessed only 1,604 whites of proper age as late as 1778, O'Reilly linked with Bayamo, some fifty miles inland, which would have 1,097. To

41. "Padrón general de la Isla de Cuba" and the abstract, 1778, AGI, SD, leg. 1525, and IG, leg. 1527.

further broaden the population base for the unit he added the district of Holguín which would count 527. Even so, in order to procure enough recruits, the subinspector general declared the Indians of the Bayamo district "white" for purposes of military service and enlisted them, despite colonial law, which viewed them as perpetual minors and thus exempt from military duty.[42] And for the entire militia, O'Reilly lowered by a half inch the minimum height of five feet required in Spain.[43]

In his report to Ricla and the crown, O'Reilly revealed very little about his recruiting methods. Spanish militia policy contained an elaborate system of classifying candidates by order of the hardship that their possible mobilization might cause. Thus, single men would be enlisted before married men, married men without children before those with children, and so on down the line until the quota was satisfied. The lottery determined choices within each group.[44] Given the limited population base available to support the Cuban militia, such fine distinctions were often superfluous. Moreover, O'Reilly claimed to have encountered widespread enthusiasm for militia duty; this assertion may have contained some immediate truth, for the memory of the British occupation was fresh.[45] In developing a policy for Cuba, the subinspector general did make a formal distinction between single and married men, and certain vassals were exempted in the public interest. The latter included those engaged in medical services, notaries, tax administrators, clerics, teachers, plantation foremen, and tobacco factors.[46] To maintain enlistment levels, the veteran lieutenants were obliged to maintain lists of the eligible candidates in the zones supporting their companies.[47] Presumably, if enough volunteers did not come forward, the choices were made by lottery.

Given the shortage of able-bodied whites in Cuba, O'Reilly, as indicated earlier, organized two battalions of mulattoes and one of free Negroes, euphemistically called *pardos* and *morenos* respectively. In the hierarchy of colonial society, men of all or partial Negro parentage were assigned a distinctly inferior social rank. White society viewed them as generally vicious, morally depraved, stupid, and untrustworthy (see Chapter 3). Yet O'Reilly was a realist. There was a shortage of able-bodied whites, and he found men of color generally robust and

42. *Reglamento para las milicias*, 1769, *estado* 1; "Padrón general," 1778, AGI, SD, leg. 1525; Kuethe, *Military Reform and Society*, 29. Neither O'Reilly nor the census indicated the size of the Indian population of Bayamo.

43. *Reglamento para las milicias*, 1769, ch. 2, art. 28.

44. *Real declaración sobre puntos esenciales de la ordenanza de milicias provinciales de España* . . . (Madrid, 1767), titles 2–3.

45. O'Reilly to Wall, Havana, Dec. 6, 1763, AGI, SD, leg. 2078.

46. *Reglamento para las milicias*, 1769, ch. 2, art. 25, *estado* 6.

47. Ibid., ch. 1, art. 9, and *estados* 6–7.

eager to serve.[48] Moreover, Cuba had traditionally maintained colored militia units.[49] Captain General Ricla also spoke enthusiastically about the potential of the three *pardo* and *moreno* battalions, predicting that they would become the best volunteers on the island.[50] Fortunately for the militia system, most of the eligible free *pardos* and *morenos* lived in the Havana and Santiago-Bayamo districts, where defense needs were the greatest. In time of war, Puerto Príncipe was to provide reinforcements for the battalion of Santiago-Bayamo and Cuatro Villas for the two in Havana.[51]

One major improvement in the new militia establishment came in the area of equipment. The crown provided firearms for all the battalions, which for convenience were stored in the buildings of the pertinent ayuntamiento.[52] Uniforms, featuring bright, distinguishing color schemes, were standardized by unit, but the crown expected these to come from local sources.[53] Although an abundance of patricians appeared who were willing to outfit units in exchange for commissions, O'Reilly wanted to preserve greater latitude in selecting officers and claimed to have persuaded the individual volunteers to provide their own uniforms. An exception was Matanzas, still impoverished at this time, where the subinspector general called upon the colonel and the captains to clothe the regiment.[54] That O'Reilly persuaded all or even most of the volunteers of the other units to pay for their uniforms seems most unlikely. To resolve the problem in the long run, the several municipalities supporting volunteer units established appropriate local levies (see Chapter 4). Dragoons and cavalrymen were expected to supply their own mounts, but the royal treasury undertook to cover losses incurred in the line of duty.[55]

Another improvement was the assignment of cadres of veteran officers and enlisted men to instruct the new units. O'Reilly developed a system for integrating these advisers into the chain of command, delicately balancing veteran and volunteer authorities. In the command and staff group of an infantry battalion, the colonel was a volunteer, but the second in command, the *sargento mayor*, was a veteran.

48. O'Reilly to Arriaga, Havana, Dec. 6, 1763, AGI, SD, leg. 2078.

49. Herbert S. Klein, "The Colored Militia of Cuba, 1568–1868," *Caribbean Studies* 4 (July 1966), 17–27. The use of colored troops was not uncommon among the Caribbean powers. See Peter Michael Voelz, "Slave and Soldier: The Military Impact of Blacks in the Colonial Americas" (Ph.D. dissertation, University of Michigan, 1978).

50. Ricla to Arriaga, Havana, Dec. 6, 1763, AGI, SD, leg. 2078.

51. *Reglamento para las milicias*, 1769, ch. 2, art. 11, *estado* 5.

52. O'Reilly to Arriaga, Havana, Dec. 6, 1763, AGI, SD, leg. 2078.

53. *Reglamento para las milicias*, 1769, ch. 8.

54. O'Reilly to Arriaga, Havana, Dec. 6, 1763, Pascual Jiménez de Cisneros to Arriaga, Havana, Feb. 11, 1767, both in AGI, SD, legs. 2078, 2121.

55. *Reglamento para las milicias*, 1769, ch. 4, art. 10.

He was the plans and training officer and usually held the rank of captain in the regular army. The *sargento mayor* was assisted by adjutants (*ayudantes*), who were generally veteran lieutenants or sergeants. The colonel was commander in chief of the unit, but he functioned under the watchful eye of the *sargento mayor*, who reported to the subinspector general.

Company commands functioned similarly. The captain was a volunteer, but the lieutenant was a veteran, usually holding the regular army rank of sergeant. At the noncommissioned level, along with volunteers of the same rank, each company possessed one veteran sergeant and two veteran corporals. These men were usually army corporals and privates respectively. Finally, one drummer per company and a drummer major for the command and staff group were placed on salary to assist in unit drills.

To enhance their effectiveness, the veteran lieutenants, sergeants, corporals, and drummers were expected to live in the district of their companies.[56] The higher rank accorded veterans entering the militia allowed them higher pay than they had received in the regular army, and O'Reilly hoped this better pay would attract qualified men. Nevertheless, the salaries for veteran militia officers were still considerably smaller than those for the same rank in the regular army. The lieutenants of veteran units earned forty-four pesos a month, for example, while veteran sergeants acting as militia lieutenants earned thirty-four. To prevent officers from atrophying while detached to the militia, O'Reilly also specified that the tours of duty for veteran lieutenants and captains functioning as adjutants and *sargentos mayores* should be limited to five years.[57]

For the *pardo* and *moreno* infantry, a separate white command and staff group functioned alongside the black command group. The top veteran official was an adjutant major with the title of subinspector, who was most often a sergeant in the regular army. Four adjutants assisted him, along with five *garzones*, who functioned much like the veteran sergeants and corporals in the white units. The small size of the veteran cadre in the black units meant that the volunteer officers and sergeants were expected to contribute more extensively to managing the details of unit maintenance and discipline than their counterparts in white units. Accordingly, O'Reilly assigned small salaries to them and to the battalion drummers and fifers.[58]

The cavalry followed a similar system. But mounted service, recalling the days of chivalry, appealed to colonial pretensions to nobility

56. Ibid., ch. 2, *estados* 1–2; Arriaga proposal, 1764, AGI, SD, leg. 2118.
57. O'Reilly to Arriaga, Havana, December 6, 1763, AGI, SD, leg. 2078.
58. *Reglamento para las milicias*, 1769, ch. 1, art. 13, ch. 2, art. 34, and *estados* 10–11.

and enjoyed special prestige among the creoles. O'Reilly was particularly pleased at his success in recruiting the finest elements of Havana
society into the cavalry regiment. Proud of its efficiency, he assigned
the regiment special responsibilities. Of the thirteen companies, four
would be integrated directly into the Veteran Dragoon Squadron of
America during wartime to form tactically a full regiment. This step
would be facilitated by Martín Esteban de Aróstegui, a Spanish resident
of Havana who by virtue of his past services had been awarded the grade
of brigadier in the regular army and who agreed to command the
volunteer regiment. O'Reilly specified that, when the colonelcy became vacant, another Spanish veteran should fill the position if
possible.[59] In contrast to the cavalry, the three mounted companies of
the Matanzas Regiment of Dragoons, which were widely scattered and
which were assigned only secondary defense obligations, received no
veteran advisers; and the three foot companies, although enjoying the
same complement of veteran sergeants, corporals, and drummers as the
infantry, possessed no veteran officers except an adjutant major who
functioned on the command and staff group.[60]

   Although the militia initially trained intensively to learn the basic
military skills, volunteers usually drilled once a week after Sunday
Mass.[61] In areas where a battalion's companies were widely scattered,
they drilled individually. Battalions were also obliged to muster every
two months for unit maneuvers and to take firing practice, except in
Santiago-Bayamo and Cuatro Villas where distance made such exercises impossible. Moreover, at year's end, units underwent review by
the subinspector general or his representative, who used the opportunity to fill vacancies and inspect the equipment.[62] O'Reilly's plan, if
upheld, promised to remedy the principal weaknesses of the earlier
system. Units were equipped, provided with standardized tables of
organization, trained by veterans, and drilled regularly.

   A final issue was the concession of military privileges to the militia.
As the several battalions and regiments took shape under O'Reilly's
direction, Ricla used his broad powers to grant them the *fuero de guerra
militar*, which permitted militiamen to present their legal causes before military tribunals.[63] In hierarchical colonial society, the *fuero
militar* conveyed special distinction and prestige and reinforced a sense

   59. Militia cost report, O'Reilly, Havana, Nov. 30, 1763, O'Reilly to Wall, Havana,
Dec. 6, 1763, O'Reilly to Esquilache, Havana, July 28, 1764, "Puntos de respuesta a Ricla y
O'Reilly," all in AGI, SD, leg. 2078; *Reglamento para las milicias*, 1769, estados 3–4, 8–9.
   60. *Reglamento para las milicias*, 1769, estados 4, 8; royal order, San Lorenzo, Nov. 7,
1767, AGI, SD, leg. 2078.
   61. O'Reilly to Arriaga, Dec. 6, 1763, AGI, SD, leg. 2078.
   62. *Reglamento para las milicias*, 1769, ch. 2, art. 32, and ch. 3.
   63. Ricla to Arriaga, Havana, Apr. 1, 1764, AGI, SD, leg. 2118.

of corporate honor and esprit de corps. It was one of some thirty-four privileged jurisdictions in the empire, which included the church and its several subdivisions; the Matrícula de Mar; artisan, mining, and merchant guilds; and the Mesta. "Such privileged *fueros* or jurisdictions were the judicial expression of a society in which the state was regarded not as a community of citizens enjoying equal rights and responsibilities, but as a structure built of classes and corporations, each with a unique and peculiar function to perform."[64]

Ricla's thinking on this issue is clear. In discharging their military duties, volunteers incurred considerable inconvenience and, worse, faced the very real possibility of mobilization. Lacking the means to reward these men monetarily, Ricla viewed the *fuero* as a form of practical compensation as well as the means to enhance their sense of corporate identity. Reporting his action to Spain, he explained, "I knew since my arrival in this colony that it would not be possible to achieve the advantageous level of discipline that His Majesty desires and that is so essential for the defense of this important island without conceding to all militiamen the benefit of the *fuero militar*."[65] The crown confirmed Ricla's action by order of August 25.[66]

O'Reilly codified his militia system into a regulation, which Ricla transmitted to Spain in June 1764.[67] In October, Charles, acting through Esquilache, approved the document for immediate use in Cuba and ordered Ricla to print it.[68] By June 1765 the first copies were ready.[69] Meanwhile, the king referred the regulation to the Consejo Supremo de Guerra for further study. The former viceroy of New Spain, the Conde de Revillagigedo, and the former captain general of Cuba, Francisco Cagigal, acted as consultants. After the Consejo Supremo had effected a number of refinements, the crown, in early 1767, sent a revised copy to the new captain general of Cuba, Antonio Bucareli, for his input.[70] The regulation finally appeared in final form on January 19, 1769.[71]

Although they had awarded the *fuero militar* to the disciplined militia, Ricla and O'Reilly refrained from codifying the privilege in the regulation that they submitted to Spain in 1764. Neither was a trained

64. McAlister, The "Fuero Militar," 5–6.
65. Ricla to Arriaga, Havana, Apr. 1, 1764, AGI, SD, leg. 2118.
66. Royal order, San Ildefonso, Aug. 25, 1764, ibid.
67. Ricla to Arriaga, with manuscript of the "Reglamento para las milicias de infantería, y caballería de la Isla de Cuba," Havana, June 15, 1764, ibid.
68. A copy of this order can be found in the *Reglamento para las milicias de infantería, y caballería de la Isla de Cuba* (Havana, 1765), in AGI, SD, leg. 2120.
69. Ricla to Arriaga, Havana, June 23, 1765, ibid.
70. Royal order, n.p., Feb. 3, 1767, AGI, SD, leg. 2125.
71. Copies of the regulation can be found in AGI, SD, leg. 2127, and AGI, IG, leg. 1885. It has been republished in José María Zamora y Coronado, comp., *Biblioteca de legislación ultramarina en forma de diccionario alfabético . . .* (Madrid, 1845), III, 285–302, 321–25.

jurist, and points of corporate privilege could be highly sensitive. O'Reilly did, however, prepare a brief on the subject, which accompanied his draft of the regulation. This document contained a compilation of the pertinent sections on military privilege from the regulation existent for the provincial militia of Spain as well as a formal report on local custom by two distinguished Cuban lawyers, Francisco López de Gamarra and Juan Miguel de Castro Palomino. The observations of these men considerably influenced the final construction of the Cuban *fuero* and, in the long run, the shape of militia privilege in much of America.[72]

The López-Castro report advocated a broadly defined privilege owing to a number of considerations. In a practical sense, the *fuero* enabled the army to retain primary control over its personnel. Those involved in criminal litigation, for example, would be confined in military prisons or be remanded to the custody of their superiors rather than be dispersed under the authority of other jurisdictions. This practice meant that in time of mobilization the full unit would be at hand for service without the interference of other authorities. Given the important mission of the disciplined militia, this consideration carried much weight. The lawyers also supported the opinion advanced by Ricla and O'Reilly that the distinction the *fuero* conferred would encourage enlistments and reward volunteers for their sacrifices. They warned that without this benefit the militia would lack the cohesion required to make it an effective component of the defense force.

Less certain was the exact definition that the *fuero* should assume. In Spain the *fuero* of the provincial militia encompassed both civil and criminal causes for officers and sergeants, but corporals and enlisted men enjoyed only the criminal privilege. In the Cuban militia before the reform, López and Castro reported, military privilege had been extended to officers and sergeants for both civil and criminal actions but enlisted men had not enjoyed the *fuero*. They urged, nevertheless, that the full *fuero*, both civil and criminal, be extended to enlisted men under the new regulation. A concession of this breadth would, significantly, give Cuban enlisted men broader privileges than their counterparts on the peninsula. The lawyers justified their recommendation by reason of the militia's critical mission and the conviction that broad privileges would enhance its ability to meet that responsibility.

The Consejo Supremo de Guerra in Spain, along with consultants Revillagigedo and Cagigal, accepted the recommendations of the report, confirming the *fuero militar*, both civil and criminal, for all militiamen. As part of its review and revision of the Cuban militia

72. This brief can be found in Ricla to Arriaga, Havana, June 15, 1764, AGI, SD, leg. 2118.

regulation, it added two chapters to the O'Reilly draft that defined the militia *fuero* and outlined the procedures to be observed in the adjudication of military causes, procedures closely following the recommendations of Castro and López.[73]

Under the new regulation, the highest ranking military officer in each district, assisted by a legal aid (*asesor*), acted as the court of first instance. In Cuatro Villas and Puerto Príncipe, where no governor resided, this officer would be the deputy governor (*teniente de gobernador*), who usually headed the local military detachment. Appeals from Puerto Príncipe went first to the governor of Santiago de Cuba and then to Havana. Elsewhere, criminal actions and civil suits involving more than a hundred pesos were appealed to the captain general, whose decision was practically final, although sentences entailing the penalty of death or mutilation could be taken to the Consejo Supremo de Guerra in Spain for review. Other appeals to Spain would have limited value, unless very substantial issues were at stake, for the captain general's decision stood in the interim, the process being redressive (*devolutivo*) rather than suspensory (*suspensivo*). In practice, because of the multiple responsibilities of the captain general, his judicial duties were delegated to an *auditor de guerra* (military judicial officer). Militiamen were thus immune from ordinary justice, subject only to their superior officers, and prisoners were detained in military facilities to provide the army direct custody over them.

In military law, however, a number of special offenses, including sedition, counterfeiting, heresy, and smuggling, as well as civil actions arising from debts contracted prior to enlistment, the disposition of entailed estates, the division of inheritances deriving from civilians, and mercantile law, were classified as instances of *desafuero*, where the common good or special considerations intervened and ordinary justice or other tribunals assumed jurisdiction. The 1769 regulation did not enumerate these instances, although they were understood to exist and would be clarified later by royal legislation.[74]

The disciplined militia also enjoyed a number of lesser privileges, called *preeminencias*. The crown, when it approved the *fuero militar* for the disciplined militia, went on to grant the new units the same exemptions and *preeminencias* as the regular army.[75] As codified by the 1769 regulation, these rights included immunity from various kinds of municipal licenses and levies, the quartering of troops, and prison cell fees.[76] Although these exemptions were not of major significance in the

---

73. *Reglamento para las milicias,* 1769, chs. 10–11.
74. Kuethe, *Military Reform and Society,* 27.
75. Royal order, San Ildefonso, Aug. 25, 1764, AGI, SD, leg. 2118.
76. *Reglamento para las milicias,* 1769, ch. 2, art. 40, and ch. 4, arts. 2, 6–7.

larger sense, any privilege, no matter how small, conveyed additional prestige. And for humble enlisted men, especially *pardos* and *morenos*, immunity from municipal levies could be important.[77]

One key point remained unresolved in the codification of 1769. The description of the *fuero* did not make clear whether it should be construed as simply passive, to apply solely when the holder was the defendant, or whether it should be understood as active, to include causes where he was the plaintiff. The active *fuero* was a rare privilege in Spanish military law. The provincial militia of the peninsula was limited to the passive construction as, indeed, was the regular army.[78] Only a few special corps such as the Royal Guard enjoyed the broader privilege. Yet there was precedent in Cuba for invoking the active *fuero* based on a judicial action that had reached Spain by appeal in 1759. The case involved an attempt by Sergeant José de Estrada, a *pardo* silver-smith who was accused of violating a contract, to plead his case before a military tribunal. Ordinary justice objected, arguing that the *fuero* did not extend to litigation arising out of business contracts. Although precedents in the case were unclear, Estrada won the decision, owing in large measure to the vigorous support of Captain General Francisco Cagigal de la Vega, who argued that the *fuero* was the only reward available to the Havana militia and that royal support of broadly inter-preted prerogatives was therefore absolutely essential. More impor-tant, however, the royal authorities went beyond the immediate issue at hand in sustaining Estrada. Although the active *fuero* was not at issue since Estrada was the defendant not the plaintiff in the case, the crown by order of May 10, 1759, declared that the officers and sergeants of the Cuban militia should be accorded the active as well as the passive privilege.[79]

The 1759 order did not fully explain the reasoning of the royal authorities, but their motives are clear enough. War was at hand; Cuba was situated on the exposed rim of the empire; and Spain, with only limited resources at its disposal, was hard pressed to motivate its forces. Under this pressure, the crown extended preferential treatment to the Cuban militia. This astonishing concession obviously had no effect on the militia's performance during 1762, because the other components for creating a viable volunteer force were missing, but during the postwar reorganization the issue arose again.

Following Ricla's concession of the *fuero militar* to the units orga-

77. For a thoughtful analysis of the social tensions generated by the disciplined militia system and in particular the colored units, see Santiago Gerardo Suárez, "Conflictividad social de la reforma militar dieciochista," *Memorias del Congreso Bicentenario de Simón Bolívar* (Caracas, forthcoming).

78. McAlister, *The "Fuero Militar,"* 7–8.

79. File on the jurisdictional dispute, 1758–59, AGI, SD, leg. 2112.

nized by O'Reilly, the officers and sergeants generally construed their privilege as active. Difficulties arose when enlisted men laid claim to the same privilege. This innovation led the crown, in a special declaration of April 15, 1771, to rule that the active *fuero* should be limited solely to officers and sergeants, but in so doing it directly confirmed a privilege for the officers of the Cuban disciplined militia more ample than that for the peninsular militia and, indeed, the regular army.[80]

The concession of a privilege of this magnitude eloquently bespoke the sociopolitical thinking in the Spain of Charles III. As has been widely observed by historians of his reign, the king was a man of the Enlightenment, an intellectual movement that increasingly questioned the legitimacy of privilege and special arrangements. The traditional, almost sacrosanct ecclesiastical *fuero*, for example, was gradually but relentlessly curtailed during Charles's reign.[81] Yet in those affairs of state where vital interests were concerned, the monarch was perfectly willing to resort to traditional structures—unenlightened though they may have been—to achieve his objectives. While the ecclesiastical *fuero* suffered unsympathetic scrutiny, reflecting the increasingly secular orientation of Spanish politics, the military privilege was sustained, indeed broadened, in strategic areas such as Cuba. A parallel example was the mercantile *fuero*, which entered directly into the struggle for imperial viability and also escaped circumscription during Charles's enlightened reign. Such pragmatism permitted the monarchy to extend a privileged corporate constitution to a broad sector of Cuban society, including *morenos*, *pardos*, and whites, whom it hoped to convert into fighting men. And the mainstream of society felt the impact of this privilege acutely, for it embraced citizen soldiers, most of whom inhabited the principal municipalities of the colony.

The military reorganization of 1763–1764, together with the definition of militia privilege, thus created a viable if politically compromising framework for arming Cubans and, by implication, other Americans. No one at the time expected the disciplined militia to perform as well as the reconstructed regular army, but 7,500 volunteers, maintained at strategically selected points on the island, would at least provide an effective reserve in Spain's preparation for yet another confrontation with the British. To establish a promising framework was the first step. The severest test would be the creation of the financial and sociopolitical means to support the system and, ultimately, make it work.

80. "Real declaración sobre puntos esenciales del reglamento para las milicias de infantería, y caballería de la Isla de Cuba . . . ," Aranjuez, Apr. 15, 1771, AGI, IG, leg. 1885.
81. N.M. Farriss, *Crown and Clergy in Colonial Mexico, 1759–1821* (London, 1968).

3. Politics

From the beginning, Charles III and Esquilache grasped the reality that a political understanding with the Cuban elite was indispensable to make the military reorganization work. The municipalities would become responsible for equipping the units of their localities, for ensuring adequate numbers of recruits, and for accommodating the pretenses of military justice as amplified by the privileged *fuero* of the volunteer units. Of more immediate importance, Cubans would have to bear heavier taxes accompanied by tighter royal administration to support the expanded regular army as well as the veteran cadres assigned to the disciplined militia. Given the traditional colonial aversion to new taxes and the implications of the shift of military—and therefore political—power to creole hands, revenue reform promised to become the most difficult challenge confronting Ricla as captain general of Cuba. To O'Reilly fell the task of shaping a militia officer corps that tie the elite to the military corporation, making it the beneficiary and supporter of the new, emerging order in Cuba.

A complex, delicate process that extended over a period of two years, the implementation of revenue reform was a striking example of the consultative character of Spanish absolutism as practiced during the early reign of Charles III. Before he left Spain, Esquilache had instructed Ricla to address the issue of finance in consultation with the Havana elite, making clear the need for new revenues but promising concessions to the island to balance the burden.[1] The Italian, who was quickly

1. These instructions were given orally. Ricla to Esquilache, Havana, July 5, 1763, AGS, Hac, leg. 2342. Usually associated with rigid, authoritarian behavior, José de Gálvez, like Ricla, openly consulted with colonial interests during the early stages of his visit to New Spain. See José Jesús Hernández Palomo, *El aquardiente de caña en México* (Seville, 1974), 68–70.

gaining a reputation for rigid, inflexible government in Spain, aspired to operate in quite the opposite fashion in Cuba where he plainly hoped to draw strategic Havana into a cooperative arrangement with the crown. In discharging the assignment that Esquilache gave him, Ricla would prove himself an uncommonly effective representative of the king, showing remarkable skills as a negotiator and as an intermediary between the interests of Havana and the court. As events developed, Ricla, working in remarkable harmony with O'Reilly in Cuba and Esquilache in Spain, would succeed in constructing a viable reform program that both underpinned the military reorganization and established the foundation for a political stability that would endure well into the following century.

The financial dilemma was staggering. The regular army, even under O'Reilly's new wage regulation, required 487,453 pesos a year for salaries alone, and housing and equipment were additional expenses. The militia's veteran cadres required another 110,121.[2] And fortification construction costs were expected to add at least half a million. Local revenues fell far short of these totals. During the 1750s, Cuba generated an average of just under 162,500 pesos a year.[3] The Havana treasury, moreover, had to cover a multitude of obligations besides defense.

New Spain had historically provided Cuba with substantial financial assistance. Under the policy that Viceroy Revillagigedo established in 1753, the Mexican treasury subsidized the island with nearly half a million pesos annually. That practice was resumed after the war, but these monies were designated solely for purposes of fortification.[4] Esquilache now expected Cuba to fund the army, a decision that implied ambitious measures to locate new sources of revenue.

Ricla, recognizing its overwhelming economic and political significance in the colony, focused his immediate attention solely on Havana. By 1763, the city's creole society was already highly structured. Connected by a network of marriages, a small nucleus of patrician families enjoyed dominance over local politics and society. Some of these families could trace their Cuban heritage to the first conquerors, but most had arrived during the seventeenth and eighteenth centuries, and at least some still maintained active relations with their Spanish cousins. Within this elite, to hold sway over vast tracts of land was, of course, commonplace, but interests in wholesale commerce or in enterprises related to the island's advantageous position on the imperial naval

2. *Reglamento para las milicias,* 1769, *estados* 8–11.
3. See Allan J. Kuethe and G. Douglas Inglis, "Absolutism and Enlightened Reform: Charles III, the Establishment of the *Alcabala,* and Commercial Reorganization in Cuba," *Past and Present: A Journal of Historical Studies,* no. 109 (Nov. 1985), 120.
4. Royal orders, Mar. 23, Apr. 25, 1764, both in AGS, Hac, leg. 2342.

routes were not rare. Men of condition regularly demonstrated their social excellence through conspicuous acts of public service and generosity, and a few held perpetual office in the ayuntamiento.[5]

An impressive number of creoles had acquired legal recognition of their social excellence. At the top, five people held titles of Castile: Juan Francisco Núñez del Castillo, Marqués de San Felipe y Santiago; Manuel José Aparicio del Manzano y Jústiz, Marqués de Jústiz de Santa Ana; Gonzalo Francisco Recio de Oquendo, Marqués de la Real Proclamación; Gonzalo de Herrera y Tapia, Marqués de Villalta; and Francisco José Chacón y Torres, Conde de Casa Bayona. Four more would gain titles during the 1760s: Agustín Cárdenas Vélez de Guevara, Marqués de Cárdenas de Montehermoso (1764); Jerónimo Espinosa de Contreras y Jústiz, Conde de Gibacoa (1764); Pedro José Calvo de la Puerta y Arango, Conde de Buena Vista (1766); and Gabriel Beltrán de Santa Cruz y Aranda, Conde de San Juan de Jaruco (1767). The first three of the latter group, apart from vast fortunes, had rendered distinguished services connected to the war. The last combined immense land holdings with an illustrious intellectual reputation, holding the position of *catedrático* at the University of San Jerónimo. During this same period, the crown granted titles to two Spaniards involved in royal service who had become "rooted" (*radicados*) into creole society, having married into prominent Havana families. Lorenzo Montalvo, Conde de Macuriges (1765), who was marine intendant, was one of the few Spanish officials in Havana whose performance during 1762–1763 satisfied the crown, and Domingo de Lizundia y Odría de Echevarría, Marqués del Real Agrado (1764), was the treasurer of the tobacco monopoly. This flood of new titles was yet another manifestation of the royal attempt to cement an alliance with the colonial elite during the postwar period. Other creoles had acquired habits in the Spanish crusading orders or had distinguished their families through the establishment of *mayorazgos* (entailed estates).[6] Not all members of the upper strata held titles, of course, but to secure such prestige was a compelling ambition.

To assist him in his consultation with Havana's elite, Ricla solicited the cooperation of Father Ignacio Tomás Butler, a prominent and respected Jesuit, whom he commissioned to act as an unofficial intermediary between himself and the colonists, thus shrewdly avoiding directly compromising either himself or his monarch. As instructed by

5. Knight, "Origins of Wealth," 235–38; Kuethe and Inglis, "Absolutism and Enlightened Reform," tables 1 and 2.

6. Rafael Nieto y Cortadellas, *Dignidades nobiliarias en Cuba* (Madrid, 1954), 71–72, 98–99, 113–15, 250–51, 294–95, 308–10, 411–13, 420–21, 480–82, 495–96, and 609–11; Tornero, "Hacendados y desarrollo," 715–37; Emilio de la Cruz Hermosilla, "Lorenzo Montalvo, figura señera de la Armada," *Revista general de marina* 202 (Jan. 1982), 17–23.

Ricla, Butler carefully explained to select leaders of the creole community the need for revenue reform and alluded to generous royal concessions for the development of the island as future compensation. The authorities were not prepared to be specific on the latter point until O'Reilly could conduct a visitation of the island in conjunction with his military duties and formulate specific recommendations, but changes in the commercial regulations governing Cuba were clearly implied.[7]

The Cuban economy had experienced a definite quickening under the early Bourbons, especially following the establishment in 1740 of the Royal Havana Company, which was founded by Cubans to stimulate exports but in which Spaniards controlled half the shares. Traditionally, tobacco and hides had ranked as Cuba's most important export products, but sugar, which had been granted duty-free access to the Spanish market upon the founding of the Royal Company, had recently made rapid strides, surpassing leather and coming to rival tobacco. The crown had made tobacco a royal monopoly for the Spanish market in 1717, arbitrarily fixing prices and quotas that discouraged new investment, and by 1763, tobacco had become the small farmer's domain. The cattle industry was similarly troubled because meat prices were usually fixed by the municipal governments at levels that discouraged production. Hides could be marketed, but because they were most often shipped as packing material, the volume of their sales was tied to the volume of exports. Sugar, by comparison, offered an attractive investment alternative, especially after 1755 when world prices began to rise sharply.[8] Shipbuilding was another major enterprise, and Havana was surrounded by small truck farms that provided foodstuffs for the port's maritime traffic.[9]

Cuba's primary problem was a lack of legal commercial outlets. After a promising start, the Royal Havana Company had fallen upon hard times owing to a multitude of reasons. In later years, it had proved unable to handle the Cuban trade and had recently lost the last of its monopolistic privileges. As matters stood in 1763, the principal concern was the inflexibility of the port system in Spain. Secure in centuries of tradition, the Consulado (merchant guild) de Cádiz enjoyed a

7. Ricla to Esquilache, Havana, Dec. 14, 1763, AGS, Hac, leg. 2342.
8. The transformation of the Cuban economy under the early Bourbons is analyzed in Marrero, *Cuba,* VI, ch. 4, VII. The appendix of the latter volume contains the charter of the Royal Havana Company. See also, Moreno Fraginals, *El ingenio,* I, 20, 55; McNeill, "Theory and Practice," 155–92, 216–45.
9. G. Douglas Inglis, "Cuban Settlement Systems and Demographic Patterns in the 1770s," in Margaret E. Crahan, ed., *Cuba: Social Transformations, 1750–1950* (forthcoming); G. Douglas Inglis, "The Spanish Naval Shipyard at Havana in the Eighteenth Century," in *New Aspects of Naval History* (Baltimore, 1985).

monopoly on the American commerce, which by law had to be conducted in the guild's ships. This arrangement had the effect of narrow-
ing markets and depressing prices. Some licensed intercolonial trade in
Cuban ships existed, principally with Veracruz, Campeche, and Cartagena de Indias, but the volume was not great. Finally, a plethora of
duties based on volume and weight further depressed legal commerce.
Smuggling, an enterprise at which Cubans had long been adept, provided some relief, but it could not be a satisfactory substitute for a
viable legal system. During the years immediately preceding the British conquest, sugar had accumulated on the docks of Havana awaiting
ships from Cádiz to transport it to market.[10] Britain's ability to exploit
this trade embarrassed the officials in Spain and goes far to explain why
the British occupation had not been entirely unpopular. Indeed, Ricla
saw fit to bring charges against two leading patricians, Sebastián Peñalver and the Marqués de la Real Proclamación, for collaborating with the
conquerors.[11]

After finding the initial creole reaction to his overtures favorable,
Father Butler added weight to the dialogue by arranging a formal meeting with thirty patricians in the home of O'Reilly, who conveniently
arranged to be absent. Most of the thirty had held municipal office at
one time or another. Three possessed titles of Castile, and five more
would be ennobled in the immediate future. Their investment portfolios reflected the diversity of the Cuban economy at this time, and at
least twenty-three owned one sugar plantation or more. Changes in the
trade regulations to the benefit of the emerging planter aristocracy was
obviously a high priority.

The creoles seemed willing to accept higher taxes but with the
strong expectation that royal concessions would follow in the area of
commerce. Butler then informed the gathering that Ricla was willing
to consult directly with a delegation to hear their viewpoint on taxation and the kind of commercial reforms that would enable them to
bear a heavier burden. Evidently believing that more could be gained by
building upon a royal initiative, the assembly declined this offer, voting
instead to await action from court.[12] The participants did, however,
express the desire to meet again, raising the intriguing possibility of
semiformalized, ongoing consultation between crown and colonists.
Not wishing to compromise the royal prerogative, Ricla warily backed
off at this point. He encouraged no further meetings, satisfied that he
had already achieved creole acquiescence to new taxation.

10. Marrero, *Cuba,* VII, 18–19, 112–51, 166–96, VIII, 9–14; McNeill, "Theory and
Practice," 276–77.
11. Thomas, *Cuba,* 49–61.
12. A list of the participants, their attributes, and their votes can be found in Kuethe
and Inglis, "Absolutism and Enlightened Reform," table 1.

To advise the crown on its options, Ricla commissioned a Catalonian, José Antonio Gelabert, the chief auditor of the colonial treasury, to prepare a brief on possible sources of additional revenue. Gelabert's report, dated December 8, 1763, outlined fourteen alternatives, the most important a plan to bring the Cuban *alcabala* to a par with the tax assessed in other colonies. The *alcabala* under current imperial practice was collectible on each sale as well as upon export, and in most colonies it was set at 4 to 6 percent.[13] In Cuba, however, the *alcabala* had not been established until 1758 and then at only 2 percent. The captain general sent the report to Spain in December, informing Esquilache that Havana understood the need for revenue reform.[14]

The Junta de Ministros took Ricla at his word but acted with a degree of restraint in appreciation of the political dangers entailed in advancing taxation too aggressively, even with prior consultation. For the moment, the Junta resolved to activate three of Gelabert's proposals. It doubled the *alcabala* from 2 to 4 percent, placed a 3 percent tax on incomes from certain types of property including land (*rentas líquidas de casas, censos y posesiones*), and established a levy on alcoholic beverages: two pesos per barrel of aguardiente and a silver real per barrel of *sambumbia*.[15] A royal order of April 25, 1764, from the desk of Esquilache conveyed this legislation to Cuba.[16]

Ideally, at least some commercial concessions should have accompanied the April order, but the need for money was pressing, and the junta still did not have the information required to act in that sphere. The ministers did not, of course, know about the troop mutiny that had just occurred as a result of O'Reilly's salary scheme, but the financial facts spoke for themselves. Changes in commercial policy, although on the mind of the junta, would have to await a study of the report from O'Reilly's *visita*, which had not yet arrived. Moreover, the Cuban problem intersected with much larger questions. Once O'Reilly's report was in hand, the Junta de Ministros would appoint a special five-man committee to examine commercial policy for the entire empire. Much more was at stake in this venture than simply finding appropriate compensation for offended Cuban taxpayers. Exploiting the crisis mentality arising from defeat in war to override entrenched vested interests and the Cádiz monopoly in particular, Esquilache envisioned a sweeping reorganization of the colonial trade laws, aiming

---

13. José Antonio Gelabert to Ricla, Havana, Dec. 8, 1763, AGS, Hac, leg. 2342.

14. Ricla to Esquilache, Havana, Dec. 14, 1763, ibid.

15. Expediente, "Acuerdo de la Junta de Señores Ministros," El Pardo, Mar. 15, 1764, ibid. *Sambumbia* was a local drink made from the fermenting of cane juice, water, and peppers.

16. Royal order, Apr. 25, 1764, AGS, Hac, leg. 2342.

to recapture a greater share of American commerce and to pull the colonies into a tighter mercantilistic dependence upon Spain.[17]

While Ricla and Esquilache took the preliminary steps toward revenue reform, O'Reilly incorporated the Havana patriciate into the militia establishment, further defining the reform equation that was unfolding in the colony. In selecting his officers, he paid close attention to the question of experience and to individual behavior during the British invasion, but social status outweighed all other considerations. To place in positions of command representatives of those families that controlled Havana's politics and economy and to make them beneficiaries of the new expenditures was indispensable. Their cooperation would be needed to support the militia, and their acquiescence to revenue reform was imperative. For Havana's hierarchy, which still looked to the feudal past for its sense of identity, military offices evoked images of nobility and reinforced pretenses of social excellence. Throughout its history, the Havana militia would never lack an abundance of elite aspirants to volunteer office. The First Battalion of the White Volunteer Infantry Regiment, the Cavalry Regiment, and the colonelcy of the Matanzas Dragoons—all offered coveted opportunities for rank, the uniform, and privileges, without a full-time commitment to service.

The officer corps that O'Reilly named, as well as the leadership that would emerge in subsequent years, faithfully mirrored the elite of Havana society. The office of colonel of the white infantry went to Luis José de Aguiar. Aguiar was a Havana creole of distinguished social reputation who had served as *fiel ejecutor* (regulator of weights, measures, and market prices) on the ayuntamiento in 1762. He held vast investments in sugar and cattle, but his appointment was in significant measure the consequence of his personal heroics during the British occupation, which impressed O'Reilly. He was the only municipal official to work directly for the reconquest of the capital, having gone inland in a vain attempt to rally resistance.[18] And during the battle itself, Aguiar's force captured a number of British cannons, mortars, and prisoners, including an officer. Moreover, when the city fell, he saved some sixty slaves, twenty-four of them the property of the crown. After the city had been restored to Spanish control, he also contributed eight slaves to assist with the crash program to fortify the Cabaña.[19]

---

17. Vicente Rodríguez Casado, "Comentario al decreto y real instrucción de 1765 regulando las relaciones comerciales de España e Indias," *Anuario de historia del derecho español* 13 (1936–41), 101, 109–13; G. Douglas Inglis and Allan J. Kuethe, "El Consulado de Cádiz y el reglamento de comercio libre de 1765," in *Jornadas de Andalucía y América* (Seville, 1985), IV, 108–15.

18. Thomas, *Cuba*, 45, 48; O'Reilly to Arriaga, Havana, Dec. 6, 1763, AGI, SD, leg. 2078.

19. Service record, Colonel Luis José de Aguiar, 1769, AGI, SD, leg. 2095.

To act as lieutenant colonel, O'Reilly named Francisco José Chacón y Torres, who combined illustrious social status with a reputation for public generosity and who, like Aguiar, held extensive sugar and cattle properties. Chacón, too, had served during the battle but without distinction. Nevertheless, when the British evacuated Havana, he contributed the substantial sum of thirty thousand pesos to repair damages and to assist the widows and families of those who had died in combat.[20] Chacón was *teniente a querra* of the town of Santa María del Rosario and would later serve as *alcalde ordinario* of Havana. His social status was commensurate with his civic leadership. He held a title of Castile as the second Conde de Casa Bayona and possessed a *mayorazgo*. Further, he had married Mariana Josefa Tomasa de Herrera y Chacón, his niece, who was the daughter of the fourth Marqués de Villalta.[21]

O'Reilly named Martín Esteban de Aróstegui to command the cavalry regiment. A native of Navarre, knight of the Order of Santiago, and brother of the former president of the Royal Havana Company (Martín de Aróstegui), Aróstegui held the rank of brigadier general in the regular army. He had served previously as deputy governor of Puerto Príncipe and Cuatro Villas, where he had been in 1762. When the British invaded Havana, he had worked vigorously to solicit aid from neighboring colonies, had later gone to Havana to fight, and following the surrender had returned to the interior to carry on the resistance. Pleased to have an officer with his experience, O'Reilly made him colonel of the cavalry regiment, although the position should presumably have gone to a volunteer. In the Cuban regulation, the latter possibility remained open, although in practice a succession of veteran officers assumed the position thereafter.[22]

For the volunteer office of lieutenant colonel, O'Reilly selected Juan O'Farrill y Ariola. Like Aróstegui, O'Farrill combined extensive military experience with a distinguished social reputation, the latter resting upon his status in Havana, where he was born, the son of a factor of the South Sea Company. O'Farrill had served in the navy during the War of Jenkins' Ear, first as a cadet, then as an ensign, and between tours aboard ship, he had seen action as a volunteer in the land expedition from Florida against the English. When he retired from the navy in 1746, the crown awarded him the grade of captain of infantry. O'Farrill had voluntarily resumed active duty to fight at Havana, returning to civilian life after the war. Meanwhile, he had amassed a huge personal fortune through commerce, sugar, and cattle.[23]

20. Service record, Lieutenant Colonel Conde de Casa Bayona, 1769, ibid.

21. Nieto, *Dignidades nobiliarias,* 115.

22. Service record, Colonel Martín Esteban Aróstegui, 1765, AGI, SD, leg. 2093; *Reglamento para las milicias,* 1769, ch. 1, art. 12.

23. Service record, Lieutenant Colonel Juan O'Farrill y Ariola, 1765, AGI, SD, leg. 2093; Thomas, *Cuba,* 32.

To command the Matanzas Dragoons, O'Reilly named Jerónimo Espinosa de Contreras y Jústiz. A Havana native and a major landowner in Matanzas, Contreras held diversified investments, including sugar and tobacco. Along with his half brother, the Marqués de Jústiz de Santa Ana, he also provided lumber for the Havana shipyard and engaged in shipbuilding himself. Contreras, who also possessed a *mayorazgo* in Havana Province, gained royal favor by contributing 108 *caballerías* of land in Matanzas to refugee families from Florida, uprooted when Spain ceded that colony to England. As an expression of royal gratitude for that and other acts of civic generosity, the crown conferred upon him the title of Conde de Gibacoa in 1764. He was married to his cousin, María Micaela Bárbara de Jústiz y Zayas-Bazán.[24]

The original leadership fashioned by O'Reilly for the three regiments endured long after he had departed. Aguiar and Casa Bayona commanded the infantry regiment until the death of the former in 1776 and the latter, who had become colonel, in 1780. Aróstegui and O'Farrill remained at their commands until 1779, and the Conde de Gibacoa led the Matanzas dragoons until his death in 1787.

To fill the company-grade offices in Havana, O'Reilly worked in conjunction with an advisory committee for each of the two regiments. The infantry committee consisted of Aguiar, Sargento Mayor José Bernet, civilians Luis Pacheco and Tomás López de Aguirre, and Alcalde Ordinario Laureano Chacón. Chacón, who held the grade of captain in the regular army, but without attachment to any unit, was known for his anti-British sentiments and for his sympathy with Aguiar's resistance.[25] He and Aguiar also served on the cavalry's junta, along with Aróstegui, O'Farrill, and Sargento Mayor Francisco Arnaiz, providing reliable political and social information to O'Reilly. The two juntas met with O'Reilly in his home, where they formally presented their recommendations to him. These he passed in turn to Ricla who accepted them without change.[26]

When he had completed the formation of the Havana militia, O'Reilly proudly reported to Spain that he had recruited the flower of Havana society into the city's two white regiments, a claim that can readily be substantiated. Most impressive was the correlation between the leaders in sugar production and the militia officer corps. In 1761 the nine largest sugar plantations measured by output were owned, in order of importance, by Pedro Beltrán de Santa Cruz (cousin and brother-in-

---

24. Service record, Colonel Gerónimo de Contreras, 1765, AGI, SD, leg. 2093; Nieto, *Dignidades nobiliarias,* 250–51; O'Reilly to Arriaga, Havana, Apr. 13, 1764, AGI, SD, leg. 2118. The Conde de Gibacoa uniformed 150 men of his regiment at his own expense. Petition, Conde de Gibacoa, Havana, Jan. 12, 1772, AGI, SD, 2129.

25. Thomas, *Cuba,* 45, 53.

26. O'Reilly to Arriaga, Havana, Dec. 6, 1763, AGI, SD, leg. 2078.

law of the first Conde de San Juan de Jaruco), Gonzalo de Herrera (the fourth Marqués de Villalta), Ignacio Peñalver, Juan Francisco Núñez del Castillo (the third Marqués de San Felipe y Santiago), Francisco Oseguera, Ignacio de Cárdenas (brother of the Marqués de Cárdenas de Montehermoso), Juan O'Farrill, José Ambrosio Zayas, and María Teresa Chacón.[27] In the militia, Juan de Santa Cruz, son of Pedro Beltrán de Santa Cruz, served as a sublieutenant in the infantry regiment; Miguel Antonio de Herrera, son of the Marqués de Villalta, was captain of cavalry; Ignacio Peñalver, the sugar magnate, was captain of infantry; the Marqués de San Felipe y Santiago was captain of cavalry; Nicolás Cárdenas, brother of Ignacio and the marqués, served as captain of cavalry; Juan O'Farrill, as discussed earlier, was lieutenant colonel of cavalry; the son of José Ambrosio Zayas, Joaquín, was a sublieutenant in the infantry; José Ambrosio's brother, Martín, was captain of cavalry; and the lieutenant colonel of infantry, the Conde de Casa Bayona, was the brother of María Teresa Chacón. Moreover, a number of other officers were related to the same families through their mothers.[28] Seen from a somewhat different angle, at least sixteen of the twenty-six men who served as colonels and lieutenant colonels of the three regiments or captains of the First Infantry Battalion or of the Cavalry Regiment, owned sugar plantations or were the sons of men who did.[29]

The close ties between the officer corps and the titled nobility were equally impressive. As already discussed, the Condes de Casa Bayona and Gibacoa and the Marqués de San Felipe y Santiago held offices in the militia as did the son of the Marqués de Villalta and the brother of the Marqués de Cárdenas de Montehermoso. Of the remaining six families that held titles in 1763 or would gain them during the 1760s, only the Marqués de la Real Proclamación, who was childless and who, in any event, was in disgrace for having collaborated too openly with the British, and the Marqués del Real Agrado, whose commitments were primarily tied to the royal tobacco monopoly, seem not to have enjoyed close familial connections to the officer corps. The Marqués de Macuriges had a brother-in-law in the militia, Captain Francisco Bruñón of infantry, as did the Marqués de Jústiz de Santa Ana, Captain Ambrosio de Jústiz of cavalry. The Conde de Buena Vista was the brother-in-law of Juan O'Farrill. Finally, the Conde de San Juan de

27. Thomas, *Cuba*, 32.

28. Francisco Xavier de Santa Cruz y Mallen, *Historia de familias cubanas* (Havana, 1940–50), I, 51, 328–33, III, 140–41, IV, 432–34, 444; service records, Volunteer Infantry Regiment of Havana and Volunteer Cavalry Regiment of Havana, 1765, AGI, SD, leg. 2093. The Havana Cavalry Regiment was so conscious of the lineage of its officers that the names of each man's parents were recorded on his service record, a most unusual practice.

29. For a census of sugar producers in 1759, see Marrero, *Cuba*, VII, 19.

Jaruco, who was childless, had a nephew in the cavalry, Francisco Xavier de Santa Cruz, whose son would eventually inherit the title.[30]

Other distinguished families also enjoyed representation in the officer corps. These included the Arangos, Armenteros, Barreras, Cocas, Duartes, Morales, Porliers, Torres, Zaldívars, and Zequeiras (see Appendix 2).[31] O'Reilly did not exaggerate when he claimed that the volunteer officer corps embraced the core of the Havana patriciate.

Havana's elite fully understood the political significance of the emerging arrangement between crown and creole. In a letter dated April 1764, the colonel and the lieutenant colonel of the Volunteer Infantry Regiment and the captains of its First Battalion thanked the crown for the distinction that it had bestowed upon them.

> The duty and the love of the vassals of such an [august] sovereign instilled in them dedication to daily training, without yielding to fatigue; [they were] fervently motivated by the wisdom of Your Majesty in condescending to make them ready instruments for the revival of this important *plaza* and the security of all the island, through the Conde de Ricla and Don Alejandro O'Reilly, whose splendid work has made all see the power of Your Majesty in America and that her [Cuba's] native sons are capable of the best military discipline and of all that furthers the well-being of the state.[32]

Exploiting their love for military rank, O'Reilly had thus drawn directly into the reform program a willing patriciate with the local political means to make the system work.

The method of selecting officers was not fully institutionalized until after O'Reilly's departure from the island, although his commitment to the elite was never questioned. In his draft of the militia regulation for Cuba, the subinspector general simply adopted the procedures defined in the 1734 ordinance for the provincial militia of Spain. This regulation provided that three nominations each for the offices of colonel and lieutenant colonel should come from the pertinent ayuntamiento, with the inspector making the selection, subject to review by the minister of defense. This procedure, however, had the unwelcome effect of limiting the latitude of the central authorities in the selection process. Consequently, when examining the Cuban regulation as drafted in 1765, the Consejo Supremo de Guerra replaced those articles that granted nominative power to the ayuntamientos with a provision placing that power in the hands of the subinspector

---

30. Santa Cruz, *Historia de familias,* II, 81—82, 228, III, 335—36; Nieto, *Dignidades nobiliarias,* 308—10, 411—14, 420—21, 495—99.

31. Service records, Volunteer Infantry Regiment of Havana and Volunteer Cavalry Regiment of Havana, 1765, AGI, SD, leg. 2093.

32. AGI, SD, leg. 2118. Also quoted in Allan J. Kuethe, "The Development of the Cuban Military as a Sociopolitical Elite," *HAHR* 61 (Nov. 1981), 700—701.

general himself. The consejo also strengthened the captain general's position by granting him the right to review the subinspector's list of nominees, three in number, and the authority to select one pending a final review by the Ministry of the Indies.[33] In subsequent years, not all Cuban militia inspectors were inclined to cooperate as fully with the captain general as had O'Reilly, and in all probability independent appointive authority at that level would have detracted from the office of captain general, weakening the fabric of royal administration on the island.

The practical political effect of the consejo's action was to introduce an important degree of centralization into the militia system. By placing the nominative power in the hands of the subinspector, the Cuban regulation as defined in the final, 1769 draft, presumably afforded the central administration a measure of gratitude from its appointees. At the same time, however, it incurred firsthand responsibility to accommodate deserving patricians with proper military honors. Had the ayuntamientos retained the right to nominate officers, individual units most likely would have come to reinforce the level of local autonomy enjoyed by the ayuntamientos and the local aristocracy that controlled them. Such a pattern developed in New Spain where the Castilian system prevailed and where chaotic consequences plagued the reformed militia throughout its history.[34] Under the Cuban system, the militia acted as a vehicle for royal penetration to the local level of community life, and the system of appointments served as a check on the political implications of arming the colonials. Although a spirit of cooperation generally prevailed, nominations were made by the subinspector, who was usually a strategically placed Spaniard conscious of larger imperial objectives, and confirmed by the captain general, who was also, obviously, conscious of the interests of the crown.

Refinements in the selection procedures would not, however, alter social patterns within the Cuban militia. Continuity was guaranteed by the mutual interests of the crown and the creole aristocracy and by the provision in the Cuban regulation that colonels be selected from "the most distinguished subjects, who have illustrious qualities, men of spirit, honor, application, and selflessness, the behavior and sufficient wealth to sustain the dignity of the position."[35] Moreover, O'Reilly established the Noble Company of Cadets to ensure an adequate supply of young men with the proper social standing to replenish the officer corps. This unit attracted youngsters of the same status as

33. *Reglamento para las milicias,* 1765, ch. 6, arts. 2–8; *Reglamento para las milicias,* 1769, ch. 6, arts. 2–8; *Ordenanza de milicias provinciales de España* (Madrid, 1734).

34. Christon I. Archer, "Bourbon Finances and Military Policy in New Spain, 1759–1812," *The Americas* 37 (Jan. 1981), 315–50.

35. *Reglamento para las milicias,* 1769, ch. 6, art. 2.

those who commanded the Havana militia.[36] On through the 1770s, therefore, men with names such as Arango, Arredondo, Basabe, Calvo de la Puerta, Cárdenas, Castillo, Coca, Duarte, Herrera, Jústiz, Montalvo, Santa Cruz, Sotolongo, Zaldívar, and Zayas would continue to dominate company commands (see Appendix 2).[37]

Below Havana's narrow elite stood the vast majority of creole society. This diverse group included small farmers from the environs of the city, who raised tobacco or produced foodstuffs. Others worked for the tobacco monopoly or in the flourishing shipbuilding industry. Many earned their livings as retail merchants or as artisans.[38] These filled the ranks of the militia as enlisted men.

The Second Battalion of the Infantry Regiment, which was based in Havana's satellite across the bay, Guanabacoa, and the Matanzas Dragoons, lacked the kind of social distinction that the units based directly in Havana enjoyed. As a municipality, Guanabacoa could claim little prestige, and the dynamic prosperity that would engulf Matanzas at the turn of the century was only beginning. The service records for the officers of Guanabacoa simply classified them as "whites." In later years these same men would be variously described as "laborers" or as "undistinguished" (sin decir).[39] In the foot companies of the Matanzas Dragoons, only one officer managed to rate higher than "good," and although the mounted captains—all from Havana—were classified as "distinguished," the lesser officers usually also rated a mere "good."[40] This pattern would change only when those districts became more directly affected by the sugar revolution, whereupon the social beneficiaries of that transformation would find their way into the militia.

Important social distinctions also existed within the officer corps of the Havana Cavalry Regiment. In selecting its second lieutenants and ensigns, O'Reilly and his junta chose men who lived on farms and haciendas in the countryside, who could help support the mounts that the units required. Although generally "distinguished," they did not enjoy the same kind of status as the captains who were, in O'Reilly's words, "all from the first families."[41]

As O'Reilly extended the military reform to the east during early 1764, he perpetuated the system he had structured for Havana. The elites were more vaguely defined in the interior than in the capital, for

36. File on establishment of the Noble Company of Cadets, 1764, AGI, SD, leg. 2118.
37. Service records, 1771, 1775, 1781, all in AGI, SD, legs. 2129, 2095, 2098.
38. Marrero, *Cuba*, VIII, 148–53.
39. Service records, Volunteer Infantry Regiment of Havana, 1765, 1768, 1775, AGI, SD, legs. 2093, 2095.
40. Service records, Volunteer Dragoon Regiment of Matanzas, 1765, AGI, SD, leg. 2093.
41. O'Reilly to Arriaga, Havana, Dec. 6, 1763, AGI, SD, leg. 2078.

the economies of those districts were less developed; but the inspector general attempted to marry the volunteer officer corps to established families as he had in Havana, while taking into account previous military service and, whenever possible, combat experience. He also personally consulted with the colonists as part of the *visita* for which he was responsible.

The creoles of Cuatro Villas, Puerto Príncipe, and Santiago-Bayamo had also diversified their investments in the face of depressed tobacco and meat prices, shifting to sugar, but far more tentatively than in Havana. Given the difficulty of marketing their products through Havana, the people of the south-central and eastern zones of the island had developed a healthy if illegal trade with Saint Domingue and Jamaica and with other Spanish colonies. They also sustained a legal trade with Portobelo and Cartagena de Indias. The ability to market salted beef, hides, and oxen in the neighboring sugar islands sustained ranching as their primary concern.[42]

O'Reilly found no titled nobility to draw upon to command the eastern battalions, although the service records of the men he chose in Puerto Príncipe and Santiago described them as "nobles," a term commonly used in the colonies to affirm high social status although no title was involved. In Cuatro Villas, the Spanish *sargento mayor* uniformly described the officers as "soldiers of fortune," which could be taken to mean nearly anything. Although the officer list included a López Silvero of Sancti Spríritus and a Sánchez of Trinidad, the present state of the local elite obviously did not impress him. The company grade officers came from families with holdings in cattle and sugar. Nearly all had served in the previous militia and had gone to Havana during the siege, seeing at least some action. Subsequently, these same men would be described as "sons of laborers," presumably small farmers, and as of "known" social status. When Juan Pablo López Silvero became colonel in 1769, he rated a "distinguished" social reputation, but interestingly, his successor, Pedro Antonio Sánchez, was merely a "laborer" until he became colonel when he suddenly enjoyed "known" social quality. In the absence of a creole magnate with illustrious credentials, O'Reilly named as first colonel a Spaniard, Francisco José Gutiérrez y Rivera, who had had experience during his youth in the Spanish regular army, had served in the old militia of Puerto Príncipe, fighting the English at Guantánamo in 1741, and had later acted as deputy governor in Sancti Spíritus.[43]

42. Marrero, *Cuba*, VII, 168–88; Moreno Fraginals, *El ingenio*, I, 18; McNeill, "Theory and Practice," 244–45, 287–89.

43. Service records, Volunteer Infantry Battalion of Puerto Príncipe, 1765, Volunteer Infantry Battalion of Cuatro Villas, 1765, 1777, 1783, Volunteer Infantry Battalion of Santiago-Bayamo, 1771, all in AGI, SD, legs. 2093, 2096, 2099, 2120, 2129.

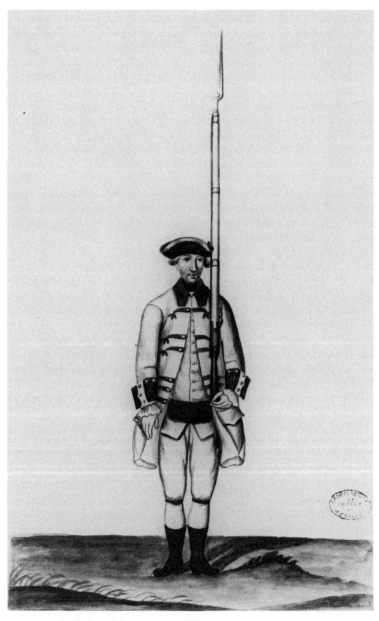

Volunteer, White Infantry Battalion of Santiago-Bayamo. Courtesy of Archivo General de Indias.

In Puerto Príncipe, the second largest city of Cuba, O'Reilly named Diego Antonio de Bringas colonel. Bringas' father, Carlos, had diversified his investments by adding a sugar plantation to his ranches. So too had the heads of the families of many other officers, although their strongest commitment was to cattle. The company officers included representatives of such prominent clans as the Agüero, Agramonte, Boza, Caballero, Castillo, Escobar, Miranda, Quesada, Socarrás, Varona, Velasco, and Zayas.[44] As in Cuatro Villas, most of the new officers had gone to Havana in 1762.

The officers of the Santiago-Bayamo battalion included small hog and cattle farmers from Holguín but also established elites such as the Cisneros, Hernández, Ferrer, and Mustelier families of Santiago. At least some of the latter had added sugar plantations to their hogs and cattle, as had the Chavarría and Vásquez families of Bayamo.[45] Lorenzo Vásquez Piña of Bayamo, who had fought at Guantánamo, commanded the unit. Although many had been mobilized for local defense in 1762, few of these officers had ever experienced combat.

Upon returning to Havana, O'Reilly with his accustomed thoroughness prepared a comprehensive report on the findings of his *visita* and sent copies of it to both Esquilache and Arriaga. Although the report touched a wide variety of topics, O'Reilly's recommendations focused upon three problems. The island, he observed, was underdeveloped economically and unproductive of royal revenues because of a lack of effective government, inadequate outlets for legal commerce, and a labor shortage. Proper changes in these areas would do much to benefit Spain and to finance the defenses of the island.[46]

In the area of royal administration, he found a widespread evasion of existing laws and an unhealthy institutional structure whereby the sole avenue of appeal beyond the jurisdiction of the ayuntamientos was the Audiencia of Santo Domingo. In practice, communication difficulties with Hispaniola made Cuba's municipal tribunals practically autonomous and went far to explain a common disregard for royal regulations in favor of local vested interests. To remedy the problem, O'Reilly urged the establishment of a separate appellate court in Cuba to streamline the administration of justice.

Regarding trade, he argued that restrictions on legal outlets had artificially depressed the Cuban economy and had turned much of its

44. Early investment patterns of these families can be found in Marrero, *Cuba*, VI, 206–9, for cattle, and VII, 9, for sugar. The genealogy of the López Silvero and Sánchez families of Cuatro Villas and many of the officers of Puerto Príncipe can be found in Santa Cruz, *Historia de familias*.

45. Marrero, *Cuba*, VI, 214, VII, 6.

46. O'Reilly's report to Arriaga can be found in AGI, SD, leg. 1509, and to Esquilache in AGS, hac, leg. 2342.

commerce over to foreigners. The Royal Havana Company's monopolistic rights had stifled trade between Spain and Cuba by overpricing Spanish goods and failing to provide an adequate market for Cuban products. This problem was aggravated because access to Spain was confined to the port of Havana, which placed interior produce at a perilous disadvantage. Moreover, according to O'Reilly, the taxes on commerce were prohibitively high. To strengthen Spain's commercial ties with Cuba and to stimulate the economic growth of the island, the subinspector general proposed that commercial outlets to Spain be broadened and that Trinidad, Puerto Príncipe, Bayamo, and Santiago be opened directly to the peninsular trade. Surely more than mere coincidence dictated that O'Reilly's selection of recommended ports were those supporting militia units; commercial concessions would obviously make the expense and burden of maintaining the volunteer battalions much more agreeable. Finally, taxes on commerce should be reduced substantially. An increased flow of legal commerce, although taxed at a lower rate, would stimulate production, discourage smuggling, and in the end, increase revenues.

As evidence that more flexible policies would work, O'Reilly alluded to the spectacular trade the British had enjoyed during the occupation, claiming that nearly a thousand merchant ships had called at Havana. The assertion was absurd. It is true that the British trade with Havana had been brisk and that there was a backlog of sugar lying on the docks of Havana in 1762, but the volume that a thousand ships could have carried was well beyond Cuba's output over many years. Nor was Cuban production elastic enough to have responded to an open market within a mere eleven months.[47] As observed earlier, the Irishman was not above exaggeration, especially when a practical purpose was to be served. He undoubtedly believed that additional revenues could in fact be generated to support his army through a liberalization of commercial policies.

Finally, O'Reilly believed that a shortage of slave labor was impeding the development of the Cuban economy. To remedy the problem, he proposed that the crown both remove all duties on the importation of slaves and issue contracts directly to foreigners as opportunity dictated. O'Reilly saw no reason to reserve this commerce to Spaniards, since Spain had no factories on the African coast; Spanish dealers simply amounted to useless middlemen who added to costs. The subinspector general predicted that adequate labor supplies and freer trade policies would lead to important growth in the sugar industry, in

47. A more reasonable figure of ninety-six merchantmen has been advanced by historian Allen Christelow using French sources. "Contraband Trade between Jamaica and the Spanish Main, and the Free Port Act of 1766," *HAHR* 23 (May 1942), 314.

tobacco, and possibly in other products such as coffee, indigo, and cotton.

Viewed politically, O'Reilly's proposals on commerce and labor promised major concessions to the Cuban patriciate. A stimulated economy and broadened trade privileges would, at least in the first instance, benefit men of property and influence, and would, in a practical sense, serve as compensation for tougher taxation. That the establishment of an appellate court, presumably an audiencia, would benefit the aristocracy seems less certain. The administration of justice would be improved; but such an institution would subject the creole-dominated ayuntamiento to closer scrutiny, hence undercutting the high degree of local autonomy that the existing arrangement entailed. O'Reilly's package, then, while envisioning broad concessions to the colonists, did not necessarily represent an unmixed blessing for the Cuban creoles. On the whole, nevertheless, O'Reilly's report could only have pleased and reassured colonial interests, especially planters. Ricla added his name to the report, thus officially endorsing the recommendation for liberalizing commercial policy in Cuba.[48]

The arrival of the April 25 order and Ricla's promulgation of the regulations implementing the new tax schedule in late September, however, quickly soured the buoyant atmosphere in Havana. The Havana patriciate had expected to receive commercial concessions in conjunction with revenue reform, but the order said nothing about trade. Because the original 2 percent *alcabala* had only just begun to be collected, the new levy in effect resembled an 8 percent increase of the tax on sugar, 4 percent on the first sale and another 4 percent at the time of export.[49] Moreover, planters remained responsible for a 5 percent harvest tax that they had accepted in 1758 in lieu of the *almojarifazgo*, and now they were also to be taxed on income from their real property. Finally, the blow assuredly caught the *habaneros* by surprise. Having had no real experience with Esquilache's tempo of government, they had undoubtedly expected the matter to drag on for years when it was referred to Madrid. Havana's reaction to the new taxes would provide Ricla with his most difficult challenge as captain general.

The ayuntamiento met repeatedly during early fall to ponder the future of the colony.[50] In an attempt to defuse this explosive situation, both Ricla and O'Reilly took a number of patricians into their personal confidence, explaining the need for the immediate changes in the tax structure while assuring them that commercial reform would come in good time. That his name and O'Reilly's were on record as favoring a

48. File on *visita general* of the Island of Cuba, 1764, AGI, SD, leg. 1509.
49. A copy of the *alcabala* regulation can be found in AGS, Hac, leg. 2342.
50. Ricla to Arriaga, Havana, Nov. 27, 1764, AGI, SD, leg. 1509.

reorganization of the trade laws undoubtedly strengthened Ricla's role as conciliator, as did the open, consultative character of his administration. The political dialogue reached a climax when the ayuntamiento requested that the captain general meet with an assembly of *habanero* patricians to explain the crown's position. Ricla instead agreed to send José Antonio Gelabert, the author of the pivotal report on taxation, to provide additional information, thus once again keeping a prudent distance from formal assemblies while remaining responsive to the political concerns of his colony.[51]

The events that followed were truly astonishing. Forty-seven patricians, including the city officials, met with Gelabert on October 24. The chief auditor assured them that commercial reform was coming but would require time. O'Reilly's report had only recently reached court. Then, to document the legitimacy of the new taxation, he opened the account books of the captaincy general. The crown's case was obvious, and the nature of Gelabert's—and hence Ricla's—political gesture flattering. The financial dilemma of the royal treasury, moreover, must have made a special impression on the twelve militia colonels and captains, the six fathers, the six brothers or brothers-in-law, and the other relatives of officers in attendance.[52] The patricians' suspicion and anger subsided somewhat, although this assembly, unlike that of the previous year, resolved to make its expectations explicit.

The gathering selected six representatives, whom it commissioned to draft a petition on commerce to the crown with the assistance of the city's solicitor and the two alcaldes. This committee completed its task on October 26, in just two days' time, and delivered the document to Ricla on the following day, the rapidity of its work suggesting that the *habaneros* had already thought out their position well in advance. The petition, although properly polite, contained strong implicit criticism of existing policy and envisioned a sweeping reorganization of the laws regulating Cuban commerce, ostensibly, of course, to help the island generate the means to bear heavier taxation.[53]

The petition declared:

1. All the ports of Spain should be opened to the island for Cuban and Spanish ships alike.

2. Cuban products should be relieved of import taxes in both Spanish and American ports, and export levies on Spanish products destined for Cuba should be lightened.

51. For the events leading up to and including this meeting, see Ricla to Arriaga, Havana, Oct. 30, 1764, AGI, SD, leg. 2188, or Ricla to Esquilache, Havana, Oct. 30, 1764, AGS, Hac, leg. 1056.

52. A list of the participants, detailing their attributes, can be found in Kuethe and Inglis, "Absolutism and Enlightened Reform," table 2.

53. Petition of Havana, Oct. 26, 1764, AGI, SD, leg. 2188, and AGS, Hac, leg. 1056.

3. No monopoly, either by company or individual, should be granted power over Cuba (except, of course, the royal tobacco monopoly). The commerce of the island should be open to all provinces of Spain and America, with Cubans free to conduct the trade.

4. Cubans should be permitted to procure slaves freely, from foreign sources as well as Spanish, and slave ships should be allowed to carry produce from the island.

5. Louisiana and Yucatán, at the very least, should be opened to Cuban aguardiente.

6. Cubans should be allowed to market surplus tobacco in Cartagena de Indias or elsewhere in the American colonies.

7. The Spanish market for Cuban sugar should be protected from foreign competition.

8. The recruitment of artisans and skilled laborers, especially for the working of hides, should be fostered.

9. A permanent Cuban deputy should be admitted to court.

These propositions closely resembled O'Reilly's conclusions on the subjects of trade and taxation, but the Cubans added a number of original angles. Perhaps the most important was their concern about the Duc de Choiseul's persistent attempts to exploit the Family Compact to gain favored entrance into Cádiz for French West Indian sugar. This prospect threatened to flood the Spanish market, undercutting Cuban development.[54] Regarding the aguardiente trade, the petitioners showed an awareness of His Majesty's special interests in selling Spanish liquor in America, but they evidently hoped to open a wedge for Cuban products by requesting access to two nearby but relatively unimportant colonies. Louisiana would have offered the opportunity to penetrate the North American Indian trade and might also have provided the means to reach the English colonies more effectively. Finally, the desire to position an official full-time lobbyist at court showed Cuba's realistic assessment of the political process in Madrid. Ricla promptly sent the petition to Spain with a strong endorsement, explaining that crucial political, military, and financial advantages would result from royal approval.[55]

On the same date that it delivered its petition on commerce to Ricla, the ayuntamiento completed a second memorial denouncing the new tax structure. Evidently fearing that this step might cool the captain general's good will and support for commercial reform, the city magistrates sent the letter directly to its part-time agent at court, Antonio Ventura Montenegro, who in turn advanced it to the Ministry of Finance along with his own remarks. After predicting economic ruin for

54. D'Ossun to Choiseul, Madrid, Mar. 8, Apr. 2, 1764, AAE, CE, vol. 540, fols. 182–86, 225–26.

55. Ricla to Arriaga, Havana, Oct. 30, 1764, AGI, SD, leg. 2188; Ricla to Esquilache, Havana, Oct. 30, 1764, AGS, Hac, leg. 1056.

the island and reminding Esquilache that Havana's finest were serving
in the militia, not to mention funding their own uniforms, and after
vaguely alluding to possible disorder among disreputable elements
should the colony's grievances go unredressed, the ayuntamiento skill-
fully advanced a counter offer on taxation. An *alcabala* of 6 percent
would be acceptable if levied solely on the first sale and if accompanied
by abolition of the 3 percent levy on property income. In a postscript,
the magistrates also asked Ventura to assist Sebastián Peñalver and the
Marqués de la Real Proclamación, who had been called to court to
answer the charges Ricla had brought against them for collaborating
with the British. This message accompanied the Havana petition to the
desk of Esquilache![56] Havana thus made its terms known on a broad
front, driving a hard bargain with serious political overtones.

During this same time in Europe, Esquilache acted to tighten the
financial management of the royal treasury in Havana. O'Reilly had
been appalled by the chaotic condition in which he found the management of military expenditures, and by letter of December 8, 1763, he
had urged Esquilache to appoint a special official to assume that responsibility. To this end, as well as to improve the collection of revenues, Esquilache devised a plan to establish an *intendente de guerra*
(intendant of the army) in Havana, based on the system that Philip V
had introduced into Spain but with adjustments to Cuban realities.[57]
The king approved Esquilache's plan without reservation in September. The Italian then sent the legislation to Arriaga, who had been cool
toward the whole idea, so that it might go out properly through the
Ministry of the Indies.[58] Arriaga complied but in a private letter warned
Ricla that he would find certain "excusable" provisions in the plan,
which, he complained, had been entirely Esquilache's doing.[59]

The introduction of the intendant system into Cuba represented the
administrative follow-through on revenue reform and amounted to a

56. Ayuntamiento of Havana to Antonio Ventura Montenegro, Havana, Oct. 27, 1764,
Ventura to the Ministry of Finance, Madrid, n.d., both in AGS, Hac, leg. 1056.

57. Instructions for the establishment of an intendancy in Cuba, San Ildefonso, Oct. 13,
1764, in Esquilache to Arriaga, San Ildefonso, Oct. 13, 1764, AGS, Hac, leg. 2342. The final
version of this document, dated Oct. 31, 1764, has been published in translation in William
Whatley Pierson, Jr., "Institutional History of the *Intendencia*," *James Sprunt Historical
Series* 19 (Chapel Hill, 1927), 113–33. The Cuban intendancy, unlike its Spanish counter-
part, did not include judicial or police powers. Ibid., 84.

58. Arriaga to Esquilache, San Ildefonso, Sept. 24, 1764, Esquilache to Arriaga, San
Ildefonso, Oct. 13, 1764, both in AGS, Hac, leg. 2342. In his work on the Cuban intendancy,
Pierson mistakenly credits Arriaga with founding the institution, because he signed the
final papers, but he also cites contradictory evidence, quoting Ricla's statement that
Esquilache had "perfected the thoughts and chosen the means." Pierson, "The Establish-
ment," 82.

59. Arriaga to Ricla, San Lorenzo, Nov. 16, 1764, AGI, IG, leg. 1630.

tougher approach toward the administration of finance. Not only was the intendant especially charged with increasing royal income and eliminating fraud and contraband, he was also responsible for managing the vast range of military expenditures, including salaries, supplies, transportation, hospitals, and fortification construction. The intendant ranked below the captain general in the administrative hierarchy, but he enjoyed near autonomy over the treasury except in emergencies. During the history of the intendancy in Cuba, jurisdictional and personal conflicts between the intendant and the captain general would be commonplace, but overall, the institution brought order to the financial administration of the island.[60] The first intendant, Miguel de Altarriba, who was selected by Esquilache, assumed his duties in early 1765.[61]

Why Esquilache did not pursue O'Reilly's plea for the establishment of an appellate court in Havana is unclear. Cuba would not acquire an audiencia until 1797 and then only because the loss of Santo Domingo to the French created the need for a new location for its tribunal. Prudence may well have been an important factor. Given the difficulties entailed in revenue reform, the simultaneous establishment of a high court might have carried the risk of placing too great a stress on the colony and alienating the very group required to lead the disciplined militia. Moreover, audiencias were expensive.

The capstone of Esquilache's program for Cuba, commercial reform, finally came in late 1765, but only after tough infighting at court. The special commission on imperial commerce, which had been organized in the summer of 1764 after the arrival of O'Reilly's statement, issued its findings in February 1765. The report touched a wide variety of issues, but its most important recommendations urged that more Spanish ports be opened to the American trade and that levies based on weight and volume be rationalized to ad valorem taxes. Of immediate interest to Cuba, it also advocated the lowering of taxes on the slave trade.[62] The Junta de Ministros deliberated these issues at length as they applied to Cuba. The conservative Arriaga opposed nearly every proposed innovation while Esquilache, supported by Grimaldi, pushed forcefully for fundamental changes. The minister of the Indies argued that Cubans were already privileged to receive a huge *situado*, that they therefore deserved no further indulgence, and that they would most certainly exploit any loosening of trade regulations to increase smuggling. Esquilache, who was so indulgent of opinion in Havana, denied the frustrated Consulado of Cádiz entry to the deliberations, showing a

60. Pierson, "The Establishment," 87–97, 108.
61. Esquilache to Arriaga, San Ildefonso, Oct. 23, 1764, AGS, Hac, leg. 2342.
62. This report can be found in AHN, Estado, leg. 2314.

perfect willingness to undercut entrenched privileges where the interests of security and the royal purse intervened. As indicated earlier, the Italian was determined to exploit the crisis mentality arising from defeat in war, and the needs of Havana in particular, to lay the foundation for a reordering of the imperial trade laws. He now advanced this cause with an insensitivity to vested Spanish interests that bordered on ruthlessness.[63] The debate reached a conclusion with a royal cedula of October 16 accompanied by a royal order of the same date, which together followed Esquilache's final written opinion almost word-for-word.

Between them, the October decrees provided Cuba with much, if not all, that it wanted. The cedula opened the island's trade to eight additional Spanish ports and, in America, to Santo Domingo, Puerto Rico, Trinidad, and Margarita, all of which, in a coattail effect, received the same privileges as Cuba. Also of major importance, Cubans could seek markets with their own ships. Spanish export duties were rationalized to a simple 6 percent on national products and 7 percent on foreign goods in a reorganization that also eliminated or reduced many hidden costs, such as inspection fees and paperwork.

The royal order amounted to an acceptance of the Havana offer on taxation. The Cuban *alcabala* was raised to 6 percent, collectible only in the first instance, and it also replaced the harvest tax. For Cuban sugar, this measure represented a consolidation and reduction of existing levies. Moreover, in another concession to Cuban agriculture, the tax on incomes from property, established by the order of March 25, was dropped. Finally, import taxes on slaves were replaced with a head tax to be collected annually on those entering under the new regulations.[64] The October laws thus provided sugar producers a broader market, reduced export duties, and lowered import costs for bulky or heavy commodities. Moreover, the exemption from Spanish import duties that Cuban sugar had received in 1740 was retained in the 1764–1765 tax reforms.

Esquilache did not implement the plea that both O'Reilly and the Havana committee had made for a free slave trade because a long-term contract with Spanish merchants had already been negotiated. Further, the new method of taxing slave holdings would have no long-range effect. So great was the confusion and the muddle of paperwork under the new regulation that by mutual consent the crown and the

63. For a detailed account of this infighting, see Kuethe and Inglis, "Absolutism and Enlightened Reform."

64. Royal cedula and instruction, and royal order, San Lorenzo, Oct. 16, 1765, AGI, SD, leg. 2188. The royal cedula and instruction have also been published in Ricardo Levene, ed., *Documentos para la historia argentina* (Buenos Aires, 1915), V, 197–98. The royal order can also be found in AGS, Hac, leg. 2342.

slaveholders of Cuba returned to the old system in 1767.[65] In practice, however, the authorities would continue to tolerate slave smuggling despite much tougher policies in other areas. Moreover, as a wartime measure, Spanish nationals in most colonies, including Cuba, were granted permission in 1780 to import slaves from the French colonies, provided that the trade be conducted in Spanish bottoms, a concession that lasted six years.[66]

The October orders said nothing about the other ports of Cuba, the request for lower Spanish import duties on products other than sugar, or possible aguardiente commerce with Louisiana and Yucatán. Looking ahead, however, the historic 1778 regulation of "free trade" would qualify both Santiago and Trinidad, bringing into effect one more of O'Reilly's recommendations. An earlier decree, dated March 23, 1768, opened the Louisiana trade to Cuba, aguardiente included, and another of April 23, 1774, reduced the levy on leather.[67] Perhaps most important of all, the government of Charles III, in a move calculated to strengthen the economic vitality of the empire, denied French sugar privileged access to the Cádiz market, a step that obviously benefited Cuban producers.[68]

That these policies helped Spain recapture a larger share of the Cuban trade and worked to sustain and, most certainly, stimulate the growth of the sugar industry seems indisputable. Annually, output grew by well over 4 percent, tripling by 1791. To attribute the steady rise of sugar production solely to the commercial reorganization of 1765 would, of course, distort reality, for other forces were also at work. Output in most of the rival sugar colonies had begun to level off or decline during this period while European demand continued to grow, pushing up prices. The market was also expanding in the thirteen English colonies to the north. When the revolution there disrupted access to the customary sources of supply in the English Caribbean, Cuba's opportunity grew, especially after that trade was legalized during the period of the Spanish intervention.[69] A large portion of Cuban production went to Spain, nevertheless. Mirroring the growth of legal trade, Cuban generated revenues, led by the *alcabala*, surged to some

65. File on slave taxation, 1767–68, AGI, SD, leg. 2515.

66. James Ferguson King, "Evolution of the Free Slave Trade Principle in Spanish Colonial Administration," *HAHR* 22 (Feb. 1942), 36–41.

67. *Reglamento para el comercio libre de España a Indias* . . . (Madrid, 1778). The Mar. 23, 1768, and the Apr. 23, 1774, orders have been reproduced in Levene, *Documentos,* V, 219–30, 354–59. Cubans generally traded aguardiente for wood. See, for example, "Relación de los barcos," New Orleans, 1773–76, AGI, PC, leg. 112.

68. Allen Christelow, "French Interest in the Spanish Empire during the Ministry of the Duc de Choiseul, 1759–1771," *HAHR* 21 (Nov. 1941), 518–37.

69. Moreno Fraginals, *El ingenio,* 40–46.

375,000 pesos annually during the 1760s, 562,500 during the 1770s, and just under 987,500 in the 1780s.[70]

The most important achievement of the accords of 1763—1765 was the political understanding that emerged between the Cuban patriciate and the crown. This understanding both minimized the political risks that arming the colonials had implied and laid the foundation for fruitful cooperation in the years ahead. A process of mutual co-optation had occurred. The crown, eager to strengthen its position on the rim of its empire, indulged Cuban patricians with special commercial privileges, more titles of Castile, new opportunities for military rank, and a *fuero* for the militia more ample than the privilege enjoyed by the regular army. For their part, the Cubans understood their advantage perfectly and realized that, if approached properly, the political system at court could continue to work to their benefit.

Yet another dimension of the emerging political equation was the black and mulatto militia. The structure of colonial society did not permit the leaders of the *pardo* and *moreno* battalions a voice in the consultation that transpired between the crown and the elite. The officers of these units, nevertheless, also stood to benefit from the economic growth that the reforms promised. To a man, they were artisans, most of them carpenters, tailors, masons, cobblers, or silversmiths. [71] Some, perhaps many, were wealthy. During the War of the American Revolution, for example, José Francisco Sánchez, a lieutenant in the *pardo* battalion, and Manuel Blanco, a *moreno*, won authorization to raise and uniform, at their own expense, hundred-man companies of artillerymen, receiving in return the rank of captain, the right to name the subordinate officers, and the *fuero militar* for their units.[72]

On another level, the privileges associated with militia service offered advantages. In hierarchical colonial society, people with all or partial Negro parentage in effect constituted a separate estate. Infamous by birthright, they lived under what amounted to a separate set of laws designed to curtail their presumed vicious and irresponsible instincts. Blacks and mulattoes were forbidden to bear arms, suffered limitations on their manner of dress, and were denied entrance to honorable professions. For equal crimes, they suffered harsher punishments than whites.[73] The stigma placed on men of color in the stratified

70. Kuethe and Inglis, "Absolutism and Enlightened Reform."

71. Service records, Pardo and Moreno Volunteer Infantry Battalions of Havana, 1765, AGI, SD, leg. 2093.

72. Captain General Diego José de Navarro to José de Gálvez, Havana, Dec. 16, 1779, royal order, Aranjuez, Apr. 16, 1780, both in AGI, SD, leg. 2082.

73. "Bando sobre prohibir el uso de armas y capas a Negros y Mulatos," by Governor Navarro, Havana, May 4, 1779, in *Boletín del Archivo Nacional 28* (Jan.–Dec. 1929), 103–4; Irene Diggs, "Color in Colonial Spanish America," *Journal of Negro History* 38 (Oct. 1953), 403, 418; Edgar F. Love, "Negro Resistance to Spanish Rule in Colonial Mexico," *Journal of Negro History* 52 (Apr. 1967), 90–92.

society penetrated the military corporation as well. The heads of the *pardo* and *moreno* battalions held the title of commander, not colonel, and enjoyed no real authority over the segregated white cadre that advised their units. They stood hat-in-hand in the presence of white instructors, a practice established early and clearly intended to remind them of their lowly estate.[74] *Pardos* and *morenos* in the militia, nevertheless, enjoyed the same military privileges as whites, including the active *fuero* for officers and sergeants. The *fuero militar* removed volunteers from the jurisdiction of ordinary justice as represented by the ayuntamientos and placed them under Spanish military authorities who were conscious of their contribution to the island's defense and, within the prescribed social limits, eager to promote morale. Moreover, their *preeminencias* relieved them from certain types of municipal labor levies, taxes, and licenses. Within their estate, these privileges conveyed prestige and probably represented meaningful material gain, for which the men involved were grateful. The officers of the Pardo Battalion of Havana thanked His Majesty for the honor and privileges that their appointments had conferred. "The Pardo Battalion of Havana humbly informs Your Majesty of its intense desire to sacrifice itself for the honor of [bearing] arms and to show its readiness to this effect with an incessant dedication to discipline . . . and [readiness to sacrifice itself] for the infinite liberties [*liberalidades*] that Your Majesty has deigned to bestow on this unit, although humble by birthright."[75]

The opportunity for advancement within the larger society through military service was, however, virtually nonexistent. In localities such as coastal New Granada, where integrated units of "all colors" existed or where men might purchase the captaincy of a white company by uniforming it, mulattoes occasionally gained acceptance as whites through good service.[76] Similar examples did not appear in Cuba, where the social structure was more rigid. The best a black officer might expect in return for high achievement was the award of a gold or silver effigy of His Majesty, a practice established in 1764 upon O'Reilly's recommendation.[77] Yet the incentives provided were sufficient. Captain General Antonio María de Bucareli, who later did much to bring the militia to a proper level of discipline, was surprised at how quickly the *morenos*, "a coarse and dull-witted people" (*gente ruda y torpe*),

74. *Reglamento para las milicias,* 1769, ch. 1, art. 13, ch. 2, arts. 13, 22, 34, ch. 4, art. 13; file on the militia commander versus the lieutenant governor of Panama, 1779, Archivo Nacional de Colombia, Milicia y Marina, vol. 40, fols. 669–87.

75. Officers of the Pardo Infantry Battalion of Havana to His Majesty, Havana, Dec. 7, 1763, AGI, SD, leg. 2118.

76. Kuethe *Military Reform and Society,* 30–31, 61–62, 161–62, 179–80.

77. Pedro Deschamps Chapeauk, *Los batallones de pardos y morenos libres* (Havana, 1976), 47–49. A steady flow of petitions for these honors came from the colored officer corps, and a fair number received satisfaction.

learned the military skills.[78] Cuba's *pardo* and *moreno* battalions consistently received high marks for their proficiency, and as will be seen later, they became a source of fear among Havana's elite.

By the time the October decrees were published in Havana, both Ricla and O'Reilly had departed the island. Charles permitted Ricla to return to the politics of court, where he became minister of war in 1772. O'Reilly sought authorization to extend his system to Mexico, but the crown had already commissioned Juan de Villalba y Angulo to that colony. Instead, O'Reilly was ordered in 1765 to Puerto Rico, where he continued the military reform.[79] He returned briefly to Spain before Charles sent him to establish effective control in Louisiana (see Chapter 4). Finally, in 1770 the king named him inspector general of the army of America, a new position created at that time for the supervision and coordination of colonial military planning.[80] Ricla and O'Reilly had spent barely two years in Cuba, but their reforms had laid the foundation for a lasting transformation of the island.

The smooth course of the colonial reorganization in Cuba contrasted sharply with the history of the reform in many parts of the empire during this period. José de Gálvez, visitor general of New Spain from 1765 to 1771, met stubborn resistance, including occasional violence, in his attempt to advance financial reforms to support the army Villalba was reorganizing. Outright rebellion confronted revenue reform in Quito, the Popayán Valley, and the Chocó of New Granada; in Guatemala; and in Santiago de Chile.[81] The reasons for this contrast to the Cuban experience were as complex as the distinct personalities of the several colonies of the American empire, but two general explanations seem evident. Cubans, who were situated on the exposed rim of the empire and had experienced conquest, plainly viewed the colonial reorganization from a much different perspective than did colonists who lived in the mainland interior and who feared the British less than they resented the outflow of monies to coastal defense complexes and the tighter administration that accompanied it. Leadership was probably a second factor. French authorities were highly skeptical that Esquilache's plan for a reorganization of the American colonies would

78. Captain General Antonio María de Bucareli to Arriaga, Havana, Jan. 4, 1768, AGI, SD, leg. 2123.

79. Torres Ramírez, *Alejandro O'Reilly*, 49, 55–94.

80. File on establishment of the inspector generalship of the Army of America, 1770, AGI, IG, leg. 1885.

81. Herbert Ingram Priestley, *José de Gálvez: Visitor-General of New Spain (1765–1771)* (Berkeley, 1916), 140–42, 150, 158, 162, 175–209; Miles Wortman, "Bourbon Reforms in Central America, 1750–1786," *The Americas* 32 (Oct. 1975), 227–29; William Frederick Sharp, *Slavery on the Spanish Frontier: The Colombian Chocó, 1680–1810* (Norman, 1976), 160–69, Guillermo Céspedes del Castillo, "La renta del tabaco en el Virreinato del Perú," *Revista histórica* 21 (1954), 149; Kuethe, *Military Reform and Society*, 49–51.

succeed, because they doubted that Spain possessed enough competent officials to make it work.[82] The events of 1765–1766 on the two American continents strongly suggest that they were correct.

The fall of the Marqués de Esquilache in March 1766, brought the early reform period of Charles III to a close. Arising from complex causes, including his insensitivity to Spanish customs and his aggressive revenue policies, riots in Madrid and the provinces forced a most reluctant Charles to dismiss and exile the controversial minister. Esquilache initially took up residence in Messina, Italy, and Charles subsequently named him ambassador to Venice, all the while thoughtfully supplying him with Cuban tobacco.[83] To replace him, Juan Gregorio Muniain became minister of war and Miguel de Múzquiz, minister of finance, but neither had the ambition or the strength of character to press forcefully ahead with the Italian's programs. Grimaldi, who had personally implemented the reform of the royal mail system, possessed such attributes, but the nativist character of the Esquilache Riots precluded the possibility that another foreigner might dominate. Another voice for innovation was stilled when Isabel Farnese, who had opposed Esquilache's dismissal, died soon afterward.[84] Arriaga, whose conservative respectability must have been a comfort to the king in those troubled times, regained stature within the government. Moreover, the decision to expel the Jesuits in 1767 disrupted the impetus for reform, while the Third Family Compact began to weaken as the French, who failed to gain privileged access to Spanish markets, began to lose their appetite for another reckoning with the British.[85] Cuba, meanwhile, continued to function under the policies established during 1763–1765.

82, D'Ossun to Choiseul, Madrid, Jan. 23, 30, Mar. 8, 1764, Choiseul to D'Ossun, Versailles, Feb. 7, 1764, all in AAE, CE, vol. 540, fols. 64, 80, 98, 182–86.

83. Esquilache to Bucareli, Messina, Sept. 11, 1771, AGI, IG, leg. 1629.

84. Bergamini, *The Spanish Bourbons*, 90.

85. The characteristics of the period following the fall of Esquilache are developed more fully in Allan J. Kuethe, "Towards a Periodization of the Reforms of Charles III," *Bibliotheca americana* 1, no. 3 (Jan. 1984), 153–57.

4. Revenge

Revenge came on May 10, 1781. After a seige of two months, Pensacola, the key British strongpoint in the Gulf of Mexico, fell to an expeditionary force under Field Marshal Bernardo de Gálvez, capping a spectacular series of victories by Spanish forces that had begun at Manchac and Baton Rouge in September 1779, extended to Mobile in March 1780, and culminated in East Florida. The triumphant army, although European in its main component, was intimately connected to the island of Cuba and its reformed defense structure. The disciplined militia's ability to replace veteran units on the home front permitted Spain to send on the offensive both the Spanish units deployed for garrison duty in Havana and troops from the fixed units. The dramatic victory at Pensacola vindicated the strategy of Ricla and O'Reilly and the persistent work of those who followed and sustained their program.

During the interlude between the Ricla mission and the outbreak of war in 1779, efforts to support the disciplined militia succeeded reasonably well. The several units were uniformed, although sometimes in rags; the volunteers had weapons, even if they seldom served for anything more than practice; and the units drilled according to schedule and produced reassuring if uneven results. Finally, the militia maintained its authorized strength remarkably well despite chronic problems with desertion, disease, and other troubles.

Under normal circumstances, the crown expected the municipalities supporting volunteer units to finance with local taxes both the cost of uniforms and the repair and replacement of firearms, as was done in Spain. As explained earlier, however, O'Reilly prevailed upon the militia to clothe itself in the beginning, and the crown furnished the weaponry as part of the initial reorganization. Out of deference to the new financial obligations that Havana and the island had recently incurred in connection with revenue reform, the crown also provided new uniforms, manufactured by Spanish contractors, in 1769 and in 1776, although in the latter instance only the units of Havana and Santiago were supplied immediately.[1] Dress for the remaining units arrived over the next three years. In theory, these garments were supposed to last for half a decade, but in the tropics reality was something else. Thus, when war broke out in 1779, all of the militia possessed uniforms, but many had begun to wear thin.[2]

Firearms were another problem. In 1779 the militia was still using the same muskets the crown had provided some fifteen years earlier. Rust had long since begun its attack, and many had begun to fall apart. Nevertheless, it made little sense to arm volunteers with new weapons simply for training purposes. Close-order drill could be mastered as well with rusty muskets as with shiny ones, and enough functional pieces could be found or assembled so that everyone had the opportunity to fire during the bimonthly maneuvers. Militia officers, naturally, complained endlessly about their equipment, but volunteers gained familiarity with the feel of weapons and learned how to fire them.[3] The crucial test for the royal administration would be to provide serviceable equipment for the militia when mobilization occurred.

Meanwhile, steps had been taken to transfer to the municipalities the responsibility for providing uniforms and firearms. In a series of royal orders issued during 1772, 1773, and 1774, the crown, noting the rapid expansion of Cuban commerce and the enormous royal expenditures for the navy, fortifications, and the regular army, ordered Captain General Marqués de la Torre to seek from local sources the means to finance regular replacement of uniforms and armaments. De la Torre instructed the ayuntamientos of the relevant municipalities to submit appropriate plans.[4]

Havana designed a program to replace the uniforms of its units every four years and the firearms every twelve years at an estimated average cost of 20,191 pesos annually. To raise this revenue, the ayuntamiento formed a bakers' guild, limited to fourteen members, to which it granted a monopoly over the sale of bread in Havana at current prices, although residents were permitted to bake bread for their own consumption. In return for his privilege, each monopolist paid the city four pesos daily, which produced a total annual revenue of 20,440 pesos,

    1. Royal order, El Pardo, Mar. 10, 1785, AGI, SD, leg. 2160.
    2. The inspection reports for the disciplined militia of Cuba for the period 1764–81 can be found in AGI, SD, legs. 2119–36. See also O'Reilly to José de Gálvez, Puerto de Santa María, July 2, 1776, AGI, SD, leg. 2132.
    3. Inspection reports, 1764–81, O'Reilly to José de Gálvez, Puerto de Santa María, July 2, 1776, all in AGI, SD, legs. 2119–36, 2132.
    4. Royal order, El Pardo, Mar. 10, 1785, AGI, SD, leg. 2160.

slightly more than the amount needed. Apparently, the law simply drove the other bakers of Havana out of business. The crown approved this scheme by order of December 7, 1774, but much more would be heard on the subject during the 1780s.[5]

The interior jurisdictions produced various schemes that reflected the peculiar characteristics of their respective economies. Because of the smaller income bases in those districts and the relatively large size of the militia establishments, all the ayuntamientos elected to reuniform their units only every six years, most paying for the uniforms with taxes on salt, butchered beef, and liquor. Matanzas established a bread monopoly like Havana's, and Bayamo an aguardiente monopoly.[6] With de la Torre's approval, these ayuntamientos petitioned for the royal treasury to bear the cost of weapon replacement. These plans laid the foundation for stable finances in later decades and provided some immediate assistance during the war years.

The primary responsibility for upholding the quality of the militia rested with the subinspector general, who was normally the lieutenant governor (*teniente de rey*) of Havana. Lieutenant Governor Pascual Ximénez de Cisneros, who held the rank of brigadier general, became inspector when O'Reilly left in 1765.[7] Later promoted to field marshall, he served until 1772 when he transferred to New Spain. At that time, Colonel Juan Dabán replaced him, serving until 1782.[8] Annually, usually in December or early in the new year, the inspector or his agent conducted battalion reviews as prescribed by the regulation. The subinspectors general themselves seldom advanced beyond Matanzas, normally assigning the militia of Santiago-Bayamo to the local governor, the lieutenant governor, or an officer from the Fijo, and the battalions of Cuatro Villas and Puerto Príncipe to the veteran officers currently serving in those districts as deputy governors.

In addition to monitoring the condition of the equipment, the subinspector examined the morale of the veteran cadre, observed unit maneuvers, and in conjunction with the local authorities filled the vacancies in the soldiery that had developed over the past year. Routine vacancies occurred because of death, old age, chronic illness, or changes of residence. On rare occasions, sergeants were promoted to officers, and on the other side of the spectrum, a few men usually had to be drummed out as incorrigibles. Desertion also quickly became a factor, albeit usually a minor one, once the initial glamour of militia

5. Marqués de la Torre to Arriaga, Havana, Aug. 2, 1772, royal order, Madrid, Dec. 7, 1774, both in AGI, SD, leg. 2160.

6. Report, de la Torre, Havana, Sept. 1, 1774, royal order, El Pardo, Mar. 10, 1776, both in AGI, SD, leg. 2130.

7. Cisneros to Arriaga, Havana, Mar. 2, 1765, AGI, SD, leg. 2078.

8. De la Torre to Arriaga, Havana, Feb. 21, 1772, AGI, SD, leg. 2128.

duty gave way to the drudgery of Sunday drills. Evidently, most deserters were men who either could not or did not bother to obtain authorization to change their places of residence. During the 1770s, they accounted for an annual manpower loss of about 3 to 3.5 percent.[9] Acting in conjunction with the municipal authorities, who were expected to produce censuses of the able-bodied men in their district between the ages of fifteen and forty-five, the subinspector filled the vacancies by admitting new volunteers or effecting a levy if necessary.

Finding replacements could be difficult, as Cisneros discovered during his review of the militia of Cuatro Villas in late 1766. Although the municipal officials had properly prepared lists of the able-bodied men and had announced his arrival, only thirty men appeared in Sancti Spíritus, twenty-eight in Santa Clara, ten in Trinidad, and none in Los Remedios. The rest of the potential "volunteers" had apparently sought refuge in the hills and forests to escape service. Cisneros simply prevailed upon the municipal officials to levy stiff fines on the delinquents to avert future embarrassments. In recruiting as in the provision of uniforms and equipment, the key to sustaining the battalions was the cooperation of the local elite, as Ricla and O'Reilly had plainly understood when structuring the reform program.[10]

Not surprisingly, the quality of the militia units varied considerably. The units in the interior all labored under less than ideal conditions. Outside of Havana, only the companies of Santiago functioned in the presence of a significant veteran garrison; the other island volunteers could only imagine what mobilization might be like. Moreover, as seen in Cuatro Villas, the lack of an immediate threat to their home districts must have dulled the motivation of many.

An additional problem arose because the companies of Santiago-Bayamo and of Cuatro Villas were so widely scattered that they could not train as battalions.[11] Similarly separated were the three mounted companies of the Matanzas Dragoons, although in this instance unit integration was less important. The mounted companies, which consisted of ranch hands from the numerous *hatos* of that district, existed to evacuate cattle from the coast and to escort convoys and supplies to Havana, tasks that did not require a high degree of expertise, and so O'Reilly had not assigned them veterans.[12] Understandably, these companies possessed little esprit de corps, a condition reflected in erratic attendance and performance at drills, and they demonstrated little

9. Militia inspection reports, 1771–72, 1774–75, 1778–79, AGI, SD, legs. 2129–30, 2133, 2135.

10. Cisneros to Arriaga with enclosure, Havana, Feb. 11, 1767, AGI, SD, leg. 2094.

11. *Reglamento para las milicias,* 1769, ch. 3, art. 15.

12. O'Reilly to Arriaga, Cádiz, Nov. 17, 1766, Bucareli to Arriaga, Havana, Mar. 28, 1768, royal order, San Ildefonso, Aug. 4, 1768, all in AGI, SD, legs. 2121, 2122.

proficiency. By contrast, the foot companies of the Matanzas Dragoons had immediate military significance. They were centrally located, drilled together, and generally earned satisfactory marks.[13]

On another level, many volunteers were frequent absentees owing to occupational obligations. The regulation, recognizing the importance of the tobacco industry, ordered the veteran cadres of the units of Cuatro Villas, Santiago-Bayamo, and Matanzas to follow their militiamen into the agricultural zones to train them during the planting, growing, and harvesting seasons, but many such volunteers still could not be reached.[14] Woodcutting and the transport of lumber to the shipyards of Havana diverted others, and many went to sea to fish or trade.[15]

By all accounts, the four units of Havana were the best on the island, no doubt partly because of their location at the center of military activity and authority where supervision was rigorous. The vital mission to defend the capital and heart of the colony must also have had a positive effect on motivation, especially among those who had investments at stake. Moreover, the concentrated population permitted battalion-level training. In 1768 Captain General Bucareli observed that the Havana infantry battalions "when mobilized differ little from regular troops," and that the Cavalry Regiment consistently enjoyed high esteem as the best militia unit on the island.[16] Less developed, however, was the Second Battalion of the Infantry Regiment, the one based in Guanabacoa and points east. Although the men of this unit often rated as individually superior to those of the First Battalion, the nine companies were so scattered that they could assemble only for bimonthly firing practice and the annual review. The quality of the battalion as a tactical unit suffered accordingly.[17]

Despite the problems that afflicted the outlying units and to a lesser degree those of Havana, a surprisingly high number of volunteers remained faithful in their service and reached satisfactory competence in the essential skills of soldiery. When Cisneros first assumed from O'Reilly the responsibility for the disciplined militia, he found that

13. See, for example, Colonel Juan Dabán to José de Gálvez, Havana, May 2, 1779, Cisneros to Arriaga, Havana, Feb. 11, 1767, both in AGI, SD, legs. 2121, 2133.

14. *Reglamento para las milicias*, 1769, ch. 3, art. 14; inspection report, Governor Juan Manuel Cagigal, Santiago, Dec. 31, 1766, AGI, SD, leg. 2094.

15. Bucareli to Arriaga, Havana, Feb. 14, 1767, de la Torre to José de Gálvez, Havana, May 11, 1776, both in AGI, SD, legs. 2094, 2130.

16. For example, see Dabán to José de Gálvez, Havana, Apr. 19, 1779, Bucareli to Arriaga, Havana, Jan. 4, 1768, and Jan. 8, 1769, Cisneros report, army of Cuba, Apr. 4, 1769, all in AGI, SD, legs. 2123, 2125, 2133.

17. For example, see Bucareli to Arriaga, Havana, Apr. 28, 1766, reports of Juan Dabán, Havana, Feb. 1, 1773, Apr. 12, 1775, all in AGI, SD, legs. 2120, 2129, 2130. *Reglamento para las milicias*, 1769, ch. 3, art. 6.

Table 4.   **Troop Strengths of the Cuban Militia, 1779**

Unit	Authorized Enlistment	Effective Enlistment
White Regiment of Havana		
First Battalion	800	576
Second Battalion	800	576
Pardo Battalion of Havana	800	628
Moreno Battalion of Havana	800	640
White Battalion of Cuatro Villas	800	592
White Battalion of Puerte Príncipe	800	560
White Battalion of Santiago	800	550
Pardo Battalion of Santiago	800	644
Cavalry Regiment of Havana	650	564
Matanzas Dragoons (foot companies)*	300	228
Total	7,350	5,558

SOURCES: Inspection report, Cuban militia, 1778–79, inspection report, White Battalion of Cuatro Villas, Dec. 1779, both in AGI, SD, legs. 2133, 2135.

*The mounted companies of the Matanzas Dragoons were dismissed as untrained and have not been factored into these calculations.

some 60 percent of the volunteers had already mastered the expected skills.[18] During his inspectorship, he raised that percentage to nearly 78, a level that his successor, Dabán, sustained with little variation.[19] Moreover, some of the absentees from the annual inspections, who therefore did not enter into the count of disciplined volunteers, were trained men who were ill or who had authorized absences, a consideration suggesting that the number actually instructed stood higher than the raw head counts of those who performed satisfactorily for the subinspector.

In the winter immediately preceding Spain's entrance into the War of the American Revolution, the militia, as usual, had been brought up to full strength during the annual inspection. At that time, slightly more than 75 percent of the authorized complement demonstrated proficiency, firing from twelve to fifteen rounds in the process.[20] When war finally came, the royal authorities, not unreasonably, counted heavily upon the Cuban militia when planning action against the enemy.

18. Militia inspection reports, 1766–67, AGI, SD, leg. 2094.
19. Militia inspection reports, 1771–72, AGI, SD, leg. 2129. Also see, for example, the inspection reports of 1774–75, AGI, SD, leg. 2130.
20. The inspection report for the Cuban militia during the winter of 1778–79 can be found in AGI, SD, leg. 2133. Unfortunately, the report for the White Battalion of Cuatro Villas is missing for that year; for that unit I have used the Dec. 1779 report, in AGI, SD, leg. 2135.

The condition of the regular army had also stabilized by 1779 although disorder had plagued the period following O'Reilly's reforms. Salary disputes, mutinies, and impractical rotation schemes—all worked against the forging of a creditable force. Moreover, the ravages of disease and local recruitment problems undermined the veteran manpower base. Often the regular army counted as a less certain component than the disciplined militia. But the difficulties that faced Spain in Cuba were essentially manageable, and eventually order and realism prevailed. When war came, the regular army, like the disciplined militia, would prove itself capable of accomplishing its mission.

As O'Reilly prepared to depart Cuba in early 1765, he boasted to Arriaga: "The veteran troops are under the best discipline. They advance their perfection daily. I must tell you of the persistent zeal of these officers, the precision with which service is performed, the rigorous subordination, and the high morale of all."[21] But like so many of his previous assurances about the regular army, O'Reilly's departing statement was woefully amiss. During the spring and summer of 1765, a series of troop mutinies exposed the still unsettled condition of the veteran forces and, in the long run, led to the dismantling of much of O'Reilly's program for the veteran Havana garrison.

In May 1765 ninety-eight men from the Second Battalion of the Fijo, which had been detached to Santiago, took refuge in the cemetery of the cathedral to protest their grievances over unpaid wages. Governor Juan Manuel Cagigal reacted by mobilizing both the white and the *pardo* militia and bringing up the remaining regulars. Although the militia fired a cannon through the gate killing several mutineers, the governor hesitated to go further for fear of leaving the port defenseless. Fortunately, the incident ended peacefully when the protesters, having made their point, voluntarily left the cathedral grounds. The embarrassed Cuban authorities moved quickly to remedy the grievances, but in the meantime a similar protest over back pay erupted in Havana on August 14, this time involving a dozen dragoons from the Regiment of America. These incidents, although arising in part from an initial shortage of funds and from short-term administrative snarls, revealed deep anger in the ranks over the new support levels and an alarming want of discipline.[22]

A more serious incident followed on August 22 when troops from both the Fijo and the Regiment of Lisbon, which had just arrived to replace the Regiment of Córdoba, mutinied en masse. Angered by official delinquency in meeting their salary claims and in the delivery of the wine rations owed them from their time at sea, and objecting to

21. O'Reilly to Arriaga, Havana, Feb. 24, 1765, AGI, SD, leg. 2120.
22. File on Santiago troop mutiny, 1765–66, Intendant Miguel de Altarriba to Arriaga, Havana, Aug. 16, 1765, both in AGI, SD, leg. 2119.

the newly reduced wage standard, over a thousand men barricaded themselves in the Monastery of San Francisco and threatened to plunder the city for food if they were not fed during the course of their protest. Diego Manrique, who succeeded Ricla as captain general, had died in early August, leaving Lieutenant Governor Cisneros in interim command of the island. Cisneros promptly mobilized the militia to contain the mutineers and, in conjunction with the bishop of Cuba, who was in Havana, dispatched Vicar General Santiago Echavarría to attempt mediation.[23]

Seeking asylum in churches as a means of protest was a standing tradition in the Cuban garrison. Now, in the more secularized climate of the Enlightenment, military authorities had won royal authorization to enter these sanctuaries to retrieve their men, but this step was still not taken lightly.[24] By involving the ecclesiastical jurisdiction, moreover, such protests opened for the troops an alternate line of communication with the crown through the Church.[25] This consideration probably increased the accuracy of the reports sent to Spain and certainly militated against any possible coverup of embarrassing revelations or developments.

After two days of tense confrontation and mediation, the soldiers won enough concessions to justify going back to their quarters. With the help of contributions from wealthy creoles, Cisneros settled the army's claim against the treasury on the spot; he had wine delivered to the barracks; and with no real alternative, he respected a promise of amnesty that Echavarría had made. Moreover, both Cisneros and Father Echavarría communicated the troops' salary demands to court, the latter reporting in detail his harrowing experiences in mediating the dispute.[26]

These confrontations, along with earlier incidents during the time of O'Reilly, profoundly affected official thinking about the army of Cuba, with important implications for the empire. The mutinies in Santiago and Havana had rendered both strongpoints momentarily vulnerable to attack; that such an incident might occur during wartime was unthinkable. Moreover, neither governor was able to punish the guilty simply because neither had the means to do so. Disorders of this magnitude suggested serious defects in the system itself.

23. File on Havana troop mutiny, 1765–66, AGI, SD, leg. 2120.

24. Royal declaration, San Ildefonso, Aug. 20, 1736, AGI, IG, leg. 1885; Arriaga to Ricla, Madrid, Apr. 12, 1763, AGI, SD, leg. 1211.

25. For an analysis of flexibility and communication within the Spanish colonial administration, see John Leddy Phelan, "Authority and Flexibility in the Spanish Imperial Bureaucracy," *Administrative Science Quarterly* 5 (1960), 47–65.

26. File on Havana troop mutiny, 1765–66, AGI, SD, leg. 2120. The intendant reported to Arriaga in Feb. 1766 that all adjustments for back pay for both veteran and militia units had been completed. AGI, SD, leg. 2121.

If the treasury had to hedge in meeting its obligations, military salaries obviously were not the place to do so, as Arriaga pointedly emphasized in a September 1765 order to the intendant.[27] But the deeper question went beyond any momentary juggling of funds. O'Reilly's salary reductions had provoked mutiny in every major unit in Cuba and during this same period had brought about a revolt of the entire garrison of Panama as well.[28] That O'Reilly had blundered in believing that such reductions were possible was obvious, but the Marqués de Esquilache was determined not to yield to the demands of the Cuban army. His fall and exile in March 1766, however, opened the way for a moderation of policy.[29] The result was yet another wage regulation for the Indies that contained timely concessions, although it did not restore the former salary levels. For example, a fusilier who earned eleven pesos a month under the 1753 regulation had seen his pay cut to eight pesos by O'Reilly. Under the new regulation he would be paid nine pesos a month. This mitigation of O'Reilly's cuts, however, was enough to end the wave of mutiny and disorder in the regular army.[30]

O'Reilly's scheme for abolishing fixed units and rotating the Cuban garrison every two years also came under criticism. The bishop of Cuba, writing to Spain immediately after the August 22 mutiny had been settled, assigned much of the blame for that incident and earlier disorders on the practice of rotating troops. Moving men across the ocean was costly, exposed them to frequent and dangerous changes of climate, and restricted their right to marry. The latter deprivation, he lamented, exposed them to the "risk of enormous sins" and dulled their interest in defending the island.[31] The crown, he argued, must show more compassion for its troops. In evaluating the events of 1765–1766, the Ministry of War reached much the same conclusion, and O'Reilly's scheme to rotate the entire garrison was quickly forgotten. The Havana Fijo remained in place and the minimum service time for those European units deployed on the island returned to three years as originally planned, rather than the two years advocated by the subinspector general.

The retention of the Fijo was paralleled by an overall improvement

27. Cisneros to Arriaga, Havana, Jan. 13, 1766, AGI, SD, leg. 2119.

28. File on troop mutiny, 1766, Archivo Nacional de Colombia, Milicia y Marina, vol. 2, fols. 673–702. For a calendar of the mutinies of the eighteenth century, see Marchena, *Oficiales y soldados,* app. 3.

29. Royal order, San Lorenzo, Nov. 6, 1765, Bucareli to [Ministry of the Indies], Havana, Mar. 25, 1766, both in AGI, SD, legs. 2093, 2121.

30. Royal order, El Pardo, Feb. 27, 1767, AGI, SD, leg. 2122; royal decree, Oct. 4, 1766, AGI, IG, leg. 1885. Although there was a basic wage standard, there were, of course, minor regional adjustments. The regulations for Cartagena and Panama can also be found in AGI, IG, leg. 1885.

31. Bishop of Cuba to Arriaga, Havana, Aug. 25, 1765, AGI, SD, leg. 2119.

in the role of Americans in the Cuban defense system. During the August 22 mutiny, the militia had responded well, patrolling the city during the night and helping to contain the insurrection. The patrician militia leadership had, after all, much at stake socially and economically in keeping the soldiery in its place and in protecting the city. In the east, the militia of Santiago had also performed well. Ironically, the disciplined militia found itself containing the regular army, which had always been seen as an important safeguard against the dangers of arming Americans. Creoles were upholding royal authority against Europeans. The crown, which officially commended the Havana militia for its loyalty and good service, fully appreciated the implications of these developments and the view of the reformed militia improved accordingly in Madrid.[32] Indeed, in a gesture surely intended to be more symbolic than substantive, His Majesty expressed his gratitude by expanding the *preeminencias* of the disciplined militia to include an exemption from the *gallina*, the fee of one hen which the *alcaldes ordinarios* traditionally exacted during their semiannual visits to the ranches and plantations of their jurisdictions.[33] Although this *gracia* represented little material gain, the prestige it accorded was what counted. In the regular army, a more vigorous effort to recruit Cubans followed the decision to retain fixed units, the earlier restrictions to 20 percent Creole enlistment never having been reinstituted after the war.

The task of restoring a semblance of discipline to the Cuban garrison fell to Lieutenant General Antonio María de Bucareli, who succeeded Diego Manrique as captain general after the latter's death. Bucareli derived from a distinguished noble line in Seville, that included, as his name suggests, a strain of Italian ancestry. He was a political intimate of Esquilache, as well as a close friend, who, even when Esquilache's power had vanished and he languished in exile, maintained the friendship through regular correspondence and gifts of Cuban tobacco.[34] Bucareli was also on close personal terms with O'Reilly, a friendship that guaranteed continued support at court. Apart from his personal connections, Bucareli possessed strong military qualifications. He had extensive and distinguished combat experience in the Italian theater during the War of Jenkins' Ear, and he had later served as inspector general of cavalry and dragoons in Spain and as inspector of coastal fortifications in Granada. Bucareli was one of Cuba's best captains general, governing until 1771 when he was promoted to vicer-

32. Royal order, Madrid, Mar. 15, 1766, AGI, SD, leg. 2120.

33. File on rewards for the militia of Cuba, 1765–66, AGI, SD, leg. 2121.

34. Charles had made provision for Esquilache's habit during his exile but his plaintive letters reveal that His Majesty had underestimated the Italian's appetite. The correspondence between Bucareli and Esquilache can be found in AGI, IG, leg. 1629.

oy of New Spain. A fatal illness in Mexico would end his promising career in 1779.[35]

Bucareli brought with him to Cuba 12 officers and 250 enlisted men from the Regiments of the Queen and Zamora to provide new leadership for the Regiment of Lisbon and to fill vacancies that had developed in the companies.[36] The officers who had been discredited during the mutinies he returned to Spain for reassignment. Bucareli's strong personal leadership, the improved officer corps, the timely royal concession on wages, and the more realistic policy on troop rotation—all worked to stabilize the garrison.[37]

Once the mutiny crisis had passed, the regular army's most persistent problem was the maintenance of authorized troop levels. Enlistments expired after six years, and it was difficult, as the authorities put it, to *reenganchar* (literally reensnare) terminating soldiers. Moreover, tropical diseases, especially yellow fever, preyed upon the army, particularly recent arrivals. Desertion was a depressingly persistent theme. And finally, there were the hopelessly incorrigible and the dangerous criminals who had to be condemned to royal labors on the fortifications. Deficiency levels in the garrison varied considerably, depending in part on the quality of individual Spanish regiments and their mortality rate during the passage from Spain and on the length of time since the last major infusion of recruits into the Fijo. During unfavorable periods, shortages could reach nearly a full battalion, numbering, for example, 641 in March 1768 and 644 in July 1773. Consequently, a steady supply of replacements was a continual necessity.[38]

Unhappily from the viewpoint of the Cuban authorities, few Cubans sought enlistment. Life for enlisted men was at once dull and dangerous and afforded little if any opportunity for material gain. Nor would most young men want to associate with the typical Spanish soldier. The Havana garrison included the most miserable of human beings. Given the conditions of military service, including the deplorable wage level, young men with other means avoided the army in Spain as elsewhere in Europe during this period. The recruits sent to America were usually the destitute and the depraved: hapless vaga-

35. María Lourdes Díaz-Trechuelo Spínola, María Luisa Rodríquez Baena, and Concepción Pajarón Parody, "Antonio María Bucareli y Ursua (1771–1779)," in José Antonio Calderón Quijano, ed., *Los virreyes de Nueva España en el reinado de Carlos III* (Seville, 1967), I, 387–90; Bernard E. Bobb, *The Viceregency of Antonio María Bucareli in New Spain, 1771–1779* (Austin, 1962), 18–20.

36. Bucareli to Esquilache, Cádiz, Dec. 6, 1765, Bucareli to Arriaga, Cádiz, Dec. 6, 1765, both in AGI, SD, legs. 2088, 2119.

37. Bucareli to Arriaga, Havana, Apr. 28, Oct. 2, 1776, AGI, SD, leg. 2120.

38. Bucareli to Arriaga, Havana, Mar. 4, 1768, Sept. 27, 1769, May 4, 1771, inspection report, army of Cuba, July 1, 1773, all in AGI, SD, legs. 2123, 2124, 2128, 2129.

bonds, criminals sentenced to the army, or captured deserters.[39] Eager to export crime and disorder, the crown customarily deployed its most wretched regiments in America, going so far as to complete their complements with malefactors transferred from the other units.[40] In Cuba, such conditions must have done much to discourage the enlistment of all but the most desperate, while concurrently the island's expanding economy provided increased opportunities for the able-bodied. Bucareli repeatedly lamented the shortage of Cuban enlistees and complained that those who did join all too often took their enlistment bonus and uniform and fled when the opportunity arose.[41] Indeed, as late as 1776, only 152 Americans served in the Fijo and not all of them were Cubans.[42]

Although an aggravation, the want of local enlistments did not pose an impossible obstacle to a proper defense, for Cuba's advantageous location on the trade routes facilitated access to men from the outside. The crown frequently permitted the recruitment of soldiers from units returning to Spain from Cuba or other jurisdictions, and it sent replacements directly from the peninsula. The first such instance occurred in 1768 when the Cuban authorities with prior approval recruited 390 men from the Regiment of America, which stopped in Havana en route to Europe from New Spain. These men were assigned to the Fijo and the artillery companies. Meanwhile, seventy Catalonians arrived from Spain to complete the light infantry.[43] Moreover, in 1775 the crown authorized the Fijo to establish a recruitment party in the Canary Islands, as had been done from 1753 to 1762 but not following the Treaty of Paris.[44]

The plan to rotate a fresh European regiment into Cuba every three years to supplement the fixed garrison worked reasonably well, although delays were commonplace. The Regiment of Lisbon replaced the Regiment of Córdoba in 1765. The Regiment of Seville arrived in August 1769 to relieve that of Lisbon. It was followed by the Regiment of Lombardy and in turn by the Regiment of the Prince, which arrived in 1777.[45]

39. O'Reilly to José de Gálvez, Puerto de Santa María, Jan. 21, 1777, Colonel Luis de Urbina to Bucareli, Havana, Mar. 9, 1770, inspection report, Fixed Infantry Regiment of Havana, June 28, 1776, all in AGI, SD, legs. 2124, 2131.

40. Marchena, *Oficiales y soldados*, 342–43. Marchena describes in detail the misery of the daily life of the American soldier.

41. Bucareli to Arriga, Havana, Mar. 4, May 5, 1768, Bucareli to Juan Muniain, Havana, Mar. 3, 1768, AGI, SD, legs. 2123, 2079.

42. O'Reilly to José de Gálvez, Puerto de Santa María, Jan. 21, 1777, AGI, SD, leg. 2131.

43. Cisneros to Arriaga, Havana, Dec. 10, 1768, Bucareli to Arriaga, Havana, Mar. 4, 1768, both in AGI, SD, legs. 2122, 2123.

44. File on manpower shortage in Cuba, 1775–78, AGI, SD, leg. 2132.

45. Bucareli to Arriaga, Havana, Sept. 27 and Dec. 5, 1769, and Cisneros to Arriaga,

Although the combination of disciplined militiamen and fixed and rotating veteran troops constituted a formidable defense force and certainly represented a great improvement over 1762, early contingency planning envisioned reinforcing the island during wartime with two to, ideally, four additional battalions. The fortified strongpoints of Havana, although covered by the forces at hand, lacked depth, and Santiago, which was garrisoned by only the Second Battalion of the Fijo, would require at least another battalion in addition to part of Havana's cavalry or light infantry.[46]

Shortly before departing Cuba, the Conde de Ricla devised a deployment strategy for the army that was still honored in 1779. Of the three available veteran battalions (one from the Fijo and two from the current Spanish regiment), one each would garrison the Cabaña, the Morro Castle, and new defense positions under construction to the west. The light infantry, all but one company of the dragoons and cavalry, and the Pardo Infantry Battalion would operate in the east to protect the approaches to the Cabaña and the Morro, while the Moreno Infantry Battalion would be deployed in the west. Ricla assigned the immediate defense of the city to the White Volunteer Infantry Regiment and the remaining company of cavalry.[47] This system relied heavily upon the militia, but there was little margin for error. The veteran infantry and dragoons, it should be remembered, also provided detachments for Cuatro Villas and for Puerto Príncipe, and those units were habitually undermanned. The authorities in both Cuba and Spain, therefore, anticipated that during wartime Cuba would require one or perhaps two additional regiments.[48]

Events between the initial military reform and Spain's declaration of war on Great Britain in 1779 provided the Cuban army with what amounted to two trial runs. The first incident tested the Cuban army's capacity to marshal trained manpower for offensive action. It arose out of Spain's acquisition of Louisiana from France as part of the settlement following the Seven Years' War. The French colonists, who had resented this transfer of sovereignty and who had developed personal antagonism toward Governor Antonio de Ulloa, rebelled in late October 1768. When he assumed the governorship, Ulloa had brought with him only ninety men, and by the time of the uprising this force had dwindled to no more than seventy-nine. There was no question of putting down the revolt. Ulloa fled the colony to Cuba and thence to

Havana, Sept. 23, 1769, AGI, SD, leg. 2124; troop review, Havana, May 31, 1773, AGI, SD, leg. 2129.

46. Royal order, San Ilfefonso, July 27, 1764, AGI, SD, leg. 1213.

47. Ricla to Field Marshal Diego Manrique, Havana, July 11, 1765, AGI, SD, leg. 2119.

48. For example, see Bucareli to Arriaga, Havana, Nov. 10, 1770, AGI, SD, leg. 2127.

Spain, where he arrived in 1769.[49] Embarrassed by this failure to secure effective control of Louisiana, Charles decided to establish Spanish authority by means of the Cuban army. To command the expedition, he selected Alejandro O'Reilly, who was, of course, not only one of Spain's top officers but a man who knew the Cuban military intimately.

Reaching Havana on June 24, O'Reilly was pleased to see the proficiency and enthusiasm of the Havana militia and the discipline that Bucareli had instilled in the veteran garrison.[50] Within two weeks, he was able to organize and launch an expedition of 2,030 men and 111 officers and command and staff group personnel. This force included 679 troops from the once mutinous Regiment of Lisbon, 567 from the Fijo, 150 from the Catalonian Light Infantry Companies, 50 from the Dragoon Squadron of America, and 91 artillerymen, 31 of whom were assigned to permanent service in Louisiana. Also included were 213 men detached in Europe from the Regiments of Aragón and Guadalajara, whom the king had sent to strengthen the Fixed Infantry Battalion of Louisiana. O'Reilly completed his force with Havana militiamen, summoning the eighty-man grenadier companies from the First Battalion of the Havana Infantry Regiment and from the Pardo and Moreno Infantry Battalions, as well as a detachment of forty cavalrymen. A number of distinguished volunteers also accompanied the expedition, undoubtedly with the hope of acquiring "merit" that could later justify petitions for royal favors.[51]

O'Reilly's force reached the Mississippi River on July 9, but difficult weather delayed its arrival in New Orleans until August 17. When O'Reilly entered the city and raised the Spanish flag, he did so with an intimidating display of military force. Moreover, he quickly arrested twelve leaders of the insurrection, ordering six of them shot and the rest confined to Havana's Morro Castle.[52] O'Reilly remained in

49. John Walton Caughey, *Bernardo de Gálvez in Louisiana, 1776–1783* (Berkeley, 1934), 9; Vicente Rodríguez Casado, "O'Reilly en la Louisiana," *Revista de Indias*, no. 2 (1941), 117.

50. O'Reilly to Arriaga, Havana, June 25, 1769, AGI, SD, leg. 2125.

51. Report on the officers and troops from the army of the island of Cuba that marched in the expedition of Alejandro O'Reilly, Havana, July 7, 1769, AGI, SD, leg. 2124. There is another account of O'Reilly's force, the "Relation of the Troops, Artillerymen, and Munitions That Have Embarked in This Port for Louisiana," n.d., AGI, SD, leg. 2656, which varies slightly from the first one. This second account places the number of Catalonian troops at 162 instead of 150, and the individual volunteers at 6 noble cadets and 8 distinguished volunteers as contrasted to the figure of 10 *caballeros particulares*.

52. There are various accounts of these events, including the previously cited works of Caughey and Rodríguez Casado. More recent accounts can be found in Jack D.L. Holmes, *Honor and Fidelity: The Louisiana Infantry Regiment and the Louisiana Militia Companies, 1766–1821* (Birmingham, 1965), 17–21, and Torres Rámirez, *Alejandro O'Reilly*, 97–183.

Louisiana only long enough to set the foundations of Spanish government firmly in place. In the military sphere, he strengthened the Fixed
Battalion with the detachments he had brought for that purpose and
with 179 volunteers from the Regiment of Lisbon. He also raised
thirteen separate militia companies, although, for want of proper support and sufficient veteran advisers, these units were not placed on a
disciplined footing. He accorded the *fuero militar* only to the officers,
observing that, there would be no ordinary justice if he granted the
privilege to the enlisted men as well.[53]

By October, O'Reilly began withdrawing the Cuban forces, a task
completed in December. He himself departed at the end of February,
leaving Lieutenant General Luis de Unzaga of the Havana Fijo in New
Orleans as governor. Charles III rewarded O'Reilly for his achievements by naming him inspector general of the army of America, giving
him the power to receive and evaluate military communications before
they reached Arriaga, to transmit royal communications back to America, and to help shape policy.[54] This appointment occurred during the
Falkland (Malvinas) Islands Crisis of fall 1770, when O'Reilly's talents
were needed to plan and coordinate troop deployments in America.
Once vested with his new powers, O'Reilly in effect became minister of
the army for the Indies and used his power ambitiously, extending, for
example, the military reform to New Granada, Caracas and Santo
Domingo.[55] In its larger meaning, the Louisiana episode convincingly
demonstrated the capacity of Spain to send forces from Cuba into
action on the North American continent, a capacity that would be
remembered in the years immediately ahead.

The first opportunity for Spain to test Cuba's ability to react defensively to a warlike situation arose during the crisis over the Falkland
Islands, which brought the Family Compact to the brink of war with
Great Britain. The dispute arose in June 1770, when Governor Francisco Bucareli of Buenos Aires, brother of the captain general of Cuba,
forcibly dislodged the British from a settlement they had established on
the islands off the coast of Patagonia at the strategic approaches to the
Strait of Magellan. A complex diplomatic crisis quickly developed in
which Charles III showed himself quite willing to resort to war to
uphold his nation's honor. Spain's diplomatic and military position

53. Holmes, *Honor and Fidelity*, 19; O'Reilly to Arriaga, New Orleans, Jan. 8, 1770,
AGI, SD, leg. 1223.

54. Royal orders, San Ildefonso, Aug. 25, San Lorenzo, Nov. 21, 1770, both in AGI, IG,
leg. 1885; Cisneros to O'Reilly, Havana, Feb. 20, Mar. 1, Apr. 1, 1772, all in AGI, SD, leg.
2129.

55. Kuethe, *Military Reform and Society*, 10–24; María Rosario Sevilla Soler, *Santo
Domingo: Tierra de frontera (1750–1800)* (Seville, 1980), 325–26; Arriaga to the governor of
Caracas, San Ildefonso, Sept. 20, 1773, in Santiago Gerardo Suárez, ed., *Las fuerzas armadas
venezolanas en la colonia* (Caracas, 1979), 160–61.

suddenly eroded in early December, however, when Louis XV, who was troubled domestically both by the desperate state of his finances and by the crisis that had enveloped the attempt of René-Nicolas de Maupeou to reconstitute the parlements, dismissed Choiseul, the author of the Third Family Compact, and urged his Bourbon cousin to seek peace. Abandoned by France, Spain found herself forced to back down, but for a brief period during late 1770 and early 1771 war had been a very real possibility.[56]

To prepare Cuba for possible British reprisals, the crown in November dispatched the Regiment of Irlanda to the island and sent some seven hundred additional men to bring the Fijo and the Regiment of Seville up to strength. These men arrived during February and early March.[57] By January, the king also resolved to deploy the Regiment of Asturias on the island, but the crisis abated before the unit had embarked.[58] Bucareli and Cisneros found the veteran units all well equipped and supplied. The viceroy of New Spain, moreover, pronounced himself ready to provide financial support and, in case of immediate need, additional supplies and manpower.[59] O'Reilly, who supervised the buildup in his capacity as inspector general, was delighted at how efficiently the several pieces of the defense structure in Europe, Cuba, and the larger empire came into play and by the confidence that the royal administration could place in Spain's capability on the rim of its empire.[60] Thus, although the crisis had weakened the fabric of the Family Compact, at another level it enhanced Madrid's faith in its own ability to react in the American theater.

The course of events that finally led to the Spanish declaration of war on June 21, 1779, permitted the royal authorities ample time to place Cuba on a satisfactory wartime footing. As early as 1775 and 1776, Spain began to adjust to the growing crisis in British North America by taking inventory of military resources, shoring up manpower and supplies, and intensifying the training and discipline of its forces. The initial thinking appears to have been defensive in the face of the British military buildup in the north, but by 1779 insurgent victories and the French intervention of the previous year made conceivable offensive action and the quest for long-awaited revenge.[61]

56. Julius Goebel, *The Struggle for the Falkland Islands: A Study in Legal and Diplomatic History* (New Haven, 1927), 271–410.

57. Royal order, San Lorenzo, Nov. 21, 1770, Bucareli to Arriaga, Havana, Mar. 2, 1771, both in AGI, SD, legs. 2126, 2127.

58. Royal order, El Pardo, Jan. 17, 1771, AGI, SD, leg. 2127.

59. Marqués de Croix to Bucareli, México, Jan. 3, 1771, Bucareli to Arriaga, Havana, Feb. 6, 1771, inspection report, army of Cuba, June 8, 1771, all in AGI, SD, leg. 2128.

60. O'Reilly to Arriaga, Madrid, June 6, 1771, ibid.

61. An excellent example of the cautious, essentially defensive character of early Spanish thinking about the British posture in North America during 1775–76 can be found

The new realities in North America coincided with important leadership changes in Spain. In January 1776 the venerable Frey Arriaga died. Charles replaced him with José de Gálvez, a man of humble birth who had risen to become visitor general of New Spain, 1765–1771, and later a minister on the Council of the Indies.[62] Gálvez, who had taken a French wife, was, like his friend O'Reilly, closely connected to the French court and strongly committed to tough but enlightened political and fiscal reforms to prepare the way for successful military operations against the British.[63] No sooner had Gálvez assumed his position than he dispatched special visitors general to Peru and New Granada and subvisitors to Quito and Chile with extraordinary powers to tighten political authority and to generate royal income. His action signaled a resumption of the work that Esquilache had left undone. In Cuba, where a fiscal reorganization and the establishment of an intendancy had already been accomplished, the new leadership in the Ministry of the Indies expressed itself principally through the severe tone of Intendant Juan Ignacio de Urriza (1777–1786).[64]

The emergence of Gálvez was paralleled by a decline in the fortunes of both Alejandro O'Reilly and Minister of State Grimaldi, owing to O'Reilly's disastrous failure in July 1775 as commander of an expedition to punish the dey of Algiers for hostilities against Spanish settlements in North Africa. Partly because of overconfidence, O'Reilly blundered badly, losing over fifteen hundred men and only narrowly saving the rest of his army. So harsh was the public outcry against the Irishman, that Charles discreetly sent him on a tour of the Chafarinas Islands off the coast of Morocco before placing him in Cádiz as captain general of Andalusia.[65] O'Reilly retained the title of inspector general until 1783, but his power in American affairs quickly diminished. When it suited Gálvez, he ignored his old friend, although he routinely did him the courtesy of referring to him the correspondence affecting

in the *dictamen* of the Conde de Ricla, Minister of War, El Pardo, Jan. 17, 1777, AGS, GM, leg. 7311.

62. Priestly, *José de Gálvez*; Mark A. Burkholder, "The Council of the Indies in the Late Eighteenth Century: A New Perspective," *HAHR* 56 (Aug. 1976), 410.

63. Aiton, "Spanish Colonial Reorganization," 273–80; Caughey, *Bernardo de Gálvez*, 61.

64. Pierson, "Institutional History," 96.

65. Torres Ramírez, *Alejandro O'Reilly*, 10–11. I have found no evidence to indicate that O'Reilly held himself to the same standards that he demanded of the defeated in Havana. Indeed, when Charles, who had a strong sense of loyalty to faithful servants, refused to see him disgraced or even investigated, O'Reilly gladly accepted his command in Andalusia and tried to rebuild his career. See also Aiton, "Spanish Colonial Reorganization," 279. For an account of the ill-fated expedition, see Servicio Histórico Militar, *Dos expediciones españolas contra Argel, 1541 y 1775* (Madrid, 1946), pt. 2.

Cuba.[66] Grimaldi, who shared the public blame for the Algiers under-taking, resigned in 1776 but managed to persuade the king to name his disciple, the Conde de Floridablanca, to replace him rather than his rival, the Conde de Aranda. Floridablanca quickly emerged as the dominant force in the government, serving until 1792, although Gál-vez, unlike his predecessor, was able to maintain dominance in his ministry. Meanwhile, the Conde de Ricla, who had become minister of war following the death of Muniain in 1772, retained his portfolio.[67]

The changing diplomatic and military realities in North America confronted Cuba at the time when Havana's military position was the weakest it had been since the time of the great mutinies. A major influx of recruits for the Fijo had not arrived since 1771 and at mid-decade a severe epidemic of yellow fever had gripped the veteran garrison. By November 1775 over three hundred men were hospitalized and many others had died. Together, the First Battalion of the Fijo, the Light Infantry Companies, and the Squadron of Dragoons managed to muster only 260 men on actual duty in Havana, and the customary detach-ments to the other island strongpoints were also severely reduced. The Regiment of Lombardy had over 1,000 effectives, but 655 of them were scheduled to complete their enlistment by the end of the year. And many who served in the Fijo were already due their discharges. The militia could have been mobilized, of course, but this action would have added substantial costs to the already burdened treasury, while disrupting normal economic and domestic life in the colony.[68]

The Marqués de la Torre, who replaced Bucareli, petitioned Madrid for a massive infusion of recruits and for the expansion of the Fijo by one battalion or the creation of a separate unit for Santiago.[69] Rather than attempt institutional reorganization during this difficult period, the crown simply rerouted to Havana the Regiment of Spain, which it had originally assigned to New Spain, thus bringing the number of infantry regiments in Cuba to three, the same number deployed during the 1770–1771 crisis. Moreover, a trickle of Spanish recruits continued to arrive and the decision to establish a recruitment detail in the Canary Islands in October 1775 promised long-term relief.[70]

66. Kuethe, *Military Reform and Society*, 65–66. The routine correspondence for Cuba during O'Reilly's inspector generalship can be found in AGI, SD, legs. 2116–20.

67. These changes are treated in José Antonio Escudero, *Los orígenes del Consejo de Ministros en España* (Madrid, 1979), I, 341–405, and in Rodríguez Casado, *La política*, 234–37.

68. Minute, file on the report of the governor of Havana, 1775–78, AGI, SD, leg. 2132.

69. Ibid.

70. Royal order, Madrid, Dec. 5, 1775, inspection report, Fixed Infantry Regiment of Havana, Havana, June 28, 1776, both in AGI, SD, legs. 2130, 2131.

Shortly after becoming minister of the Indies, Gálvez took additional action. By order of February 28, 1776, he called for a full report on
Cuba's military capability, citing the unsettled nature of world affairs
and the potentially dangerous British military buildup in the Western
Hemisphere. Because the Regiment of Spain had not yet arrived, de la
Torre's observations on the regular army amounted to a reiteration of
his earlier statement, although he was able to report that the epidemic
had begun to subside and that the number of men on duty had therefore
increased somewhat. The defense plan that he advanced, however,
encompassed unprecedented levels of veteran manpower. He asked for
nine full veteran infantry battalions, including the Fijo, from which he
intended to employ 3,480 infantrymen along with 50 dragoons, 120
militia cavalrymen, and 344 artillerymen to defend the *plaza* and the
fortified strongpoints. The remaining veteran infantrymen and dragoons, the light infantry, another 56 artillerymen, and the disciplined
militia, including the rest of the cavalry, would be employed as a
mobile strike force (*campo volante*), bringing his total projected army
to 10,930 men. Perhaps mindful of the fate of Governor Prado, the
captain general was clearly hedging his bets, and neither Gálvez nor
O'Reilly took his request seriously.[71] De la Torre's report, nevertheless,
underscored the urgent need to strengthen Havana's veteran forces.
Gálvez addressed the problem promptly, sending 273 captured deserters from Spain to the fixed units in 1776 and relieving the Regiment
of Lombardy with the Regiment of the Prince in 1777.[72] Moreover, in
August 1778 he promised an additional regiment if international conditions warranted.[73] Meanwhile, a steady inflow of recruits continued to
strengthen the fixed units. By the end of December 1779, the Fijo would
have 1,004 men, the light infantry 157, and the dragoons 140.[74]

De la Torre calculated that he could count upon roughly two-thirds
of the authorized militia force in the event of mobilization, taking into
account routine losses of manpower and the impediments imposed by
occupational conflicts.[75] To Gálvez, who had witnessed firsthand the
woeful deficiencies in the Mexican militia, this estimate must have
been good news indeed.[76] As indicated earlier, new uniforms for the

71. De la Torre to Gálvez, Havana, May 11, 1776, AGI, SD, leg. 2130. De la Torre's
successor, Diego José Navarro García advanced a similar plan in Feb. 1778, AGI, SD,
leg. 2132.

72. De la Torre to José de Gálvez, Havana, June 8, 1776, troop report, Jan. 31, 1778, both
in AGI, SD, legs. 2130, 2132.

73. Royal order, San Ildefonso, Aug. 16, 1778, AGI, SD, leg. 2132. It will be recalled that
in 1771 the crown was preparing a third regiment for Cuba when the crisis abated.

74. Ricla to José de Gálvez, El Pardo, Feb. 1, 1779, troop inspection report, Dec. 1779,
both in AGI, SD, legs. 2133, 2134.

75. De la Torre to José de Gálvez, May 11, 1776, AGI, SD, leg. 2130.

76. For the shortcomings of the reformed army of New Spain at the time of Gálvez, see
Archer, *The Army in Bourbon Mexico*, 12–16.

militia began arriving in 1776, and Gálvez also sent 4,411 muskets to the Havana armory, some of which were assigned to the regular army.[77] The Regiment of the Prince had arrived with its equipment in unsatisfactory condition and the Catalonian Light Infantry also had to be reequipped. The Regiment of Spain, however, had come to Cuba heavily armed and the equipment of the Fijo and the dragoons was, as usual, in good condition.[78] Plenty of new muskets therefore remained for the militia in the event of actual mobilization.

When ordering de la Torre to report on Cuban preparedness, Gálvez had urged caution so as not to arouse domestic anxiety or undue suspicion. Yet even the most casual observer must have sensed the change that was transpiring. Besides the obvious marshaling of manpower and supplies, a new emphasis on discipline appeared. Under pressure from Gálvez, de la Torre in 1776 issued a new, tough edict on desertion that also declared the visibly unemployed liable for forced induction. And during that same year, Gálvez approved the execution by firing squad of Corporal Isidro Antonio Franco of the Fijo, who had abandoned guard duty in the act of deserting. Although consistent with existing regulations, capital punishment in such instances was uncommon, for even the most incorrigible soldier could contribute through banishment to royal labors.[79] On another level, the crown in early 1779 ordered Cuban militia and veteran officers on license in Spain to return to their units and cancelled further leaves.[80]

Despite the dangerous example that the English colonies represented for its own empire, Spain had actively encouraged the American Revolution from an early date by providing money and supplies to the insurgents. By 1779 Charles could no longer resist the temptation to strike a blow at his besieged enemy. In February, Gálvez ordered the Regiment of Navarre to Havana, bringing the veteran infantry in Cuba to the full crisis strength of four regiments, and on May 18, he notified the Cuban authorities that war was to be declared, a communication that reached Havana on July 17.[81]

Spain's primary American objectives were to drive the British from the Gulf of Mexico and the shores of the Mississippi and to dislodge

77. Minute, file on the report of the governor of Havana, 1775–78, AGI, SD, leg. 2132.

78. Dabán to Navarro, Havana, Nov. 11, 1777, AGI, PC, leg. 1235; inspection report, Fixed Infantry Regiment of Havana, June 28, 1776, AGI, SD, leg. 2131.

79. Royal order, Madrid, July 1, 1776, de la Torre to José de Gálvez, Havana, July 6 and Aug. 1, 1776, both in AGI, SD, legs. 2129, 2130; *Ordenanzas de S.M. para el régimen, disciplina, subordinación, y servicio de sus ejércitos* . . . (Madrid, 1768), vol. I, trat. 8, título 10, art. 97.

80. Navarro to José de Gálvez, Havana, Feb. 16, 1779, minute of May 12, 1779, both in AGI, SD, leg. 2133.

81. Navarro to José de Gálvez, Havana, Mar. 8, July 28, 1779, both in AGI, SD, legs. 2133, 2082; Buchanan Parker Thompson, *Spain: Forgotten Ally of the American Revolution* (North Quincy, Mass., 1976), chs. 1–5.

them from their enclaves in Central America.[82] Having recently settled
its differences with Portugal in the Treaty of San Ildefonso, October 1,
1777, Spain had little to fear in Europe and eventually committed an
expeditionary force six regiments strong to the American theater.[83]
This step was delayed, however, by an unsuccessful attempt to seize
Gibraltar. The main component of the Army of Operations, as it was
called, did not reach Havana until August 1780.[84] The delay forced the
royal authorities in America to rely entirely upon local resources
during the early phases of the war.

Minister of the Indies José de Gálvez had placed two of his close
relatives in positions where significant military action was most
likely. He made his brother, Matías, captain general of Guatemala, and
he sent Matías' son, Bernardo, to New Orleans in 1776 as colonel of the
Fixed Battalion, shortly thereafter elevating him to interim governor.
Although only thirty at the time of his appointment to govern
Louisiana, the younger Gálvez already possessed broad military experience. He had fought in Portugal in 1762, had accompanied his uncle
José to New Spain where he commanded forces against the Apaches,
and had served in the ill-fated O'Reilly expedition to Algiers. In these
actions, Bernardo had demonstrated strong leadership qualities and
great personal fortitude, suffering serious wounds both at the hands of
the Apaches and in North Africa.[85] He would exhibit these same qualities repeatedly throughout his career. A royal order of August 29, 1779,
named Gálvez, who had earlier been made brigadier general and proprietary governor, commander of the expeditionary forces against British
Florida.[86] In the meantime, Field Marshal Diego José Navarro García, an
elderly but well-intentioned officer, had replaced de la Torre as captain
general.[87]

Because of New Orleans' dangerously exposed position, Captain
General Navarro reinforced the enfeebled Louisiana garrison in May
1778 with forty-nine men from Havana's Fixed Infantry, forty-six from
the Regiment of the Prince, and ninety-three from the Regiment of
Spain. And during mid-August 1779, in response to Gálvez' alarm over
British movements upriver, he sent the Second Battalion of Spain to
New Orleans, bringing the total relief force to 826.[88] To cover these

82. Navarro to José de Gálvez, Havana, Aug. 11, 1779, AGI, SD, leg. 2082.
83. Dauril Alden, "The Undeclared War of 1771–1777: Climax of Luso-Spanish Platine
Rivalry," *HAHR* 41 (Feb. 1961), 73–74.
84. Navarro to José de Gálvez, Havana, Aug. 28, 1780, AGI, SD, leg. 2082.
85. Caughey, *Bernardo de Gálvez*, 61–68.
86. Royal order, San Ildefonso, Aug. 29, 1779, AGI, PC, leg. 2351.
87. For a brief biography of Navarro, see Francisco Girón María, *Espejo de gobernadores: Biografía de don Diego José Navarro* (Seville, 1942).
88. Dabán to Navarro, Havana, May 9, 1778, Aug. 5, 1779, both in AGI, PC, legs. 1234,
1235; Navarro to José de Gálvez, Havana, Aug. 11, 1779, AGI, SD, leg. 2082; Bernardo de

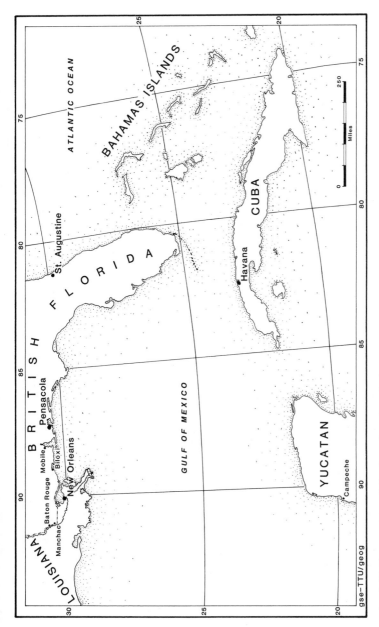

The Gulf Theater, War of the American Revolution

manpower losses for Cuba, Navarro, according to plan, called upon the disciplined militia. He mobilized 601 men from the First Battalion of the White Infantry Regiment of Havana to replace the Battalion of Spain while also recalling to Havana veteran detachments in Matanzas, Puerto Príncipe, and Cuatro Villas. To replace the latter, he mobilized a full company of the Matanzas Dragoons and one 50-man company each from the White Volunteer Battalions of Puerto Príncipe and Cuatro Villas. And to cover deficiencies in the Second Battalion of the Fijo, the governor of Santiago ordered to service two companies from his battalion of whites. Throughout the war, the authorities carefully limited the number of men they mobilized both to curtail costs and to minimize domestic disruption.[89]

In the area of equipment, Navarro approved a scheme by Dabán to provide each company of the Havana, Matanzas, and Santiago-Bayamo volunteer infantry with eight new muskets to enhance their training. Cuatro Villas and Puerto Príncipe still possessed enough usable firearms to function without such assistance.[90] And for the Havana infantry, the municipal uniforms and weapons fund financed new knapsacks and utensils.[91]

Even before the Battalion of Spain had arrived from Havana, Gálvez struck at the British strongpoints of Manchac and Baton Rouge to establish Spanish control over the Mississippi and to secure New Orleans from attack. Gálvez left New Orleans on August 27 with an army of 667 men, 500 of them regulars, the rest Louisiana militiamen and volunteers. Although recently reinforced from Mexico and the Canary Islands, the Louisiana garrison was so badly understrength owing to disease that it could muster only 370 untrained recruits, some of whom had to be left behind pending the arrival of more troops from Havana. Key components of Gálvez' army were 160 of the Havana veterans and a small corps of local artillerymen. On his way up river, moreover, Gálvez also managed to incorporate some 160 friendly Indians and another 600 colonists, some of them outlying militiamen, others raw recruits.[92] Gálvez' victories at Manchac on September 7 and against the main British force at Baton Rouge on September 21 were in

Gálvez to Navarro, New Orleans, Apr. 14, 1778, in Lawrence Kinnaird, ed., *Spain in the Mississippi Valley, 1765-1794* (Washington, D.C., 1949), I, 265-66.

89. Navarro to José de Gálvez, Havana, Aug. 7, Sept. 1 (twice), 1779, all in AGI, SD, legs. 2133, 2134; Dabán to Navarro, Havana, Aug. 23, 1779, AGI, PC, leg. 1235.

90. Navarro to Dabán, Havana, Aug. 15, 1779, AGI, PC, leg. 1235.

91. Dabán to Navarro, Havana, Nov. 2, 1779, ibid.

92. Bernardo de Gálvez to Navarro, New Orleans, July 3, 1779, AGI, SD, leg. 2082; Bernardo de Gálvez to Navarro, New Orleans, Aug. 17, 1779, AGI, PC, leg. 2351; Navarro to José de Gálvez, Havana, Aug. 11, 1779, AGI, SD, leg. 2082. For efforts of Gálvez to expand the Louisiana garrison to a regiment, see Holmes, *Honor and Fidelity*, 24-26.

the main a credit to his imaginative leadership and to the veteran and volunteer troops of Louisiana. Cuban forces constituted a prominent although not dominant component of the expedition.[93]

Before he had left to clear the lower Mississippi of British forces, Bernardo de Gálvez by letter of August 17 had urgently solicited four thousand additional troops from Cuba to carry the war to Pensacola. Spanish intelligence estimated that victory would require seven thousand men, but the governor, who also planned to bring a thousand men from Louisiana as well as the Battalion of Spain hoped to catch Pensacola before the British could reinforce it.[94] Aware of the limited size of the veteran forces at Havana, Gálvez reminded the governor of the value of the Cuban militia. "These 4,000 men," he wrote, "should be chosen from the units of that garrison, both veterans and militiamen. The latter have a good reputation in that *plaza* (the whites as well as the colored) to the point that they are are held in as much confidence as the veterans."[95] Damage to his forces from a hurricane on August 18 led Gálvez to increase his request to five thousand men.[96]

Unfortunately, Governor Navarro could not provide Gálvez the support that he sought. Earlier, when he dispatched the Second Battalion of the Regiment of Spain to New Orleans, the captain general had complained to the crown of manpower deficiencies. The core problem was that the veteran infantry units of Havana, including the Regiments of the Prince and Navarre, the First Battalions of the Fijo and Spain, and the Light Infantry Companies, were short a total of 1,184 men. In large measure, this difficulty arose from the condition of the Regiment of the Prince, down 623 men, which had arrived badly understrength and continued to deteriorate. Taken together, these losses left the garrison nearly a regiment under its wartime footing, not including the troops already deployed in Louisiana. Navarro had only 3,107 veterans left in Havana—far less than the number Gálvez sought—and 3,500 volunteer infantrymen, including the foot companies of the Matanzas Dragoons. The militia, which was already partially mobilized could, of course, have been exploited more fully to replace departing veterans or to accompany the expedition, but to have sent 5,000 men would have left

93. An account of this action can be found in Caughey, *Bernardo de Gálvez*, 153–57, 163. Also see Holmes, *Honor and Fidelity*, 30–31. The British side of these battles and the subsequent action in the Gulf Campaign has been nicely presented in J. Barton Starr, *Tories, Dons, and Rebels: The American Revolution in British West Florida* (Gainesville, 1976).

94. See John Caughey, "The Panis Mission to Pensacola, 1778," *HAHR* 10 (Nov. 1930), 480–89. Also see Panis to Bernardo de Gálvez, New Orleans, Apr. 29, 1779, in Kinnaird, ed., *Spain*, I, 336–38.

95. Bernardo de Gálvez to Navarro, New Orleans, Aug. 17, 1779, AGI, PC, leg. 2351.

96. Caughey, *Bernardo de Gálvez*, 172; Navarro to José de Gálvez, Havana, Sept. 11, 1779, AGI, SD, leg. 2082.

Havana nearly defenseless, with only 1,607 infantrymen and no reserve, a risk that Navarro clearly found unacceptable.[97] Instead, by advancing his own alternative proposals, the captain general stalled Gálvez while awaiting further help from Spain.[98]

José de Gálvez reacted to Navarro's delay with uncommonly harsh criticism, and historians who have focused upon these events from the perspective of Bernardo de Gálvez and his expedition have generally shared that impatience.[99] The opportunities in Florida where the British were badly unprepared and highly vulnerable and where sudden, decisive action could easily have gained the advantage, go far to justify the criticism. Certainly, Navarro's behavior emerges as something less than a model of daring, courageous leadership. He undoubtedly could have spared two or three thousand men, if not the five that Gávez wanted, but it should be remembered that his first duty was to the island, a point that José de Gálvez himself had emphasized in his instructions of October 1778.[100] And Charles himself must bear part of the responsibility for Navarro's caution. The example that he had made of Governor Prado must have weighed heavily on Navarro's mind, particularly since a British strike beneath Florida into Cuba appeared a very real possibility.[101]

In the meantime, the basis for further action against the British took shape. On October 3 the minister of the Indies responded to the Cuban governor's August troop report by promising a fourth Spanish regiment to depart in November on the next convoy, accompanied by a large quantity of supplies.[102] In the north, Bernardo de Gálvez elected to narrow his immediate objective to an attack on Mobile, an undertaking that would require fewer men. To procure support from Havana, he sent Colonel Esteban Miró to intervene personally, now asking more realistically for two thousand men or at the very least thirteen to fifteen hundred.[103] By the time Miró arrived on January 24, Navarro had learned of the new plan and had already organized additional forces for the expedition.[104]

Navarro drew primarily upon his veterans, although with some

97. Dabán to Navarro, Havana, Nov. 11, 1777, AGI, PC, 1235; Navarro to José de Gálvez, Havana, Aug. 11, 1779, AGI, SD, leg. 2082.

98. Caughey, *Bernardo de Gálvez*, 173–74.

99. Royal order, El Pardo, Jan. 11, 1780, AGI, SD, leg. 2082. See for example, Caughey, *Bernardo de Gálvez*, 172–74, 192; Thompson, *Spain: Forgotten Ally*, 204–5.

100. Navarro to José de Gálvez, Havana, Aug. 11, 1779, AGI, SD, leg. 2082.

101. For example, see Navarro to Viceroy Martín de Mayorga, Havana, Feb. 7, Mar. 5, 1780, both in Kinnaird, ed., *Spain*, I, 368–70, 374–75.

102. Royal order, San Lorenzo, Oct. 3, 1779, AGI, SD, leg. 2082.

103. Caughey, *Bernardo de Gálvez*, 174; instructions of Bernardo de Gálvez to Miró, New Orleans, Dec. 31, 1779, in Kinnaird, ed., *Spain*, I, 366–68.

104. Navarro to José de Gálvez, Havana, Jan. 2, 1780, AGI, SD, leg. 2082.

militia support. From his Spanish units, he called upon the Regiment of the Prince, which had dwindled to 620 men, and upon 121 men from the Regiment of Navarre. From the permanent garrison the Fijo was to contribute 51, the Catalonian Light Infantry 100, and the Artillery Corps 42. In addition, Navarro ordered the Pardo and Moreno Militia Battalions to provide 139 troops each and the two Volunteer Artillery Companies, which had just been formed, 50 apiece. Completing the personnel for the expedition were 100 fortification workers. As part of the supplies for the expeditionary force, Navarro provided the militiamen with new waistcoats and trousers and sent along five hundred extra muskets.[105]

Preparations for the expedition were completed by mid-December 1779, but a combination of bad weather and timid naval leadership delayed its departure. Navarro heeded Miró's counsel to the extent that he increased the contingent from the Regiment of Navarre to a complete battalion—689 men—bringing the total force to 1,166 troops, their officers, and 100 laborers.[106] Gálvez had specifically asked for the Regiment of Navarre, whose colonel, José de Ezpeleta, was a friend and comrade from the ill-fated Algiers expedition. When committing these forces to action in Florida, Navarro stressed to Bernardo de Gálvez the danger of a British counterattack and pleaded for the prompt return to Havana of as many of the troops as possible.[107]

Ships carrying at least three companies from the Regiment of Navarre, but not Ezpeleta, set sail on February 10. The main force did not embark until the fifteenth and even then did not depart for another three weeks owing to a seemingly endless line of excuses from the officers of the fleet.[108] The advance troops from the Regiment of Navarre arrived in time for the siege of Mobile, but the others, including Ezpeleta, did not.[109]

Apart from the veteran and militia forces that it contributed to

105. Navarro to José de Gálvez, Havana, Jan. 5, 1780, ibid. For the formation of the new artillery companies, see Navarro to José de Gálvez, Havana, Dec. 16, 1779, royal order, Aranjuez, Apr. 16, 1780, both in AGI, SD, leg. 2082.

106. Navarro to José de Gálvez, Havana, Feb. 22, 1780, AGI, SD, leg. 2082. Two white noncommissioned officers, assigned to the *pardos* and *morenos*, were also added, but the Regiment of the Prince had diminished to 604 men by Feb. 10.

107. Instructions of Bernardo de Gálvez to Miró, Dec. 31, 1779, agreement of Navarro and Juan Bautista Bonet, Havana, Jan. 31, 1780, both in Kinnaird, ed., *Spain*, I, 364–66, 370–73; Eric Beerman, "José de Ezpeleta," *Revista de historia militar* 21 (1977), 99. For an exhaustive treatment of Ezpeleta's contribution to the Florida campaign, see F. de Borja Medina Rojas, *José de Ezpeleta, gobernador de la Mobila, 1780–1781* (Seville, 1980).

108. Navarro to José de Gálvez, Havana, Feb. 22, 26, 1780, both in AGI, SD, 2082; diary of Lieutenant Colonel Esteban Miró, AGI, PC, leg. 2351. Beerman, "José de Ezpeleta," 100, indicates that Ezpeleta accompanied the forces that left on Feb. 10. He did not. See Navarro to Bonet, Havana, Feb. 22, 1780, AGI, SD, leg. 2082.

109. Bernardo de Gálvez to Navarro, Río de los Perros, Feb. 27, 1780, AGI, PC, leg. 2351.

Gálvez' army, Cuba also provided personnel for the navy. In response to a request from the commandant general of the Havana squadron, Juan Bautista Bonet, Navarro ordered four companies of seventy-seven men each from the Volunteer Infantry Regiment to serve aboard ships of war as marines, replacing veterans who were returned to their units. Navarro equipped them with new muskets and provided three of the companies, which were assigned to ships detailed for the invasion, with winter clothing. The planning that went into the military reform did not anticipate naval duty, but the military authorities plainly had to improvise with the resources available.[110]

The army that Gálvez advanced toward Mobile from New Orleans derived principally from the Cuban garrison, the Regiment of the Prince contributing 49 men, the Fijo 48, and the Second Battalion of the Regiment of Spain 683. The artillery and fixed infantry of Louisiana provided another 143 and the Louisiana militia 454. Twenty-four slaves and 26 English-American auxiliaries completed the expedition, bringing its total force to 1,427.[111] Gálvez began a deliberate descent down the Mississippi River on January 11, reaching Mobile Bay on February 10. With the support of those troops from the Regiment of Navarre that arrived on time, Gálvez won a surrender on March 14.[112]

At the time that Navarro committed the additional 1,866 troops from his garrison to the service of Gálvez, he petitioned the viceroy of New Spain for a regiment to reinforce Havana and inquired if the French at Guarico, Saint Domingue, might render assistance.[113] Although immediate support from these sources was unlikely and did not in fact develop, the captain general must have taken comfort in the promise of José de Gálvez to send Cuba another regiment with the November convoy. The minister of the Indies, however, who showed so little patience with Navarro's reluctance to support his nephew, did no better himself in furnishing troops. The promised unit, the Im-

---

110. Juan de Urriza to José de Gálvez, Havana, Feb. 20, 1780, Navarro to José de Gálvez, Havana, Feb. 22, 1780, both in AGI, SD, leg. 2082; Dabán to Navarro, Havana, Feb. 9, 1780, AGI, PC, leg. 1235.

111. Troop report, New Orleans, Jan. 11, 1780, in Navarro to Gálvez, Havana, Jan. 31, 1780, AGI, PC, leg. 2351. Bernardo de Gálvez in his diary of the expedition against Mobile gave slightly different figures for the Regiment of the Prince (43), the Fijo of Havana (50), the Louisiana artillery and fixed battalion (154), and militia (456). His account has led to confusion because he omitted a comma between the Regiment of the Prince and the Second Battalion of the Regiment of Spain. This led Caughey in his *Bernardo de Gálvez* to state the contingents as "43 men of the Regiment of Príncipe of the Second Battalion of Spain," 174. Holmes, *Honor and Fidelity*, 32, omitted the Second Battalion of the Regiment of Spain altogether.

112. Caughey, *Bernardo de Gálvez*, 175–86.

113. Navarro to José de Gálvez, Havana, Jan. 11, 1780, AGI, SD, leg. 2082.

memorial Regiment of the King, did not depart Spain until April, moving with the main Spanish expeditionary force to America.[114]

The depature of the expedition to Mobile left Havana with an effective force of only 1,443 regulars, placing major responsibility for home defense on the militia. Despite those incorporated into the expeditionary force and the navy, Havana still retained 2,714 volunteer infantrymen. Navarro mobilized these troops in sufficient numbers to man the defenses of the city and its outer fortifications. Elsewhere, the governor called upon the three hundred foot soldiers of the Matanzas Dragoons to cover that city and its adjacent defense points and upon the Battalion of Cuatro Villas to provide troops for the Castle of Jagua in the south.[115] A buildup of British forces in nearby Jamaica to the strength of eight battalions was causing grave concern in Santiago, as was the condition of the Second Battalion of the Fijo, which was more than two hundred men understrength. The disciplined militia made possible a semblance of a respectable defense force as both white and *pardo* companies helped man the fortifications.[116] Navarro's fears subsided when the main body of the expeditionary force returned to Havana on May 20, bringing with it part of the troops originally deployed in Louisiana, but leaving in Mobile supplies, José de Ezpeleta, and in conjunction with the Louisiana units a small garrison.[117]

Meanwhile, the authorities continued to upgrade the equipment of the disciplined militia. On February 9, the day before the first ships left Havana for Mobile, the captain general ordered defective firearms replaced for the Volunteer Cavalry Regiment.[118] And during the course of 1780, the replacement of equipment became routine for the units of Havana and Santiago, Havana's municipal fund covering at least part of the cost.[119] The crown also authorized the outfitting of the Volunteer Cavalry Regiment with the same uniforms as those worn by the veteran squadron so that militia companies might merge with the veterans to function tactically as a regiment in the event of an invasion as O'Reilly had originally planned.[120] The militia thus continued to stand

114. Lieutenant General Victorio de Navia to José de Gálvez, aboard *San Luis*, Apr. 28, 1780, AGI, SD, leg. 2086.

115. Navarro to José de Gálvez, Havana, Feb. 22, 1780, AGI, SD, leg. 2082; Dabán to Navarro, Havana, Apr. 18, 1780, AGI, PC, leg. 1235.

116. Navarro to Commander of the Army of Operations Victorio Navia, Havana, May 31, 1780, royal orders, El Pardo, Feb. 17, 19, 1780, all in AGI, SD, legs. 2082, 2083; Dabán to Navarro, Havana, Apr. 28, 1780, AGI, PC, leg. 1235.

117. Navarro to Navia, Havana, May 30, 1780, AGI, SD, leg. 2083.

118. Navarro to Dabán, Havana, Feb. 9, 1780, AGI, PC, leg. 1235.

119. Dabán to Navarro, Havana, July 24, 1780, Feb. 24, Mar. 29, 1781, all in AGI, PC, leg. 1235.

120. Dabán to Navarro, Havana, May 6, 1780, AGI, PC, leg. 1235.

ready as a home guard while attention turned to Spain's primary objective—Pensacola.

The army of Cuba, which had contributed prominently at Manchac and Baton Rouge and had constituted the dominant component at Mobile, would also occupy a central position in the conquest of Pensacola, but in conjunction with a major army from Spain. Under the command of Lieutenant General Victorio de Navia, the Army of Operations departed Cádiz on April 28, 1780, with the strength of six regiments totaling 7,637 men and 100 artillerymen. Accompanying this expedition were the Immemorial Regiment of the King, destined for the Havana garrison; the Regiment of the Crown and four hundred recruits for Puerto Rico; and a separate company for Guatemala.[121] As explained earlier, the deployment of this force had been delayed by an abortive attempt to seize Gibraltar, but when the British navy broke the Spanish blockade and immediate hopes for victory faded, the more promising targets of the American theater assumed priority.[122] Navia's army bore orders to assist Gálvez in the conquest of Florida, if that objective had not already been realized, and then to join French forces in Guarico to strike at Jamaica.[123] Alejandro O'Reilly, who was still the captain general in Cádiz, executed the administrative responsibilities for the final preparation and embarkation of the army, once more contributing to the preparation of Spain's blow against the British.[124]

At the time of its departure, the Army of Operations possessed sufficient strength to complete the conquest of Florida on its own, but tragedy intervened twice to diminish its contribution and to place major responsibility again on the army of Cuba. First blockaded in port, then devastated by disease, the main convoy did not reach Havana until August 3, over three months after embarking. The sick were put ashore as the transports moved among the French and Spanish Antilles, leaving more than nine hundred men scattered from Guadeloupe to Guarico. Another 478 died during the crossing, and 47 found the opportunity to desert. Worse, the epidemic continued to ravage the weakened army once it arrived in Cuba, leaving the majority hospitalized and many others dead. Although the scattered components gradually made their way to Havana, Commander Navia had only 2,321 able-bodied

121. Included were the regiments of Soria (1,377), Guadalajara (1,358), Hibernia (1,115), Aragón (1,377), Catalonia (1,248) and Flanders (1,162). Navia to José de Gálvez, aboard *San Luis*, Apr. 28, 1780, AGI, SD, leg. 2086. Another report, Havana, Aug. 20, 1780, varied somewhat: Soria (1,376), Guadalajara (1,375),Ibernia (1,096), Aragón (1,366), Catalonia (1,249), Flanders (1,133), and the artillery (106), AGI, SD, leg. 2086.

122. LaFuente, *Historia general*, XIV, 329–31.

123. Royal order, Aranjuez, June 24, 1780, AGI, IG, leg. 1578.

124. Minutes, Expeditionary Junta, Cádiz, Mar. 28, 1780, AGS, GM, leg. 7303.

men in mid-October when Gálvez launched his first expedition against Pensacola.[125]

To prepare for the final step in the conquest of the Gulf Coast, Bernardo de Gálvez had come personally to Havana, arriving August 2, the day before the Army of Operations reached port. Following the victory at Mobile, some consideration had been given to carrying the war to Pensacola immediately, but the smallness of Gálvez' force, even including the late arrivals from Havana; the navy's fear of the fortifications at the entrance to Pensacola Bay; and the news of British reinforcements—all persuaded the governor of Louisiana to delay.[126] Once in Havana, Bernardo met in a series of juntas with the various military authorities to chart a final strategy.

Given the condition of the Army of Operations, major responsibility again fell to the Havana garrison. Although calling upon the viceroy, Puerto Rico, and Santo Domingo for support, the junta resolved to launch an attack with 3,800 men from Cuba.[127] For this force, the junta summoned only 799 men from Navia's army, many of them individuals from a portion of the convoy that had reached Havana at the end of June and who, consequently, were healthier than the later arrivals. Even so, only 594 actually accompanied the expedition, the remainder falling ill and having to be replaced by Cuban forces.[128] Cuba contributed 3,239 troops, 2,761 of them from the veteran garrison, 139 each from the Volunteer Battalions of Pardos and Morenos, 100 *pardo* and *moreno* artillerymen, and 100 fortification workers, bringing the total expeditionary force to 3,833.[129]

Although the new levy severely drained the Havana garrison, the situation was not as desperate as it had been in March, April, and May. Apart from the remnants of the several veteran units of the garrison,

---

125. Navia to José de Gálvez, Havana, Feb. 16, 1781, Urriza to Gálvez, Havana, Aug. 27, 1780, Navarro to José de Gálvez, Havana, Aug. 28, 1780, Navia to Navarro, Havana, Oct. 14, 1780, all in AGI, SD, legs. 2082, 2083, 2086; casualty report, Guadeloupe, July 7, 1780, "Etat des [sic] detachement . . . ," Guarico, Sept. 25, 1780, both in AGI, IG, leg. 1578.

126. Caughey, *Bernardo de Gálvez*, 187–91, confused the follow-through from Havana on the Mobile expedition, and the limited probes toward Pensacola, with a separate, major expedition against Pensacola.

127. Ibid., 192–93.

128. Navarro to José de Gálvez, Havana, Oct. 17, 1780, Navia to José de Gálvez, Havana, Jan. 17, Feb. 16, 1781, all in AGI, SD, legs. 2083, 2086.

129. Navarro to José de Gálvez, Havana, Jan. 17, 1781, AGI, SD, leg. 2083. From the veteran garrison the Regiments of Navarre contributed 810 men; Spain, 753; the Prince, 394; the King, 353; and the Fijo, 288. There were 87 artillerymen, 23 light infantrymen, and 53 dragoons. The numbers attached to the units of the Cuban garrison from the Army of Operations can be found in Navia to José de Gálvez, Havana, Jan. 17, 1781, AGI, SD, leg. 2086. Caughey, *Benardo de Gálvez*, misread Navarro's troop report, placing the expeditionary force at 3,829, a figure that excluded 4 men who died at sea.

over fifteen hundred able-bodied soldiers remained from the Army of Operations. Although these men were too weakened to participate in an amphibious operation, they were strong enough to stand behind fixed fortifications and in fact did assume garrison duty in lieu of those who left for Florida.[130] Moreover, the Immemorial Regiment of the King, which Gálvez had sent to reinforce Havana, was now available. Although afflicted like the other units that crossed on the convoy, it nevertheless managed to contribute 353 troops for the expedition and some 300 more for the defense of Havana.[131] And as always, the disciplined militia stood ready to fill gaps and to function as a reserve.

Despite tedious preparations, the long-awaited conquest of Pensacola continued to elude Spain. Tragedy struck in the form of a hurricane that caught the invasion fleet soon after its departure from Havana on October 16. The violent winds drove the transports out into the Gulf of Mexico and scattered them from Mobile to New Orleans and Campeche. The tenacious Gálvez, however, refused to be dissuaded from his objective. In mid-November, he returned to Havana to begin anew.[132]

As of January 17, 1781, 3,829 of the troops were accounted for, 862 of them in Havana, 1,771 in Campeche, 831 in New Orleans, and 365 in Mobile. The authorities in Havana attempted to retrieve the large component beached in Campeche but abandoned the idea of regrouping the entire army as costly, time-consuming, and impractical.[133] On the positive side, the forces in Mobile and New Orleans were close enough to Pensacola to be sent directly into action in coordination with a new expedition from Havana. The problem with such a scheme, however, was that a strong force from Havana would be needed to lead the way. Although the Havana garrison counted 2,561 able-bodied men by early February, the sickness in the Army of Operations continued into the new year.[134] Thus, as preparations for another invasion advanced, the importance of the disciplined militia once again came to the foreground.

On November 30, Gálvez met with the Junta de Generales in Havana. The commander asked for three thousand troops to embark as soon as possible. Although such a contingent would leave few men behind, he realistically minimized the danger to Cuba. The British forces in Jamaica, recent intelligence had reported, were themselves

130. Navia to Navarro, Havana, Oct. 14, 1780, AGI, SD, leg. 2083.
131. Navarro to José de Gálvez, Havana, Aug. 28, 1780, AGI, SD, leg. 2082.
132. Caughey, *Bernardo de Gálvez*, 193.
133. Navarro to José de Gálvez, Havana, Jan. 17, 1781, AGI, SD, leg. 2083. Also see Navarro's report on the expedition, Havana, Feb. 12, 1781, ibid.
134. Navia to José de Gálvez, Havana, Feb. 16, 1781, troop report, Havana garrison, Havana, Feb. 12, 1781, both in AGI, SD, leg. 2086.

gripped by disease, and although the United Kingdom continued to enjoy naval supremacy, it was unlikely that a major attack could be mounted on Cuba. In the event that some sort of invasion did materialize, the junta reasoned, the island should be able to depend upon the militia "instructed on the footing of veterans, which after all the fortifications [had been manned] would retain a mobile strike force of several thousand men." Further, the French in Guarico had now contributed to the Spanish effort two thousand troops under the command of the captain general of Santo Domingo. Governor Navarro and the other authorities generally supported Gálvez' scheme but differed on timing, preferring to wait until March, which would bring more favorable weather and which would permit greater time for preparation.[135]

Meanwhile, sensing Spanish vulnerability, the British in a series of minor actions in conjunction with Indian allies began to probe Gálvez' hold on Mobile. Upon learning of the threat, the Junta de Generales resolved to deploy fifteen hundred veteran troops to reinforce Mobile, a thousand of them from the Army of Operations, the remainder from the Havana garrison, the latter to depart at once. The first 500 troops left on December 7, although 219 of the men from the Regiment of the King had to be replaced with troops from the Army of Operations for want of proper winter clothing.[136] The commander of the relief expedition, José de Rada, took the force to New Orleans rather than to Mobile, however, claiming that a shift in the channel into Mobile Bay made an entrance too risky. Fortunately for Spain, José de Ezpeleta and his garrison, assisted by some 365 men who had blown ashore in October, managed to repulse a substantial British attack in early January.[137] News of this clash strengthened the hand of Bernardo de Gálvez, who continued his efforts to organize additional forces for the campaign in East Florida.

Gálvez' actual motive for organizing the "relief" force was to mount an early attack on Pensacola. Besides the remaining one thousand troops destined for Mobile by the Junta de Generales, he prevailed upon Navarro to supply five 63-man companies of grenadiers, two from the

---

135. Minutes, Junta de Generales, Havana, Nov. 30, 1780, AGI, SD, leg. 2083. An account of this meeting can be found in Caughey, *Bernardo de Gálvez*, 196–98. See also royal orders, El Pardo, Feb. 17, 1780, Aranjuez, Apr. 30, 1780, both in AGI, SD, leg. 2082.

136. Navarro to Navia, Havana, Dec. 6, 1780, Navia to José de Gálvez, Havana, Jan. 13, 1781, both in AGI, SD, legs. 2083, 2086. The expedition included troops from regiments of Soria (109 men), Guadalajara (55), Aragón (55), Spain (60), the Prince (60), Navarre (60), and the Fijo (60). The Squadron of Dragoons of America contributed a 41-man company.

137. Caughey, *Bernardo de Gálvez*, 194–95; Navarro to Gálvez, Havana, Jan. 17, 1781, AGI, SD, leg. 2083. Contingents from the Regiments of Navarre, Spain, the Prince, the Fijo, and the Louisiana militia saw action and suffered casualties. Medina Rojas, *José de Ezpeleta*, 151–54; Beerman, "José de Ezpeleta," 102.

Regiment of the King and one each from the Regiments of Navarre, the Prince, and Spain, and he also incorporated into his force an additional 50 veterans from the Royal Corps of Artillery and 102 fortification workers. To avoid rival authorities and conflicting ambitions, Gálvez embarked with his army on February 14, thus placing the troops under his exclusive control as supreme commander for the Florida theater. He then landed the troops a short distance from Havana, at Santuario de Regla, where he organized his forces for an attack on the British.[138] He departed for Pensacola on February 28, began landing his troops on Santa Rosa Island at the entrance to the port on March 9, and with a spectacular, well-known display of heroism and leadership penetrated the bay nine days later. Meanwhile, just before leaving Havana, he had ordered the acting governor of New Orleans, Pedro Piernas, to proceed with his forces by sea to Pensacola, and on March 1 he sent instructions to José de Ezpeleta in Mobile to advance by land with as many men as possible.[139]

As Gálvez prepared for a long siege, a formidable army took shape with uncommon efficiency. From Mobile, Ezpeleta arrived on March 22 with 905 men, including the 365 stranded in Mobile by the October hurricane and those left behind in May as a garrison. The following day, a convoy entered the bay carrying 1,390 troops from New Orleans. This force included the 500 men originally sent to relieve Mobile and 831 from the hurricane—minus casualties and deserters—and small components from the Louisiana garrison and militia.[140] And in mid-April, the authorities in Havana, fearing that a British fleet sighted in the area

138. Navarro to Gálvez, Havana, Mar. 1, 1781, AGI, SD, leg. 2083. From the Army of Operations, there were 231 men from the Regiment of Soria, 77 from Guadalajara, 308 from Ibernia, 77 from Aragón and 307 from Flanders.

139. Bernardo de Gálvez, "Journal of the Operations of the Expedition against the Fortified Town of Pensacola . . . ," in N. Orwin Rush, ed., *The Battle of Pensacola, March 9 to May 8, 1781* (Tallahassee, 1966), 43.

140. Ibid., 62–64; Francisco de Saavedra to José de Gálvez, Havana, Apr. 7, 1781, AGI, IG, leg. 1578. Unfortunately, we do not have a complete roster of the expedition from Mobile. Those deposited there by the hurricane included 123 men from the Regiment of Spain, 122 from Navarre, 105 from the Fijo, and 15 fortifications workers. Navarro to José de Gálvez, Havana, Jan. 27, 1781, AGI, SD, leg. 2083. See also Medina Rojas, *José de Ezpeleta*, ch. 11. Detailed reports exist for the expedition from New Orleans but as usual there are discrepancies among the reports. According to Lieutenant Colonel Cayetano de Salla, New Orleans, Feb. 28, 1781, the expedition contained from the Regiment of the King 132 men, the Prince 60, Soria 109, Guadalajara 55, Spain 60, Aragón 55, Navarre 281, Catalonia 93, and the Fijo 59, and from Havana's Squadron of Dragoons of America came 57 troopers. The Havana battalion of *pardos* contributed 130, the *morenos* 134, the Louisiana Fijo 125, and the Louisiana militia dragoons 40. AGI, PC, leg. 83, also published in Kinnaird, ed., *Spain*, I, 421–22. Holmes, *Honor and Fidelity*, 33, cites a later Salla report that placed the number of men in the army at 1,409. Holmes errs, however, in believing that the *pardo* and *moreno* militia were Louisiana troops. They were part of the October expedition out of Havana that was deposited in New Orleans.

bore aid for Pensacola and now confident about weather conditions, dispatched Field Marshal Juan Manuel Cagigal with 1,600 reinforcements, 640 of them from the Havana garrison and the remainder from the Army of Operations.[141] Moreover, French forces in Guarico had linked up with the Spanish in Cuba and provided four frigates for the convoy and 725 troops. Finally, Squadron Chief José Solano, Marqués del Socorro, who commanded the convoy, sent ashore 1,350 gunners and crewmen from his fleet, bringing the total attack force to some 7,437 men.[142] Spain's achievement in amassing an army of this strength on enemy soil, crowned by the long-awaited surrender on May 10, was eloquent evidence of the successes of the military reform and, concurrently, of the resurgence of Spanish military power.

Despite earlier concern, Cuba actually experienced less strain during the final months of the Gulf campaign than during the earlier actions. The Army of Operations had gradually continued to recover its health, although as late as mid-February 618 men were still sick and 813 convalescing, while 1,797 had died and nearly 500 more had been captured or remained scattered throughout the Lesser Antilles.[143] In addition, most of the men attached to the October expedition who had been blown to Campeche had returned to Havana.[144] Thus, even after Gálvez left with 1,000 of its company, the Army of Operations still had 2,544 able-bodied men in Havana, and the authorities in a series of juntas began charting plans for an invasion of Jamaica (see Chapter 5).[145] The Havana garrison itself still possessed 2,196 men, not enough to cover all the local points, but with the other Spanish troops, the disciplined militia, and the rapidly declining fortunes of the British in America, there was little cause for concern, even when Cagigal took another 1,600 regulars with him in April.[146]

Throughout this campaign, the disciplined militia, as determined by long-range planning, acted principally as a strategic reserve, although it also made direct, if small, contributions to the action at Pensacola. Apart from the *pardo* and *moreno* infantry and artillery companies, some 232 men from the White Infantry Regiment again served aboard ship. When the navy sent its forces into action during the siege, these components presumably also saw action.[147] But the principal contribution of the militia was to free regular forces for offensive duty by serving as a home guard.

141. Navia to José de Gálvez, Havana, Apr. 8, 1781, AGI, SD, leg. 2086.
142. Caughey, *Bernardo de Gálvez*, 208.
143. Navia to José de Gálvez, Havana, Feb. 16, Mar. 3, 1781, both in AGI, SD, leg. 2086.
144. Navia to José de Gálvez, Havana, Nov. 28, 1780, Feb. 16, 1781, both ibid.
145. Juntas of generals, Havana, Feb., Mar. 1781, ibid.
146. Troop report, Havana garrison, Havana, Feb. 12, 1781, ibid.
147. Dabán to Navarro, Havana, Feb. 28, 1781, AGI, PC, leg. 1235.

Supply did not pose significant problems for the militia. Weapons continued to be replaced routinely as they wore out. Indeed, as late as March 1781, during the midst of the siege of Pensacola, Havana still possessed a surplus of 2,199 muskets.[148] And drawing upon the municipal equipment fund, the authorities continued to reuniform the militia.[149]

How well the disciplined militia might have performed had the British actually managed a blow at Cuba cannot, of course, be determined. The Spanish authorities, from the king to José and Bernardo de Gálvez and on down, believed that it was a dependable force, and they shaped their strategies accordingly. This confidence underpinned the breadth of Spanish military action and the ultimate victory in Florida.

148. Navarro to Dabán, Havana, Feb. 24, 1781, ibid.; Urriza to Navia, Havana, Mar. 13, 1781, AGI, SD, leg. 2083.
149. Dabán to Navarro, Havana, Mar. 29, 1781, Cagigal to Dabán, Havana, Nov. 19, 1781, both in AGI, PC, leg. 1235.

5. Continuity

During the decade following the Spanish victory in Florida, a high degree of continuity characterized the Cuban militia, its place in society, and the relationship of that society to the authorities at court. The regiments and battalions of horse and foot that O'Reilly had established remained; substantially the same families continued to dominate the officer corps; and Cuban planters successfully renewed their quest for special commercial privileges in return for their military services. Some innovation occurred in the regular army where the responsibility to defend newly acquired Florida prompted an expansion of the fixed garrison and where creoles increasingly penetrated the officer corps. But even there, change was more apparent than real. The stability of the Cuban experience contrasts with the upheavals that plagued the other colonies and with the changing strategies and priorities at court following the death of José de Gálvez in 1787.

Gálvez could not have been pleased with the behavior of the South American colonies during the War of the American Revolution. His attempt to raise monies through a cadre of regents-visitor failed utterly, politically embarrassing the royal administration while leaving a huge debt in the treasury. The work of José Antonio de Areche in Peru and Juan Francisco Gutiérrez de Piñeres in New Granada provoked upheavals on a massive scale. Initial creole resistance to revenue and administrative reform in Peru had quickly spread down to the Indian masses where it sparked an uprising that sought to redress centuries of abuse. The rebellion swept the uplands, reaching as far north as the Quito border, and spilled over into northern Chile and modern-day Argentina in the south. Royal authority was restored only after the eventual arrival of two armies from Buenos Aires and a host of humbling, conciliatory measures.¹ In the interior of New Granada, a creole-led protest during the spring of 1781 had brought the royal administration to its knees. Faced by a huge, angry *comunero* army at the gates of Santa Fe de Bogotá, the colonial authorities agreed to humiliating terms to placate the revolutionaries and save the viceregal capital.² Only the arrival of an army from Cartagena—half veteran, half white and *pardo* militiamen—permitted the administration to nullify its surrender.³ And in Chile, where a resourceful elite turned reform to its political and financial advantage, Subvisitor Tomás Alvarez de Acevedo failed to improve the financial position of the treasury in the slightest.⁴ Only the cleverly ruthless José García-Pizarro, the subvisitor of Quito, managed to produce a significant surplus for the royal treasury while maintaining domestic peace. Gálvez called him home to a place of honor on the Council of the Indies.⁵

As with the resistance of 1765–1766, the full causation for these failures was complex and deeply rooted in the peculiar histories of the several colonies. Nevertheless, a number of general observations help explain this divergence from Cuban behavior. Violent resistance was almost exclusively a highland phenomenon. As Esquilache had discovered earlier, inland elites were loath to pay for coastal defense against what appeared to them a very remote threat. Political failure was a second factor. Under the pressure of war and its enormous costs, the work of Gálvez' regents-visitor became radical to the point of ignoring the traditional consultative processes and ruthless in its implementation. The anti-American tone of the *visitas* was unmistakable, especially in Peru and New Granada where Areche and Gutiérrez de Piñeres sought to open the way for a sweeping reorganization of colonial finance by dislodging entrenched clans of creole office holders from the royal treasury and the audiencias, replacing them with Spanish-born officials.⁶ The kind of pragmatic trade-offs that had characterized Ricla and O'Reilly's work in Cuba was nowhere to be found. Although the contingencies of war might provide some justification for this mode of behavior, it should also be noted that the Gálvez administration had shown a severe approach to reform from the beginning. By all appearances, the French observation that Spain lacked enough com-

    1. Campbell, *The Military and Society*, 144–46.
    2. Phelan, *The People and the King*, chs. 3–14.
    3. Kuethe, *Military Reform and Society*, 86–87.
    4. Jacques A. Barbier, *Reform and Politics in Bourbon Chile, 1755–1796* (Ottawa, 1980), ch. 6.
    5. Kuethe, *Military Reform and Society*, 90–92, 117–23.
    6. For an analysis of the breakdown of the consultative process, see Phelan, *The People and the King*, chs. 1–3.

petent men to make Esquilache's system work still retained a measure of validity in the late 1770s.

Apart from the exposed position of their island and whatever instinctive loyalty they may have had to the Spanish crown, Cubans had strong reasons to support the war effort and behave as faithful vassals. The accord of 1763–1765 had produced visible benefits to the economy in the form of a booming sugar industry. The harsher taxation, although producing more revenues for the king, paled in comparison to Cuban gains. Significantly, Cuban-generated income never came close to financing the island's needs, reaching during the 1770s only 15 percent of total expenditures, although by 1778 local revenues at least covered the salaries of the veteran garrison and the advisers for the disciplined militia.[7] The remaining funds came from the Mexican *situado* as millions upon millions of pesos were poured into ever more ambitious fortification projects. Cuba thus stood as a net beneficiary of the colonial spending patterns. Exactly whose pockets were enriched by the Mexican monies remains an open question, but it is inconceivable that the Havana elite did not absorb its share and quite probable that the *situado* helped finance the rapid expansion of the sugar industry.[8] It is most instructive that, while the elites of Peru and New Granada bridled at the exigencies of war, Havana within six hours provided a loan of half a million pesos to special agent Francisco Saavedra, who bore instructions to raise money for the French forces in America. These funds, which reached the fleet of Admiral Paul de Grasse off the Cuban coast as he sailed north, went far to finance Louis XVI's armies at the Battle of Yorktown.[9]

The performance of the South American and Mexican armies could not have provided Gálvez with much comfort either. In Peru so little had been accomplished by the eve of the war toward placing the militia

7. Kuethe and Inglis, "Absolutism and Enlightened Reform."

8. A statistical exposition on the Mexican *situado* can be found in John J. TePaske, "La política española en el Caribe durante los siglos XVII y XVIII," in *La influencia de España en el Caribe, la Florida, y la Luisiana* (Madrid, 1983), table 1. During the last two war years, 1782–83, the Mexican treasury sent Havana over nine million pesos a year. A far-flung support apparatus emanated from Havana, of course, and not all of this money was spent in Cuba; but even during the relatively calm decade preceding the First British War, 1787–96, Mexico sent the island an average of over 2,718,000 pesos annually. For a recent analysis of the interplay between the *situado* and creole businessmen, see Marchena, *Oficiales y soldados*, ch. 5. In *El ingenio*, I, 65, Moreno Fraginals logically identifies fortification finance as a major source of capital for the expansion of the sugar industry.

9. The French, short of money in America at the same time that the Spanish faced a similar predicament in Europe, arranged a continental transfer while Saavedra raised funds to pay Louis XVI's troops in America. James A. Lewis, "Las Damas de La Habana, el Precursor, and Francisco de Saavedra: A Note on Spanish Participation in the Battle of Yorktown," *The Americas* 37 (July 1980), 83–86, 90–98.

on a disciplined footing, that Viceroy Manuel Guirior had to reclassify the existing units as urban (nondisciplined) and begin the process of reform anew. In the absence of a workable relationship with the colonial elite, especially given Areche's behavior in the colony, little in fact was achieved to improve the militia, and when the news arrived that war had been declared, Peruvians showed a shocking reluctance to answer the call to arms, even in Lima. When rebellion gripped the uplands, the militia generally proved inept or, worse, was all too frequently drawn into the insurgency itself.[10] In New Granada, when Viceroy Manuel Flores descended to the coast to assume personal command of the viceroyalty's defenses, he found much of the militia understrength, without uniforms, and untrained, especially in the outlying small towns and rural districts. By contrast, the white and *pardo* battalions of the city of Cartagena were able to contribute effectively to garrison duty and, as representative of coastal interests, supported the work of the regular army in reestablishing royal control in the interior. Moreover, an impressive correlation developed between political fidelity and those inland zones that supported veteran and militia forces.[11]

In Mexico the army that Villalba had attempted to reform also showed little preparedness for war in 1779. A depressingly large number of units were woefully untrained or existed only on paper.[12] The military reorganization had preceded the reform *visita* in that viceroyalty, owing to the untimely death aboard ship of the first visitor general, Francisco de Armona. This development created a disjuncture between the two processes, while the endless jurisdictional snarls arising from the hostility of Viceroy Marqués de Cruillas to the work of both Villalba and Gálvez had created problems on another level. Not surprisingly, the reform commission had never managed to establish an understanding with the creole elites of the kind that had emerged in Cuba.[13] Mexico, in any event, was so large and the interests of its several elites so diverse that even under the best of conditions results were likely to have been uneven. Moreover, the crown was not immediately prepared to extend commercial concessions to New Spain as part of a reform package. Desirous of developing the peripheries of its empire, concerned that Mexico would overwhelm and stifle the lesser colonies in the Spanish trade, and less fearful about smuggling in New Spain than elsewhere, Spain would not bring that colony into the system of "free trade" until 1789.[14] Finally, the Mexican militia was

10. Campbell, *The Military and Society*, 76–77, 87–94, ch. 5.

11. Kuethe, *Military Reform and Society*, 23–24, 86–92.

12. Christon I. Archer, *The Army in Bourbon Mexico*, 20.

13. Ibid., 10–12; Priestley, *José de Gálvez*, 156–64.

14. From the earliest planning of the colonial reorganization, the Junta de Ministros had excluded Mexico from its scheme to extend "free trade" to the empire, at least in part

organized under the Spanish ordinance of 1734 and the Cuban regulation of 1765, thus allowing the ayuntamientos rather than the subinspector general to nominate officers.[15] This system remained, denying the central authorities the kind of political leverage that might have produced political and military behavior more aligned to royal aspirations.

The result of these disappointments was a further reorganization and reform of the American military establishments. In both Peru and New Granada, Gálvez sought to purge the upper militia officer corps of creoles as he had already done for the royal administration. In Peru, moreover, he abolished the upland units that had performed badly and were suspect politically, deploying veteran regiments in their place to maintain order.[16] In New Granada, he extended the disciplined militia system to Santa Fe, albeit with carefully tailored leadership, and established a veteran garrison at the strength of a regiment to defend the capital and to police the interior, while authorizing the reorganization of the coastal militia.[17] In Mexico, Subinspector General Francisco Crespo, searching for the means to transform the disciplined militia into an effective reserve, attempted yet another sweeping reorganization.[18] The decade of the 1780s thus featured a continuing struggle to turn the American army into a reliable military instrument.

Cuba experienced none of this. Every unit had contributed to the war effort and, at least indirectly, to the victory in Florida. Their achievement, given his record elsewhere, may well have saved Gálvez' job. Moreover, Florida was far from the limit of the Cuban contribution. After the fall of Pensacola, the Junta de Generales sent the Army of Operations and 425 men from the Havana garrison to Guarico to join French forces for an invasion of Jamaica. This venture stalled, however, when the English fleet under Admiral George Rodney inflicted a crushing defeat on the French in April 1782. In the meantime, Juan Manuel Cagigal, who had replaced Navarro as captain general, led a two-thousand-man assault on Providence Island. This force included 688 troops from the Army of Operations who had remained behind; 326 Mexican regulars destined for Guarico; 704 veterans from the Havana garrison; 202 *pardo* and *moreno* militiamen; and 80 laborers. With

---

because it feared smuggling less in that jurisdiction than in other colonies. D'Ossun to Choiseul, Madrid, Jan. 23, 1764, AAE, CE, vol. 540, fols. 64–66. See also John Fisher, "Imperial 'Free Trade' and the Hispanic Economy, 1778–1796," *Journal of Latin American Studies* 13 (May 1981), 21–23.

15. Christon I. Archer, "Charles III and Defense Policy for New Spain, 1759–1789," in Gaetano Massa, ed., *Paesi mediterranei e America Latina* (Rome, 1982), 193.

16. Campbell, *The Military and Society*, 154.

17. Kuethe, *Military Reform and Society*, 98–107.

18. Archer, *The Army in Bourbon Mexico*, 21–27.

2,390 of Havana's regulars also deployed in Pensacola, Mobile, New Orleans, and in the fleet, 1,554 of Havana's white volunteer infantrymen stood mobilized during 1782, fulfilling a role that they had accepted since the beginning of the war.[19] Gálvez had every reason to be pleased with the Cuban volunteers. As a result, the minister of the Indies made no attempt either to reorganize the system of units that O'Reilly had established or to purge the officer corps of the creole elite that exercised command.

Throughout the 1780s and on into the 1790s, essentially the same families controlled Havana's volunteer officer corps, although the O'Farrill family, aided by a network of marriages, increasingly dominated the colonelcies. All things equal, promotions were supposed to derive from a combination of merit and time in grade, and the system frequently functioned in that fashion, especially for promotion from sublieutenant to captain in the infantry. Social merit was, nevertheless, an equal and at times greater consideration, for the colonial authorities sought to adorn the officer corps with the flower of Havana society. In the cavalry, where the ensigns and sublieutenants were selected because of their ability to maintain horses on their farms and ranches around Havana, junior officers generally lacked the social rank for promotion to captain. New captains, therefore, very frequently lacked previous experience, save possibly as officers in the Noble Company of Cadets. After that unit was disbanded in the late 1760s for lack of proper instructors, few of the new captains had any previous experience.[20] In all cases, the several colonelcies were reserved for men of the highest social rank, usually titled nobles or O'Farrills.

In the Volunteer Infantry Regiment of Havana, the first opportunity for advancement to a major officership came with the death of Colonel Aguiar in 1776. According to form, Lieutenant Colonel Casa Bayona became colonel and Francisco de Cárdenas, the highest ranking captain, advanced to lieutenant colonel. Both men had impeccable social credentials as well as time and merit in rank. When Casa Bayona died in 1780 and Cárdenas became colonel, however, Antonio José de Beitía y Castro, Rentería y Espinosa, who was the second Marqués del Real Socorro, became lieutenant colonel. At the time of his promotion, the marqués was only twenty-nine years old. He had begun military service as a cadet in 1765, had made sublieutenant in 1769, and had advanced to captain in 1773, bypassing a number of others with greater time in

19. Troop report, Havana, in Dabán to Gálvez, Havana, May 6, 1782, AGI, SD, leg. 2084. For a roster of the units committed to the Providence expedition, see Urriza to Gálvez, Havana, Apr. 12, 1782, ibid.

20. Those cadets who did not receive immediate commissions were permitted the use of the uniform after the company was dissolved and at least some of them eventually acquired offices. Inspection report, Dabán, July 1, 1773, AGI, SD, leg. 2119.

grade. At the time of his promotion to lieutenant colonel, there were other captains with greater seniority and there was no evidence that he had yet demonstrated much service merit. Indeed, the veteran officer who evaluated him on his service record in 1781 found that "He has no military experience, nor noteworthy love for this profession; yet he is young with good qualities and capable of acquiring all the essential attributes [of military leadership]."[21]

As his service record suggested, the young marqués would indeed someday become a responsible officer and a dominant figure in the Cuban colony, but what counted at the moment were his social credentials. Beitía, who had inherited one of the fastest growing estates in Cuba, succeeded to his title of nobility (a title that his father had established in 1770) the same year that he became lieutenant colonel. He was also *regidor perpetuo* on the Havana ayuntamiento and in 1781 acquired a habit in the Order of Santiago. Moreover, he was married to María Luisa Josefa de los Angeles O'Farrill y Herrera, Arriola y Chacón, the daughter of Lietuenant Colonel Juan O'Farrill of the cavalry regiment and the granddaughter of the fourth Marqués de Villalta.[22] When Cárdenas died in 1783, Real Socorro duly became colonel. Meanwhile, the third Conde de Casa Bayona, who had risen rapidly to the rank of captain, became lieutenant colonel, a position that his father had held so long. He was only twenty-eight at the time of his promotion and bypassed many captains with greater seniority. Like Real Socorro, he had married a daughter of Juan O'Farrill, María Catalina.[23] The Marqués del Real Socorro and the Conde de Casa Bayona would command the unit until well past the turn of the century.

Similar patterns of privileged advancement occurred in the cavalry and the dragoons. When Lieutenant Colonel Juan O'Farrill of the Havana Cavalry Regiment retired in 1779, he was replaced by Esteban José de la Barrera, the cousin of the Conde de Gibacoa, colonel of the Matanzas Dragoons.[24] The captain with the most seniority, Ambrosio de Jústiz, failed promotion because he lacked sufficient fortune. Meanwhile, José Ricardo O'Farrill, the son of the former lieutenant colonel, was rising rapidly in rank. He had started as a sublieutenant in the Noble Company of Cadets at age fourteen, became a captain in the cavalry five years later, advanced to the grade of lieutenant colonel in 1784 while still functioning as a captain, and acquired the rank of

21. Service records, Regiment of White Volunteers of Havana, 1775, 1781, AGI, SD, legs. 2095, 2098.

22. Nieto, *Dignidades nobiliarias*, 427–28; Thomas, *Cuba*, 1502.

23. Service records, Regiment of White Volunteers of Havana, 1787, AGS, GM, leg. 7259; Dabán to Navarro, Havana, Oct. 9, 1778, AGI, PC, leg. 1234; Santa Cruz, *Historia de familias*, III, 336–37.

24. Santa Cruz, *Historia de familias*, V, 41, 98–99.

lieutenant colonel in the regular army in 1788 despite his continuing service in the militia. When Barrera retired in 1791, O'Farrill advanced to the position of lieutenant colonel which his father had occupied twelve years before.[25]

In Matanzas the command and staff group was expanded to include a lieutenant colonel during the war, a position filled by Ignacio Pedro José María de los Angeles Montalvo y Ambulodi, Montalvo y Arriola, the first Conde de Casa Montalvo. Montalvo, who without previous experience had entered the Volunteer Cavalry Regiment of Havana as a captain in 1774 at age twenty-four, was one of the primary beneficiaries of the sugar boom, the holder of a *mayorazgo*, and among the wealthiest men in Cuba. The eldest son of the second marriage of Lorenzo Montalvo, Conde de Macuriges, he had acquired his own title of Castile in 1779 and would add a habit in the Order of Santiago in 1786. He was married to María Josefa de Jesús O'Farrill y Herrera, the daughter of Lieutenant Colonel Juan O'Farrill, which made him the brother-in-law of the Marqués del Real Socorro (infantry), the Conde de Casa Bayona (infantry), and José Ricardo O'Farrill (cavalry). Casa Montalvo became colonel when the Conde de Gibacoa died in 1787.

At the time of Casa Montalvo's promotion, the second Conde de Gibacoa, José María de Jesús Espinosa de Contreras y Jústiz y Zayas-Bazán, became lieutenant colonel. He had entered the Noble Company of Cadets at age twelve and later served four years as sublieutenant in the Regiment of Asturias. His Majesty permitted Contreras to leave the army but to retain the use of the uniform when his elder brother died and he was needed to attend to the family *mayorazgo* and his four unmarried sisters. When the lieutenant colonelcy became vacant, only one captain from the Matanzas Dragoons contended for the position, the rest lacking "sufficient means to sustain the decency of the office." José Antonio Arredondo y Ambulodi, Conde de Vallellano, who was captain in the Volunteer Cavalry Regiment with twenty years service, however, made a strong bid for the office. Vallellano might well have received the appointment had not one of Gibacoa's sisters, who through marriage had become the Baronesa de Kissel and now resided at court, intervened personally with Minister of the Indies Antonio Valdéz to secure the office for her brother.[26]

It is evident that, on the whole, O'Reilly's original commitment to the Cuban aristocracy was upheld in subsequent decades. By 1791 the sons of three of the four original volunteer colonels and lieutenant

25. Service records, Volunteer Cavalry Regiment of Havana, 1787, 1792, AGS, GM, legs. 7259, 7261.

26. Service records, Volunteer Dragoon Regiment of Matanzas, 1785, AGI, SD, legs. 2100, 1792, AGS, GM, leg. 7261; Nieto, *Dignidades nobiliarias*, 72–73; Thomas, *Cuba*, 1502; file on colonelcy of the Matanzas Dragoons, AGS, GM, leg. 6868.

colonels—the Conde de Casa Bayona, José Ricardo O'Farrill, and the Conde de Gibacoa—had all acquired lieutenant colonelcies in their fathers' units. And the two powerful sons-in-law of Juan O'Farrill, the Conde de Casa Montalvo and the Marqués del Real Socorro—who were therefore the brothers-in-law of José Ricardo O'Farrill as well as the Conde de Casa Bayona—had acquired colonelcies (see Appendix 3).

The grip of the inner elite of the Havana aristocracy on the upper militia officer corps was even tighter. The death of Martín Esteban de Aróstegui in 1778 led to the appointment of another Spanish veteran, Juan Bautista Vaillant. In the meantime, Francisco José María Calvo de la Puerta y O'Farrill, Arango y Arriola had entered the officer corps as a captain. He was the eldest son of the first Conde de Buena Vista and, significantly, Catalina Josefa O'Farrill y Arriola, the sister of Lieutenant Colonel Juan O'Farrill. Calvo de la Puerta, who inherited his father's title in 1781, was a knight in the Order of Santiago and married to the daughter of the second Marqués de Jústiz de Santa Ana, heiress to her father's title. Although remaining attached to the militia, Buena Vista acquired the grade of lieutenant colonel in the regular army in 1783 and colonel in 1787. When Vaillant was named governor of Santiago in 1788, the conde assumed command of the Volunteer Cavalry Regiment. Colonel Conde de Buena Vista was, then, the nephew of Juan O'Farrill, who had served as the first lieutenant colonel of the unit, and the cousin of José Ricardo O'Farrill, who became its lieutenant colonel in 1791![27]

The company grade offices of the cavalry regiment and the first infantry battalion had their usual quotas from the Armenteros, Arango, Arredondo, Basabe, Cárdenas, Chacón, Coca, Cruz, Molina, Morales, Santa Cruz, Sotolongo, Zaldívar, and Zayas families, as well as a younger Chacón and a Beitía (see Appendix 2). The captains of the second battalion, based in Guanabacoa, continued to be an undistinguished lot apart from one "noble" from Havana. Change, however, was apparent at the lower levels. By 1792 three sublieutenants and five cadets enjoyed noble reputations.

The Matanzas Dragoons registered a somewhat faster rate of change. In the foot companies only two of the ten officers could claim noble status in 1792, but the mounted contingent had six, including Sublieutenant Juan Francisco del Castillo, son of the Marqués de San Felipe y Santiago, and the cadets included a Beitía and an Arango. The increasing level of distinction among the officers of the militia of Guanabacoa and Matanzas reflected the eastward advance of the sugar revolution, which was beginning to have an impact in those districts.

---

27. Service record, Conde de Buena Vista, 1792, AGS, GM, leg. 7261; Nieto, *Dignidades nobiliarias*, 72–73.

Looking ahead, the volunteer officers of Matanzas would all rate classification as either noble, the son of an officer, or *honrada* (honorable) by 1809, and all eleven cadets would enjoy status in the first two categories. Again, the Second Infantry Battalion would lag but nevertheless move in the same direction. As late as 1811, it would still possess only one noble captain, but the number of sublieutenants who could claim that reputation would increase to four, and the number of cadets to fifteen of twenty.[28]

One important name, however, was missing from the officer corps of the Havana militia: Francisco Arango y Parreño, who never became associated with the Cuban military. Born in 1765, educated in law in Spain, Francisco was well on his way to becoming Cuba's most vocal exponent of planter interests and in particular laissez-faire economics. He had recently been accepted at court as Havana's representative (*apoderado*) where, as will be seen shortly, he achieved wonders for the island's sugar interests. Half owner of a vast sugar plantation, brother of Lieutenant Ciriaco Arango, and nephew of Captain Anastasio Arango, both of the Volunteer Infantry Regiment, he could have acquired a militia post, but he would have none of it. Tied to the enlightened intellectual current sweeping the Western world and now beginning to penetrate Havana, he showed no interest in military rank or privileges.[29] As will be seen, his distance from the military corporation would carry important implications for the future of the Cuban colony.

In the three white infantry battalions of Cuatro Villas, Puerto Príncipe, and Santiago-Bayamo, the young sublieutenants of 1764 had become the aging captains of 1790, while many sons of the first colonels and captains appeared as sublieutenants and cadets. The volunteer officers of the battalions of Puerto Príncipe and Santiago-Bayamo continued to enjoy a uniformly noble reputation, deriving principally from the sugar and ranching aristocracy of the east. This pattern would sustain itself past the turn of the century.

Cuatro Villas possessed the least distinguished officers. As late as 1792, sons of laborers shared the captaincies equally with men whose social quality was "known" (*conocida*), hardly a laudatory description under the circumstances. Colonel Pablo Antonio Sánchez, who had advanced from sublieutenant, commanded the battalion, rating a mere "known" reputation. Yet subtle change was visible as sugar began to penetrate the region bringing new economic opportunity, outside investors, and social stratification. Captain Pablo Pérez, a newcomer

28. Service records, Volunteer Cavalry Regiment of Havana, Volunteer Infantry Regiment of Havana, and Volunter Dragoon Regiment of Matanzas, 1792, all in AGS, GM, legs. 7261, 1809, AGI, PC, legs. 1772–73; Moreno Fraginals, *El ingenio*, I, 139–41.

29. William Whatley Pierson, Jr., "Francisco de Arango y Parreño," *HAHR* 16 (Nov. 1936), 451–60.

from Havana, brought a "noble" status to the officer corps. One sub-lieutenant, also from Havana, and two cadets possessed "distin-guished" reputations, a portent of future direction. By 1809, when the battalion authorities elected to classify officers by occupation, all of the volunteer officers except one rated description as *hacendado*, a term that implied substantial investments in cattle or sugar or both and reflected increasing social pretentiousness. Interestingly, three of the captains and one of the sublieutenants were Spanish born, presumably individuals who moved to the region to exploit the new economic opportunities.[30]

Black and mulatto officers and soldiers continued to occupy an unexalted position in the military hierarchy, a position that, if any-thing, declined during the 1780s. Despite the important contribution that the *pardo* and *moreno* volunteers had made to the reconquest of Florida and despite the performance of the Pardo Infantry Battalion of Santiago-Bayamo in assuming its share of garrison duty, the service records of those units contained no individual documentation for black officers during this period, encompassing only the white command and staff groups. This omission must be taken as evidence that the personal military histories of *pardos* and *morenos* were not considered impor-tant in the larger sociomilitary equation. By contrast, service records for black officers were kept much more faithfully in New Granada and in 1765 had been completed in Havana itself. As the sugar revolution fastened its grip on Cuban society, the status of slaves declined in terms of both their legal protections and their ascribed dignity as human beings. The character of the service records for the *pardo* and *moreno* battalions strongly suggests that this deterioration came to affect free blacks and mulattoes as well.[31]

An incident arising during 1789 that involved four captains and two lieutenants of the Moreno Battalion of Havana is most instructive.[32] In a protest to the crown, the *morenos* levied grave charges against the head of the white command and staff group, Subinspector Antonio Seidel and his assistant *Garzón* Manuel Faus. The *morenos* accused

30. The 1792 service records for these units can be found in AGS, GM, leg. 7261. For 1777 and 1781–83, see AGI, SD, legs. 2096, 2099, and for 1809, AGI, PC, leg. 1772. For the advance of sugar into Cuatro Villas, see Moreno Fraginals, *El ingenio*, I, 41–45.

31. The 1765 service records for Cuba are in AGI, SD, leg. 2093 and for the 1780s in AGI, SD, legs. 2093, 2101, and AGS, GM, leg. 7259. *Pardo* and *moreno* service records for Panama and Cartegena, Viceroyalty of New Granada, can be found in the Archivo Nacional de Colombia, Milicia y Marina, vol. 13, fols. 242–80, vol. 26, fols. 869–965, vol. 27, fols. 202–59. For an analysis of the deterioration of the treatment of Cuban slaves with the advance of the sugar revolution, see Franklin W. Knight, *Slave Society in Cuba during the Nineteenth Century* (Madison, 1970), ch. 4.

32. The documentation for the account that follows is in the file on the *moreno* complaint, AGS, GM, leg. 6853.

Volunteer, Moreno Infantry Battalion of Havana. Courtesy of Archivo General de Indias.

these officials of treating them like slaves; of persistent abuse by word and deed, including the killing of a soldier; of failing to seek justice in the homicide of another; of capriciously confining black officers; and of numerous other misdeeds. They urged His Majesty to suspend the white officers and proposed the creation of a second battalion under a *moreno* colonel and lieutenant colonel, the white instructors subordinate to their authority. The lengthy *moreno* testimony sent to court showed that the officers of that unit indeed had grievances but also that they plotted an ambitious improvement of their status. It is equally evident that no one in a position of authority in Havana was inclined to take the grievances seriously.

Seidel enjoyed a good reputation as an officer, and his battalion consistently received high efficiency ratings. His rigorous training methods included abusive language replete with racial slurs and blows to delinquent soldiers. Indeed, *Garzón* Faus whacked one volunteer so hard when he strayed out of line during drill that he killed him. Although O'Reilly had specifically forbidden the beating of militiamen in his regulation, blows were probably viewed as indispensable for motivating blacks. Within this context, the death of the soldier was simply seen by the local authorities as a "training accident." The murder of José Antonio Colón at the hands of a prominent merchant, Manuel de Quintanilla, equally failed to arouse official concern. Although the *morenos* did not explain the reasons for Quintanilla's behavior in their complaint, later evidence revealed that Colón had raped the merchant's wife. Quintanilla's men quickly captured him and brought him to their employer, who had him tied to a post and flogged. After an ordeal of five hours, Colon died. Seidel declined to bring charges against Quintanilla.

The petitioners plainly hoped to exploit these incidents to overthrow the authority of the white command and staff group. The officers of the Moreno Battalion, proud of its war record, had shown signs of discontent with their status as early as 1785 when they unsuccessfully attempted to gain parity in salary with the *pardos*. Now they sought effective command authority within their unit. They objected that the *moreno* "commander" was in reality a mere figurehead and that the lowliest ranking whites enjoyed authority over him. As agents of the subinspector, whose authority was supreme, even the *garzones* customarily issued commands to *morenos* of all ranks. During unit exercises, Seidel retaliated against those who showed discontent by placing them in stocks or prison and applying regular beatings to encourage the expected subordination. These punishments ranked high among the charges of malfeasance that the *morenos* brought against the subinspector. The petition asked that whites be commanded to show respect to *moreno* officers and that a second battalion be formed in which a black could be placed in effective command. Interestingly, in seeking Seidel's dismissal, the *morenos* urged that his replacement be a Spaniard, not a creole, a request that revealed a deep mistrust of planter officers. Seidel was a Catalonian but had married the niece of the Marqués de Jústiz de Santa Ana, whose influence over the subinspector the *morenos* blamed for his harsh behavior.

Minister of the Indies Antonio Valdéz took the *moreno* charges seriously. He first requested a confidential report from Juan Bautista Vaillant, the former commander of the cavalry volunteers, who had just been named governor of Santiago. Vaillant was unable to shed light on the complaints but suggested that Valdéz name a secret agent to investigate. The minister then turned the matter over to incoming Governor Luis de Las Casas, who arrived in 1790. After an interview with Seidel, Las Casas contemptuously dismissed the *moreno* complaint, describing it as "cavalier, a mixture of ignorance and malice," and he recommended a strong reprimand for the protesters. Although ordered to interview the officers of the unit to get to the bottom of the matter, he never did so, explaining that a recent unit review by Colonel Felipe Cotarro, who had substituted for aging and ailing Subinspector Domingo Cabello, had produced no complaints. By this time, the Conde del Campo de Alange had replaced Valdéz, and he chose not to pursue the matter. Las Casas, who would soon emerge as a staunch defender of the black militia units on another level, was obviously not concerned about internal disciplinary matters, and neither he nor anyone else took the *moreno* aspiration for actual command authority seriously. Together with Seidel, he soon purged the battalion of its troublemakers, including all six petitioners. Meanwhile, the unit remained at full strength and continued to earn outstanding marks for its mastery of military skills.[33]

In the regular army, Cubans continued to strengthen their grip on the officer corps. By 1779 creoles achieved a majority of one in the Fixed Infantry Regiment, although Spaniards still dominated the higher offices. By 1788, 51 of 87 officers were creoles, and half of these held the rank of captain or above.[34] Lieutenant Colonel Juan Lleonart, a Havana *hidalgo*, commanded the Second Battalion. The commander of the Third Battalion, which had just been created, was Lieutenant Colonel Francisco Montalvo, brother of the colonel of the Matanzas Dragoons. The *sargento mayor* of the First Battalion, which a Spaniard commanded, was Antonio María de la Torre, another Havana *hidalgo*. And Lieutenant Colonel Ignacio Peñalver y Calvo, a knight in the Order of Santiago, was attached to the command and staff group. Lleonart and de

33. Inspection report, June 1793, AGS, GM, leg. 6852.
34. Service records, Fixed Infantry Regiment of Havana, 1779, AGI, SD, leg. 2134, 1788, AGS, GM, leg. 7259.

la Torre, like the creole captains and junior officers, had begun their careers as cadets or militia officers and when the opportunity arose had acquired commissions, advancing steadily as vacancies occurred and Spain failed to produce enough replacements from the peninsula. Montalvo and Peñalver, whose families enjoyed greater status, had been able to jump directly to captaincies after youthful experience in the Company of Noble Cadets and the navy respectively.[35]

Although Gálvez frequently discriminated against creoles to strengthen royal authority, especially in New Granada and Peru, the Americanization of the colonial regular army had become a nearly irreversible process, and Cuba, where no reason for political concern had developed, was no exception. Enlisting as cadets in impressive numbers, creoles throughout the empire clamored for commissions while their families made emergency war loans or financed the army during peacetime pending the arrival of the ever tardy *situados*. The crown attempted to supply peninsular replacements, but this slow, costly process could not discharge royal indebtedness to American investors. Gálvez, above all, appreciated the risks, but it was precisely during his ministry that creoles assumed a majority of American offices.[36] His options were frightfully limited.

Spain, of course, might have reoriented its diplomatic strategy with appropriate adjustments in colonial policy. A normalization with Great Britain, as under Ferdinand VI, though not a substitute for a sound defense, might have provided leeway for a more manageable military and political posture. Smaller garrisons, for example, could have meant a larger percentage of Spanish officers, especially if moderation in fortification expenditures accompanied lowered outlays for troop salaries, reducing the importance of the *situados* and the inevitable debilitating loans from creole investors. Although colonial revenues reached an all-time high as Gálvez continued to advance revenue reform and extend the intendancy system, the costs of the large colonial armies, the ongoing fortification projects, and the ever-growing bureaucracy, absorbed such a large share that remissions to Spain from the colonial treasuries showed little improvement and large debts remained in New Granada, Peru, Chile, and in all probability other colonial treasuries, not to mention Spain itself.[37]

35. Santa Cruz, *Historia de familias*, III, 290–91.
36. The interplay between military finance and the Americanization of the colonial regular army has been analyzed in Marchena, *Oficiales y soldados*, ch. 3, and in his "La financiación militar en Indias: Introducción a su estudio," *AEA* 36 (1979), 93–110.
37. Remissions to Spain may well have declined below the levels reached in the final years of Ferdinand VI. Barbier, "Towards a New Chronology," 336, 341–44. For data on the indebtedness of the Spanish treasury, see Jacques A. Barbier, "Venezuelan *Libranzas*, 1788–1807: From Economic Nostrum to Fiscal Imperative," *The Americas* 37 (Apr. 1981), 460–61. Marchena, "La financiación," 83–84, estimates that 80 percent of the expenditures

Charles and his government never seemed to have seriously considered such an alternative. Spain possessed the world's second largest navy, an expanding army, and a productive empire and, not unreasonably, considered itself a power of the first order. The victory in Florida had simply whetted its appetite for further gain. War planning during the 1780s envisioned the reconquest of Jamaica, Belize, and Gibraltar and contemplated, in conjunction with the French fleet and army, an invasion of England through Wales and Plymouth.[38] Although its power in America had been severely damaged by the loss of the thirteen colonies and Florida, Great Britain still possessed the means through its navy and Jamaica to strike with impressive force against the empire. Spain thus continued to pour huge sums into imperial defense and prepared for its military objectives by tolerating an ever-growing Americanization of the colonial armies.

An adjustment to the financial and strategic realities of the 1780s with important implications for Cuba was the decision in 1786 to cease employing Spanish battalions in America to reinforce the fixed garrisons. The cost in manpower and transportation entailed by rotation had proved prohibitively high. The alternative was an expansion of the fixed garrisons, a step that reversed the O'Reilly dictum of 1763–1764 and implied an acceleration of the Americanization of the colonial garrisons. As usual, the first adjustments occurred in Cuba, were extended to New Spain, and thereafter gradually applied to the rest of the empire.[39]

Apart from the larger imperial considerations, special local conditions called attention to Cuba. The Cuban army had acquired responsibility for garrisoning Florida following the conquests of 1779–1781, an obligation that exceeded normal peacetime resources. After the war, Spain had retained the Immemorial Regiment of the King in Cuba and had added the Regiment of Hibernia in 1783, which in conjunction with the Fijo provided makeshift detachments for Florida pending a permanent solution. Apart from these new responsibilities, the need for a permanent garrison in Santiago remained a problem.

In April 1786 Gálvez initiated plans to reorganize the Fixed Infantry

---

of the treasuries of Mexico and Peru, which provided an ongoing outflow of *situados*, were intended for military purposes. For a long-range view of the income and expeditures of the Mexican treasury, see TePaske, "La política española," 61–87. For New Granada, see Kuethe, *Miliary Reform and Society*, 114, 144, 146.

38. Instrucción reservada, Palace, July 8, 1787, AHN, Estado, vol. 1, fols. 182–85.

39. The file on the decision to replace rotating units with fixed units and the formation of the Infantry Regiment of Cuba is in AGS, GM, leg. 6880. See also, Archer, *The Army in Bourbon Mexico*, 27; Kuethe, *Military Reform and Society*, 147; Laurio H. Destefani, "La defensa militar del Río de La Plata en la época hispana," *Memoria del Tercer Congreso Venezolano de Historia* (Caracas, 1979), I, 515.

Regiment of Havana into three battalions of 615 men each (not including officers and command and staff group personnel), one of which
would permanently reside in Santiago de Cuba as a fixed garrison. A
new unit, the Regiment of Cuba, would replace the two Spanish battalions that had routinely been deployed in Havana since 1763 and,
through its third battalion, would establish a permanent garrison for St.
Augustine. On the advice of Captain General José de Ezpeleta, companies of forty-nine artillerymen and forty-three dragoons would replace the sixth and seventh companies of the Florida unit. The net
effect of the plan for Cuba was to replace two regiments of 1,358 men
with five battalions of 615, representing a gain of 359. The Squadron of
Dragoons, the Light Infantry Companies, and the Artillery Corps
would remain unchanged.

The manpower for the new regiment and the extras needed to
complete the Third Battalion of the Regiment of Havana came principally from Spanish sources. In 1787 Sargento Mayor Martín de Ugarte, a
Cuban career officer who had transferred to the new unit from the
Regiment of Guadalajara, took three hundred raw recruits with him
from Cádiz to Havana, where, with little success, he attempted to
enlist Cubans. He added to this force by drawing from the Regiments of
the King and Hibernia, which returned to Spain, and from the Regiment
of Zamora, temporarily garrisoned in Cuba en route from New Spain to
the peninsula. Another seven hundred men were drawn from seven
peninsular units, from which the inspector of Spanish infantry, Ventura Caro, proposed culling troublemakers and those who did not
measure up to the army's standard for height. Caro believed that it was
in Spain's national interest to keep large, robust men in the peninsula
while exporting smaller specimens to the colonies. The king instead
ordered Caro to select only volunteers, but he did agree that men under
five feet one-half inch could be encouraged to go. The method that Caro
actually employed is unclear. Despite His Majesty's wishes, a deplorable number of incorrigibles found their way to Havana, where many
were concentrated into the Third Battalion and promptly sent on to
Florida.[40] In 1789 another 450 men arrived from Spain. Meanwhile,
recruitment continued in the Canary Islands, and by 1791 the garrison
of Cuba had reached nearly full strength.

The majority of the Regiment of Cuba's officers were drawn from
the peninsula, including Colonel Felipe Cotarro, although Cubans
made an impressive beginning. In planning the regiment, Inspector
Caro urged that Spaniards who had learned proper military discipline in
peninsular units should be preferred for offices at the rank of captain

---

40. Juan Marchena Fernández, "Guarniciones y población militar en Florida oriental
(1700–1820)," *Revista de Indias*, nos. 163–64 (Jan.–June 1981), 133.

Table 5.   The Cuban Veteran Garrison in 1788

Unit	Authorized Strength *
Infantry Regiment of Havana	1,845
Infantry Regiment of Cuba	1,230†
Catalonian Light Infantry (3 companies)	306
Dragoon Squadron of America	160
Artillery Corps (2 companies)	240
Total	3,781

* These figures do not include officers or command and staff group personnel.
†This total does not include the Third Battalion, assigned permanently to Florida.

and above. In the future, creole officers meriting promotion to captain should be transferred to Spain. Caro's explicit reasoning derived from his conviction that service in Spain was more likely to produce capable officers than would service in America, but the unspoken political realism of his recommendation was clear enough. Gálvez, however, who had enough serious problems elsewhere, did not attempt to implement the recommendation, as the appointment of Lieutenant Colonel Martín de Ugarte as *sargento mayor* suggests. Native sons serving in peninsular units—usually those previously garrisoned in Cuba—as well as in the Fijo managed to transfer to the new regiment in significant numbers. By 1792 creoles held eighteen of thirty-nine offices.[41]

The most important Cuban to secure a commission was Sebastián Nicolás Calvo de la Puerta y O'Farrill, Arango y Arriola, the first Marqués de Casa Calvo, who opportunely was in Spain when plans for the regiment were being made and who won appointment as lieutenant colonel. Sebastián Calvo was the younger brother of the Conde de Buena Vista, who commanded the Volunteer Cavalry Regiment of Havana, and the nephew of Juan O'Farrill; like his relatives he had compiled a long list of royal services.[42] He had begun his career in 1763 in the Company of Noble Cadets; had volunteered to accompany O'Reilly to New Orleans, receiving the grade of captain in the volunteer cavalry before departing and a commission in the regular army as captain in the Regiment of Dragoons of the King upon his return; and acquired a habit in the Order of Santiago in 1771. When the Regiment of the Prince was deployed in Havana, he effected a transfer with promotion to lieutenant colonel. During the war, he served with his unit and donated the labor of thirteen slaves to the royal fortifications and two thousand pesos to the royal treasury. Upon receiving his title in 1785,

41. Service records, Infantry Regiment of Cuba, 1792, AGS, GM, leg. 7261.
42. Santa Cruz, *Historia de familias*, IV, 119–21.

he contributed another ten thousand pesos to the king. Following his appointment to the Regiment of Cuba, Calvo continued his generosity, offering to clothe his unit in attractive white uniforms that he had designed, an offer that Gálvez promptly accepted. Calvo used this contribution, along with his labors in planning and raising the unit, to secure promotion to the grade of colonel in 1790, although still functioning as lieutenant colonel. Meanwhile, Cubans began enlisting their sons in the regiment as cadets.

The death on June 17, 1787, of José de Gálvez, who had dominated the Ministry of the Indies as few, if any, had before him, opened the way for a reorganization of the Spanish government and brought a softening in the kind of confrontation between crown and colonial elites that had characterized his administration in most of America. Charles divided the portfolio for the Indies between two men, Minister of the Navy Antonio Valdéz, who added War, Finance, and Commerce for the Indies to his duties, and Antonio Porlier, who became minister of grace and justice. These appointments were accompanied by the establishment of the Junta de Estado, which was designed to coordinate the affairs of Spain and the Indies in a fashion reminiscent of the Junta de Ministros during the Esquilache era. Within the framework of the Junta de Estado, all ministers met regularly to chart imperial policy. This process led in 1790 to the incorporation of responsibility for the Indies directly into the appropriate Spanish ministries, a climactic step towards coordinating the government of Spain and America.[43]

The Junta de Estado, Valdéz, and Porlier reoriented colonial policy, introducing pragmatic adjustments designed to consolidate the gains Gálvez had made but to lower the political and financial costs, thus increasing the remission of colonial revenues to the metropolis while reassuring the colonial elites. Gálvez' revenue reforms and his intendancies remained in place, but accommodation replaced confrotation in the execution of colonial policy. The large veteran garrisons of inland New Granada and Peru were reduced, the bureaucracy pared, and anti-Americanism relaxed. Royal revenues might fall but so too would expenses, it was hoped faster than income. A spirit of economy prevailed as the junta sought to reduce its debts and draw a greater percentage of colonial revenues to the peninsula. The same foreign policy objectives remained, but if the next war were to be fought principally in Europe, as contingency planning had it, wisdom dictated that money be invested in the fleet or in the peninsula rather than in Pacific and inland colonial armies and fortifications. In the midst of this reorientation of colonial policy, Charles III died unexpectedly in December 1788, but the new directions in policy continued during the

43. Barbier, "The Culmination of the Bourbon Reforms," 51–68.

reign of his mediocre son, Charles IV, until disaster intervened in 1793.[44]

In Cuba where hostile confrontation between royal and colonial interests had not developed, the orientation of the Junta de Estado found expression in a reaffirmation of the principle of cooperation through the concession to Cuba of the major unattended demands of 1764 and the continuing provision of military honors for the planter elite. Cuban military services during the last war were still remembered at court, and as much was hoped for during the next. With the talented Francisco de Arango y Parreño at court to lobby their cause,the aggressive Cuban elite was prepared to exploit its opportunity to the fullest.

As Cuba looked to the future, the restraints on economic expansion were essentially the same as they had been in 1763, albeit at a different level. The demand for slave labor still outran supply, and broader sugar markets held the key to further expansion. During the interlude since 1763, perhaps as many as sixty to seventy thousand slaves had been imported into Cuba, but the rapid growth of the plantation economy demanded ever more. The liberalization of commercial regulations, as defined in 1765, had significantly contributed to this growth, but the possibility of broader outlets, especially in the promising market in the United States of America, was a high priority. Cuba now ranked as the world's fourth largest producer of sugar, as compared to eleventh in 1760, and had experienced the advantages of legal trade with its northern neighbor when that commerce had been sanctioned on an emergency basis during the last war.[45]

Arango immediately began to lobby for a completely free slave trade as recommended by the 1764 O'Reilly report and as articulated by the Havana commission that same year. Almost from the start of its deliberations, the Junta de Estado took the issue under sympathetic consideration that culminated in a royal cedula of February 28, 1789. In

44. Ibid. For additional perspectives on the reorientation of colonial policy following the death of Gálvez see, John Fisher, "Critique of Jacques A. Barbier's 'Culmination of the Bourbon Reforms, 1787–1792,'" *HAHR* 58 (Feb. 1978), 83–86; Allan J. Kuethe, "More on 'The Culmination of the Bourbon Reforms': A Perspective from New Granada," *HAHR* 58 (Aug. 1978), 477–80. For Valdéz' views on defense, especially his skepticism about the value of pacific-oriented establishments, see the minutes of the Consejo de Estado, Aranjuez, May 28, 1792, AHN, Estado, vol. 5. For the high priority that he attached to naval spending, see Barbier, "Indies Revenues and Naval Spending: The Cost of Colonialism for the Spanish Bourbons, 1763–1805," *Jahrbuch für Geschichte von Staat, Wirtschaft und Gesellschaft Lateinamerikas* 21 (Cologne, 1984), 181–84.

45. Thomas, *Cuba*, 61–62. Moreno Fraginals, *El ingenio*, I, 50, estimates that 50,000 of the slaves imported during this period were destined for the sugar industry. Saint Domingue, Jamaica, and Brazil continued to outproduce Cuba. See Moreno Fraginals, *El ingenio*, I, 39–46.

a sweeping concession to Cuban planters, the cedula granted to all Spanish subjects the right to engage directly in the slave trade and, perhaps more significantly, permitted foreigners to participate for a period of two years, a concession later extended for another six and, as events developed, in effect indefinitely. However, Havana and Santiago were the only ports authorized for this commerce, and access to the Santiago market was limited to Spanish subjects, apparently out of fear that the British would exploit any opening to expand their already strong illicit connections. Slave ships were permitted to carry cargoes on their voyages from the island, thus providing Cubans with access to previously forbidden foreign ports. Finally, the order abolished import taxes on slaves.[46] Planters thus found themselves with an unrestricted access to slave labor, lower costs, and a wider market for their produce.

In 1789, of course, the full potential of the Cuban sugar industry was still unknown, for French Saint Domingue dominated the world market until the slave revolution of 1791 destroyed that competition. Although the revolution sent a wave of revulsion and apprehension through Cuban creole society, it also created seemingly unlimited opportunity if planters were willing to take the risk. Within this context, Arango lobbied successfully for a series of additional dispensations relating to the importation of mill implements and utensils, minor individually but significant compositely, calculated to permit the sugar aristocracy and Spain to capitalize on the French losses.[47] He also won approval by royal cedula of April 27, 1792, for the founding of the Patriotic Society of the Friends of the Nation to promote the acquisition and dissemination of scientific and practical knowledge, one of a number of such organizations throughout the empire.[48] And finally, he persuaded the Junta de Estado, in recognition of the commercial significance of the island, to approve on October 18, 1792, the establishment of a *consulado* in Havana to administer and promote trade, a decision implemented by royal cedula of April 4, 1794.[49]

Apart from Arango's work in Madrid, the Havana patriciate led by planter-officers such as Juan Manuel O'Farrill and the Conde de Casa

46. Minutes, Junta de Estado, Feb. 19, 1789, AHN, Estado, vol. 3. The cedula has been published in Levene, ed., *Documentos*, VI, 394–99. The cedula, in a typical coattail effect, also encompassed Santo Domingo, Puerto Rico, and Caracas and, as with so many other major pieces of legislation affecting Cuba, was subsequently extended to many other colonies. See James Ferguson King, "Evolution of the Free Slave Trade Principle," 49–53.

47. Ramiro Guerra y Sánchez, et al., *Historia de la nación cubana* (Havana, 1952), III, 507.

48. Santiago had established a chapter in 1787. José Manuel Pérez Cabrera, "Don Luis de Las Casas, fundador de la 'Sociedad Ecónomica,'" *Revista bimestre cubana* 24 (Nov.–Dec. 1926), 899–900. For Arango's work at court see, Pierson, "Francisco de Arango," 465, 471–72.

49. Minutes, Consejo de Estado, Feb. 1, 1793, AHN, Estado, vol. 6.

Montalvo, with the sympathetic support of Captain General Luis de Las Casas, lobbied for this same legislation through normal bureaucratic channels. Montalvo, who would soon accompany Arango on a fact-finding tour of Portugal, England, Jamaica, and Barbados, was also at court in 1792, where Charles IV personally handed him the cedula establishing the Patriotic Society.[50] Cubans thus acquired the legal machinery to exploit the growing opportunities of the world sugar market.

While the Junta de Estado affirmed Cuba's privileged status within the framework of imperial commercial policy, it also retained the original disciplined militia. This action, like Gálvez' Cuban policy during the immediate postwar period, was exceptional within the larger American context. As an early expression of its economy-mindedness, the junta had sent Rear Admiral Francisco Gil y Lemos to New Granada to set that viceroyalty's finances in order. Gil quickly took steps to disband the interior militia, which he found to be useless and probably counterproductive as well as costly; to reduce the veteran military forces and reorient them to the coast; and to halt the fortification of the capital.[51] Gil's report on his work in New Granada led to a circular royal order, January 12, 1790, which instructed the military authorities of the several colonies to review their militia establishments, reducing inland units to an "urban" status, a measure that would strip them of their veteran advisors, royally financed equipment, and most of their military privileges. The order justified this reversal of policy in the name of economy and the hope that His Majesty's subjects might be spared the disruptions that militia service caused their lives. As a result, the militia establishments of much of America underwent yet another reorganization during the early 1790s.[52]

In Cuba, Captain General Las Casas, who was, incidentally, the brother-in-law of Alejandro O'Reilly, made no changes. He quite accurately classified all the units as essentially coastal in function and through a report by Subinspector Domingo Cabello, painstakingly justified each in terms of past services and future expectations. Moreover, Cabello noted that the annual cost for the veteran advisors of the entire establishment came to only 112,323 pesos, 4 reales, substantially less than half the expense of maintaining a single seven-company battalion of veterans. The junta accepted Las Casas' report without question, thus leaving in place the military titles of rank,

50. Pérez Cabrera, "Don Luis de Las Casas," 899–900.

51. Kuethe, *Military Reform and Society*, 146–57.

52. Campbell, *The Military and Society*, 210–12; Archer, *The Army in Bourbon Mexico*, 28–32.

uniforms, and privileges that had come to mean so much to the planter patriciate.[53]

Militia finance, apart from the veteran cadres, was no longer a problem. All units were uniformed by the municipalities, except Matanzas, which failed to sustain its program and resorted to improvisation. Havana also provided the weapons for what amounted to over half of the island's total force. Indeed, by 1790 the Havana support fund was showing large surpluses as the result of a reorganization during 1785 that replaced the system based on the Bakers' Guild with small levies on imports of flour, vinegar, wine, and aguardiente and on sugar exports.[54]

The bakers' monopoly organized in the mid-1770s had indeed produced money to reequip the Havana volunteers during the war, but it soon became widely unpopular. The bakers, not content with the golden opportunity that the municipality had handed them, sought to maximize their profits so avariciously that they quickly destroyed support for their privilege.

The central difficulty arose over the amount that the guild was willing to pay for flour and the quality of the bread that it placed on the Havana market. Fearful of abuses, the crown had frozen the price of bread at the level existing before the establishment of the monopoly. Determined, nevertheless, to exploit its hold on the market, the guild simply fixed the price that it would pay for flour, thus driving down costs. Angry flour merchants and shippers reacted to this arrogance by providing the worst possible flour. The guild was soon making bread out of near rotten ingredients. When by chance it did acquire wholesome materials, it used its deteriorating supplies first, thus perpetuating the outrage. Consumers complained that the bread had a dark color, a foul smell, and a horrible taste. Naturally, sales declined, shippers avoided Havana unless they had cargoes that they could not sell elsewhere, and customs revenues suffered, arousing the concern of the intendant and other treasury officials. The situation could not have improved when war broke out, interrupting the normal sources of flour and driving up costs, while the retail price of bread remained frozen. Merchants from the United States moved into the Havana market, but the Bakers' Guild had to compete against buyers for the wartime army.[55]

---

53. Captain General Luis de Las Casas to Conde del Campo de Alange, Havana, Sept. 22, 1790, AGS, GM, leg. 6844.

54. File on uniform support fund, 1772–1819, AGI, SD, leg. 2160.

55. For an analysis of the wartime flour trade see, James A. Lewis, "Anglo-American Entrepreneurs in Havana: The Background and Significance of the Expulsion of 1784–

The first protest reached court in early 1780. José de Gálvez, who was loath to permit such an embarrassment in time of war, instructed Governor Navarro by order of January 31 to summon a *cabildo abierto* to address the problem and to discuss alternative sources of finance. For reasons not clear—presumably the diverse pressures arising from the war—Navarro did not execute the order, nor did his successor, Juan Manuel Cagigal, who spent part of 1782 off conquering Providence. When he returned to Cuba, Cagigal, exceeding his instructions, silenced the clamor in Havana by simply abolishing the monopoly in October 1782 without bothering to summon Havana's patricians to devise an alternative. When Brigadier Bernardo Troncoso assumed his duties as subinspector general in December of that same year, he pressed Cagigal for a solution to the problem but, inexplicably, received no response. Finally, in January 1784, Troncoso complained to Bernardo de Gálvez, who had returned to court, and Bernardo brought the matter to his uncle's attention.

The minister of the Indies promptly addressed an order to the new governor of Cuba, Luis de Unzaga, that nullified Cagigal's action, thus reestablishing the bread monopoly, but that again called for a *cabildo abierto*. On July 28 Governor Unzaga complied, summoning the titled nobility and a large number of wholesale merchants to meet with the municipal authorities. Although the assembly produced no immediate solution, the merchant representatives continued to pursue the issue, finally producing a plan, which they presented to a second gathering on September 20. This plan advocated the establishment of municipal levies of three silver *reales* per barrel of imported flour, vinegar, wine, and *aguardiente* and two *reales* per crate of exported sugar in return for the abolition of the bread monopoly. The merchants used the captain general's records on commerce, which he made available to them, to make their calculations. They believed that the levies they advocated would produce a slight surplus over the militia's actual needs. Sugar producers complained about the tax on their product, but Gálvez quickly approved the plan, abolishing the Bakers' Guild as a menace to public health.

The plan may have worked too well. The merchants had made conservative recommendations, failing to anticipate the phenomenal future growth of Cuban trade. Revenues soon surpassed what the militia could absorb in equipment, and the surplus became the source of contention among those who had schemes to spend the money. Captain General José de Ezpeleta built a barracks for the militia, while the ayuntamiento turned the fund to public works during the 1790s and

---

1785," in Jacques A. Barbier and Allan J. Kuethe, eds., *The North American Role in the Spanish Imperial Economy, 1760–1819* (Manchester, Eng., 1984), 112–26.

Table 6.		Militia Equipment Fund of Havana		
Year	Revenue		Year	Revenue
1785*	24,199		1795	43,088
1786	50,749		1796	73,396
1787	48,483		1797	58,075
1788	69,222		1798	61,178
1789	39,629		1799	78,209
1790	60,433		1800	65,080
1791	57,665		1801	74,739
1792	51,658		1802	101,082
1793	53,686		1803	82,397
1794	59,792		1804	87,991

SOURCE: AGI, SD, leg. 2160.
*Beginning July 8, 1785.

beyond, constructing government buildings, resurfacing streets, and improving the water supply. By 1790 the merchants were petitioning for a readjustment of the levies while, on another level, Intendant Rafael Gómez Roubaud, who found himself bereft of money during the Second British War, unsuccessfully attempted to expropriate the surplus. Adjustments were not finally effected until 1819.

The other jurisdictions of Cuba, except Matanzas, also showed surpluses, and regularly reuniformed their battalions.[56] When Subinspector General Cabello reported to Las Casas on the Cuban militia in 1790, therefore, the only militia cost that he recorded for the royal treasury was the salaries of the veteran cadres.

In one sense, the Junta de Estado, through omission rather than commission, did not fully satisfy Cuban aspirations, for it failed to adjust the number of militia offices to a level commensurate with the growth of the Cuban sugar aristocracy. As the economy grew, so too did the number of patricians who achieved the proper social status for military honors. By 1790 twenty men held titles of Castile. Some came from new families, although most were close relatives of those already ennobled.[57] Men with titles, moreover, were not the only members of the elite. The regular army increasingly provided opportunities for young creoles, but not all aspirants to title of rank desired a full-time commitment to service. Military honors through the militia were, however, difficult to obtain. The regiments of Havana and Matanzas

56. Unfortunately, specific figures are not available for the individual outer jurisdictions. Cuatro Villas during the 1780s averaged approximately 6,000 pesos a year from its taxes on salt and slaughterhouses, far more than needed. File on the proposal for a fixed company for Trinidad, 1786–87, AGS, GM, leg. 6840.

57. Nieto, *Dignidades nobiliarias.*

supported only six colonelcies, the Cavalry Regiment twelve captaincies, and the First Infantry Battalion nine. And most occupants held their offices until death or advanced old age intervened. New offices and the opportunity for advancement thus seldom materialized.

The result was a minor, although potentially dangerous, sociomilitary crisis. Plans to manufacture military offices abounded and unfulfilled petitions for military honors accumulated in the Ministries of the Indies and, later, War. In 1789 the Conde de Casa Montalvo, colonel of the Regiment of Matanzas Dragoons, petitioned to increase the size of his unit to 650 men with, of course, a corresponding enlargement of the number of offices.[58] In 1791 the Conde de Buena Vista, colonel of the Havana Cavalry Regiment, proposed that six supernumerary captaincies be added to enhance the social luster of his unit.[59] And during this same time, in yet another scheme to provide heraldic honors for the elite, the future Conde de San Juan de Jaruco, captain of cavalry, supported by the Marqués de Montehermoso, the Conde de Casa Barreto, and José de Armenteros, urged the creation of a *maestranza* (equestrian brotherhood) on the model practiced in Seville. The Ministry of War approved this last scheme but only if membership were restricted to military officers. It had no intention of detracting from the glory of the militia by permitting an organization that might outshine the volunteer cavalry in pomp and uniform.[60]

From a modern perspective, this frantic search for title of rank may appear humorous, pitiful, or even disgusting, but its political significance should not be underestimated. The *habaneros* so frequently had their way during this period that it is surprising at first glance that these petitions enjoyed no success. Havana had the capacity to equip its own units and the growing population and economic importance of the island might well have allowed the disciplined militia to expand by a regiment or two. Such a concession, however, would have been inconsistent in the extreme with current policy elsewhere in the empire, and the cost of veteran advisers, although small, weighed on the minds of the authorities at court. As the 1790s progressed the crown would find subtler but effective means of coping with the problem.

---

58. File on petition of the Conde de Casa Montalvo, 1789–92, AGS, GM, leg. 6848.

59. File on petition of the Conde de Buena Vista, 1791–92, AGS, GM, leg. 6847.

60. File on Havana petition for a *maestranza*, 1789–94, AGS, GM, leg. 6844. For an account of an earlier attempt to establish a *maestranza*, see José Manuel de Ximeno, "Los caballeros maestrantes de La Habana," *Revista de la Biblioteca Nacional* 4 (Oct.–Dec. 1953), 111–27.

6. Crisis

Spain's unfortunate entanglement in the War of the First Coalition opened a period of crisis for the imperial system. Defeat in Europe at the hands of republican French armies, followed in rapid succession by two damaging wars against superior British naval power, placed a strain on Spain's Old Regime that it was ill prepared to handle either financially or politically. The crown's options in the management of colonial affairs narrowed perilously as it found its mercantilistic pretenses shattered, survived by hand-to-mouth on scarcer and scarcer revenues, and tolerated an ever-growing Americanization of the colonial armies. Spain's misfortune, nevertheless, worked very much to Cuba's advantage. The burgeoning sugar industry, which enjoyed unparalleled marketing opportunities, entered its golden age, while office-hungry creoles found new opportunities both in the disciplined militia and the veteran garrison. When the legitimate government disappeared in 1808, the planter-officer corps of the Cuban army, mindful of its harmonious and profitable relationship to the crown and benefiting from its current advantage, would hold fast, eschewing tempting revolutionary schemes to embrace the remnants of a system that had served it so well.

A palace coup of February 28, 1792, led to the dismissal of the Conde de Floridablanca and his replacement by his old enemy, the Conde de Aranda, who had long intrigued against him at the head of a disaffected aristocratic faction. At the behest of the victorious clique, Charles IV in a parallel action replaced the Junta de Estado with the Consejo de Estado, where outsiders outnumbered ministers. Aranda held his portfolio only eight and a half months before finding himself dispossessed in turn by Manuel Godoy, the young lover of Queen María Luisa. The Consejo de Estado pursued essentially the same colonial policies as the junta, but the administrative stability that had characterized the reign of Charles III eluded his son.[1] Lacking the toughness, will, and constancy of his father and unable to manage even his own household, Charles IV would find his reign beset by favoritism and court intrigue, and a seemingly endless succession of officials would rotate in and out of the several ministries, including war.[2] Godoy was minister of state until 1797 when a momentary rift with the royal family cost him his job, but with the support of María Luisa he soon returned, again to dominate, although without portfolio. Despite his venality, Godoy was by no means an incapable leader. After an inflamed revolutionary France declared war in March 1793, however, he had little room for maneuver in colonial affairs as he and those around him struggled to preserve Spain's American empire.

The central development in the Cuban army during this troubled period was the precipitous decline in the strength of the veteran garrison. As soldiers died, deserted, or completed their terms of enlistment, few appeared to replace them. The recruiting party in the Canary Islands yielded meager results, and native Cubans, as always, proved difficult to enlist. With the abandonment of the system of rotating troops to America, Cuban units also lost the opportunity to procure men out of regiments returning to Europe. Only a steady flow of replacements from the peninsula could have sustained the desired troop levels.

The Ministry of War, of course, attempted to send recruits from the peninsula whenever possible, but the nature of the European conflicts, not to mention considerations of finance, made that proposition difficult from the start. To the astonishment and horror of the Godoy government, the small Spanish army, organized along lines of birthright, privilege, and special arrangement, proved no better a match for the mass forces of republican France than those of the other monarchies. Spain's defeat weakened the peninsular army and conveyed a harsh reminder of the wisdom of keeping peace along the Pyrenees. The reluctant, uneasy alliance that followed, first with the Directory and then with Napoleon, led to two British wars, 1796–1802 and 1804–1808, where naval inferiority made the movement of troops to America hazardous, especially following the disaster at Trafalgar in October 1805.

In a parallel development, the financial situation deteriorated steadily. As was the case in the other states of the Old Regime, Spain's capacity to increase tax revenues on short notice was essentially inelas-

---

1. Barbier, "The Culmination of the Bourbon Reforms," 66–68.
2. For a catalog of the ministerial changes, see José Antonio Escudero, *Los cambios ministeriales a fines del antiguo régimen* (Seville, 1975).

tic. Even the costs of the relatively brief intervention in the War of the American Revolution had severely strained the royal treasury. Now, three major wars in succession placed a burden on royal finances they could not sustain. Reluctant—and in any event unable—to attempt a reorganization of the tax system that would have threatened privileged, traditional structures, the monarchy resorted to massive borrowing, principally through the issuance of redeemable, interest-bearing, moneylike certificates (*vales reales*). As royal income faltered owing to the disruption of trade and to the loss of the tax revenue that it generated, the value of these notes depreciated, and the royal capacity to borrow became severely limited. To back these notes and to strengthen its position in the domestic money markets, the crown resorted to desperate measures, such as the seizure of religious founda- tion funds in Spain and America, while employing neutral trade as a means to transfer American revenues to the peninsula through bills of exchange. Clearly, these financial difficulties demanded that costs be cut by every available means, an imperative that badly restricted the Ministry of War's ability to maintain the American regular army. Following Trafalgar, the condition of royal finances plummeted, reaching a state of virtual bankruptcy by 1808.[3]

Under these circumstances, the units of the Cuban garrison grad- ually became empty shells. The Regiment of Havana, which at full strength had 1,879 men, including the command and staff group, accounted for nearly half of the authorized complement of the island. By August 1795, following service in Hispaniola during the French War, it possessed only 976 men. By June 1797 it had dwindled to 895, and two years later to only 801 men. Following the First British War, Spain managed to reinforce the regiment modestly, but even so the first two battalions had only 510 men in August 1805, and the entire unit had shrunk to a mere 553 by April 1810. The battalions of the Regiment of Cuba that garrisoned Havana followed a similar course. Five com- panies of the First Battalion remained in Hispaniola until 1799; so complete data are available only for the Second Battalion which, in- cluding command and staff group personnel, had an authorized strength of 626. By October 1796 it retained only 273 men, 203 by late 1798. When the two battalions were reassembled in early 1799, they counted 467 between them. Some replacements arrived after the First British War, but the two battalions had a mere 484 effectives by 1805 and 332 by April 1810. By that same date, the Catalonian Light Infantry Companies retained only 63 effectives out of their complement of 306,

3. Jacques A. Barbier and Herbert S. Klein, "Revolutionary Wars and Public Finances: The Madrid Treasury, 1784–1807," *Journal of Economic History* 41 (June 1981), 315–39. See also Jacques A. Barbier, "Peninsular Finance and Colonial Trade: The Dilemma of Charles IV's Spain," *Journal of Latin American Studies* 12 (May 1980), 21–37.

the Havana artillery, which had recently been expanded to two brigades, 196 of 440, and the Dragoon Squadron of America, faring somewhat better, 97 of 160.[4]

Demands upon Cuba from the vulnerable Louisiana and Florida colonies contributed to this attrition. In the early 1790s, the authorities transferred 462 men from the fixed regiments to strengthen the Louisiana garrison.[5] Moreover, the Third Battalion of the Regiment of Cuba, which was deployed in St. Augustine, consistently enjoyed a much higher percentage of effectives than the first two. This discrepancy resulted from the preference given to Florida in the assignment of recruits and from the transfer of troops from the Cuban-based battalions to sustain its small garrison. With its trained reserve, Cuba was in a stronger position than either Louisiana or Florida to absorb manpower shortfalls, but these losses nevertheless contributed to the withering of the Cuban army.[6]

To make matters worse, the Havana garrison had become a kind of repository for the depraved and the desperate. The regular army under the best of circumstances was far less than a model of civic virtue, but the volume of criminal actions involving men of the Regiments of Havana and Cuba during the early 1800s was spectacular by any standard and especially impressive in light of the smallness of their numbers. The soldiery inflicted upon Havana and itself innumerable murders, beatings, and robberies and even engaged in counterfeiting, to mention only a few varieties of delinquency. Inspector Caro had apparently succeeded in exporting to Cuba a good share of the Spanish army's criminal element during the expansion of the garrison, but in all probability economic considerations were another factor. Inflation eroded real wages during this period while the intensive demands placed upon the dwindling soldiery reduced the opportunity for gainful auxiliary enterprises. The steady stream of convicts sentenced to royal labors on the fortification works further diminished the strength of the fixed units.[7]

4. The inspection reports for the Cuban garrison during the 1790s can be found in AGS, GM, leg. 6882. Those for Aug. 1805 and Apr. 1810 are in AGI, PC, legs. 1580, 1583, 1614. The artillery complement was increased at the end of 1804. Inspection report, Jan. 1, 1805, AGI, PC, leg. 1507A.

5. Royal order, San Ildefonso, Sept. 7, 1792, Las Casas to Campo Alange, Havana, Feb. 18, 1793, both in AGS, GM, leg. 6850.

6. Authorized strength of the Florida battalion was 396 men. In Oct. 1793 the battalion actually had 322; in Aug. 1794, 311; in Aug. 1796, 325; in Nov. 1796, 287; in June 1797, 350; in Dec. 1798, 333; and in Apr. 1810, 240. See AGS, GM, leg. 6882, AGI, PC, leg. 1583.

7. See AGI, PC, leg. 1662. For a description of the woes of garrison duty during this period, see Conde de Mopos to Marqués de Someruelos, Havana, Dec. 18, 1799. AGI, PC, leg. 1576. For an analysis of military wages, see Marchena, *Oficiales y soldados*, 20–21, 322–27.

The tragic history of the Regiments of Mexico and Puebla, which were sent to Cuba during the French War, illustrates the desperate manpower dilemma that gripped Havana. As has been seen, standard policy entailed the deployment of two additional regiments to reinforce Havana during wartime to bring the garrison up to full crisis strength. Because the principal theater of action was in Europe, it was, of course, impossible to send Spanish regiments, but troops from New Spain were available. The chance that France might mount a major invasion of the American colonies was remote, a consideration that limited Mexico's wartime needs; but Cuba served as a springboard for an abortive attempt to subdue the slave insurgents of Saint Domingue, thus justifying a military buildup in conformity to traditional standards. Following the close of the war, however, Captain General Las Casas balked when ordered to return the Mexican regiments, arguing with some justification that the Cuban garrison was too weak to permit their departure. By the time the bureaucratic process finally caught up with him, the First British War had engulfed the empire, thus justifying emergency measures to retain the units. In the peace that followed, Las Casas stalled again, and again Spain was soon at war with Britain. Consequently, the unfortunate Mexicans who were deployed in Cuba during the French War, or what was left of them, were still serving at the end of the Second British War and, indeed, remained for some time thereafter. Like the Regiments of Havana and Cuba, the Mexican regiments dwindled away—to half their authorized strength by 1803 and to a mere 20 percent of it by 1810.[8]

The corollary to the decline of the veteran garrison was the rise in the relative importance of the disciplined militia until it became the dominant combat force on the island. During the French War, as in the preceding war, the major portion of the veteran garrison operated outside of Cuba. Early in the conflict, a battalion from the Regiment of Havana, along with the Catalonian Light Infantry Companies, reinforced Louisiana. Later this task fell to a battalion from the Regiment of Mexico, but in the meantime the Regiments of Cuba and Havana were deployed in Hispaniola while the Catalonian Light Infantry reinforced Florida. Moreover, the two Mexican regiments sent to Cuba from New Spain arrived in segments, the last five companies of the Regiment of Puebla not reaching Havana until near the end of the war, and hundreds of these Mexicans were sent to garison the fleet. To fill the resulting gaps on the home front, Las Casas mobilized the First Battalion of the Volunteer Infantry Regiment and, as the need arose, parts of the Bat-

8. The involved correspondence concerning the plight of these regiments can be found in AGI, PC, legs. 1664, 1711–12. See also the troop review, May 3, 1803, royal order, León Island, Oct. 16, 1810, both in AGI, PC, legs. 1590, 1730.

talion of Pardos, the Matanzas Dragoons, and the Battalion of Puerto Príncipe. The governor of Santiago made similar use of his white and *pardo* battalions.[9]

As the campaign in Hispaniola developed, Spain simply did not possess the manpower to achieve its objectives, a failure shared by the British and later Napoleon. Martial glory thus escaped the army of Cuba, but the traditional role of the disciplined militia was nevertheless reaffirmed. Because a full battalion of the Regiment of Cuba remained in Hispaniola until 1799 and Cuba continued to reinforce Louisiana and because the remaining units were deplorably understrength, the First Battalion of the Volunteer Infantry Regiment remained mobilized during the ensuing peace, as did portions of the militia of Santiago-Bayamo.[10] More of the militia was mobilized during the two British wars and the interlude between them.[11] Indeed, by 1808 the Cuban "volunteers" had served so regularly that they could scarcely be distinguished from veterans.

The volunteer forces themselves, not surprisingly, suffered from the stress of nearly continuous war and ongoing mobilization. The disciplined militia system was designed to provide a trained reserve to support the regular army during siege or to relieve it for short periods during offensive actions; it was not well suited to meet the responsibilities it faced after 1793. As long as the price of soldiery was relatively low, the system functioned reasonably well, but during the wars of Charles IV, the burdens became insufferable. The captains general in conjunction with the subinspectors general attempted to minimize domestic disruption by rotating the responsibility for garrison duty at frequent intervals, giving preference to married men whenever possible. These humanitarian gestures seem to have sufficed during the War of the American Revolution, but Spain's endless entanglements after 1793 and the large numbers of militiamen required to compensate for the shrinkage of the regular garrison translated into long, bitter months away from home for the enlisted man year after year. Men could barely support themselves on their meager wages, let alone their families. Businesses were disrupted and farms left unattended. To the militiamen entrapped by these circumstances, the honor of the uniform and military privileges must have seemed poor compensation indeed. Besieged by pleas for relief from the mobilized portion of his regiment, the

9. Las Casas to Campo Alange, Havana, May 7, Aug. 10, 1793, Jan. 3, Feb. 18, 1794, Jan. 17, 1795, Mar. 3, Oct. 17, 1796, royal orders, San Ildefonso, Aug. 2, Sept. 24, 1794, all in AGS, GM, legs. 6850–53, 6855, 6857.

10. Las Casas to Campo Alange, Havana, June 23, 1795, Mar. 3, 1796, both in AGS, GM, legs. 6854–55.

11. For militia mobilization during the First British War, see AGI, PC, legs. 1526, 1576–79, 1711; for the Second British War, legs. 1580–82, 1667.

Conde de Gibacoa, for example, reported in 1799 that most of the remaining dragoons from his regiment refused to appear for drills. Enlistees became hard to find even in Havana, and some young men, Subinspector Conde de Mopos complained, even went so far as to enroll in the university to escape service. By 1806 the use of the lottery to find recruits for the Havana regiments became standard practice.[12]

In September 1802, when the empire was momentarily at peace, Interim Subinspector Cayetano Fantini reflected upon the hardship that militia service had come to entail:

> Because the number of troops serving in this garrison and the other points on the island is small, militiamen are almost always mobilized as at present despite the conclusion of the war and the extreme care that our captain general takes not to burden them unnecessarily; white, *pardo*, and *moreno* militiamen are serving, the first of these in the *plaza*, the second and third aboard ships of the King. Imagine the hardships that the families of these men endure for want of the husbands and sons who support them by means of their labors, whose fruits are denied them when they are mobilized. This also occurs with the cavalry because of deficiencies in the Squadron of Dragoons. The same happens in the Plaza of Cuba [Santiago], Matanzas, Puerto Príncipe, and Trinidad.

Fantini went on to advocate the abolition of the disciplined militia and an expansion of the veteran garrison to 6,328 men, including 501 for Florida. This proposal was obviously absurd from the point of view of cost alone and did not receive serious attention.[13]

Despite the cracks opening at its foundation, the disciplined militia system held together. The militia was, after all, sustained by the elite, as represented by the volunteer officer corps, which possessed the political and economic means to muster "volunteers." In the instance of Matanzas, the authorities simply called upon the district captains (*capitanes de partido*) to use their muscle to exact compliance.[14] Indeed, throughout the early 1800s the several units functioned at nearly full strength. When, for example, the governor of Santiago ordered both of his battalions to active duty on short notice in early 1808, the *pardos* mustered 677 men and the whites 757.[15] At a time when the regular army itself was withering, the militia, significantly, retained nearly a full complement of veteran advisors, although O'Reilly's admonition

12. Mopos to Someruelos, Havana, June 24, Aug. 14, 1799, Mar. 8, 1800, all in AGI, PC, leg. 1576; Mopos to the Príncipe de la Paz (Godoy), Havana, Sept. 6, 1797, MN, Mopos, vol. 1, fols. 187–209; Someruelos to Mopos, Havana, Sept. 16, 1806, AGI, PC, leg. 1627.

13. Cayetano Fantini to Someruelos, and report to the King, Havana, Sept. 9, 1802, AGI, PC, leg. 1578.

14. Mopos to Someruelos, Havana, Aug. 14, 1799, AGI, PC, leg. 1576.

15. Troop reviews, Pardo Battalion, Feb. 29, 1808, White Battalion, Mar. 15, 1808, both in AGI, PC, leg. 1582.

that the veteran sergeants who served as lieutenants be rotated periodically had long since been forgotten and morale suffered accordingly.[16]

Cubans were heartened, moreover, when news arrived that the
Puerto Rican militia, acting in concert with a small veteran garrison,
had repulsed a major British attack on San Juan during April 1797.[17]
Fearing a similar assault on Cuba, the authorities raised numerous
urban militia companies on a provisional basis throughout the island, a
practice repeated during the Second British War. According to one
troop report, the outer jurisdictions of Cuba possessed 3,154 urban
militiamen, including 1,728 for Santiago-Bayamo, 258 for Puerto Príncipe, 968 for Cuatro Villas, and 200 for Matanzas. Havana, of course,
had many more. Like their counterparts during the Seven Years' War,
these companies generally lacked equipment, were poorly organized,
and seldom if ever trained.[18] Their existence was more a testimony to
the siege mentality that had gripped the island than a meaningful step
toward improving its military posture, although every man who
showed a willingness to contribute was a potential asset on a perilously
thin defense line. The defense of Cuba, in essence, had become a
colonial responsibility.

Not unexpectedly, the political significance of the shift of military
and political power to the Havana patriciate carried a price. In a strong
position to exact acquiescence to their wishes, Cubans demanded
access to neutral trade and, with only brief interruptions, enjoyed
unrestricted commerce from 1793 onward, except, of course, with
enemy nations. While other colonies enjoyed similar arrangements
during wartime, Cubans were uniquely successful in extending their
privilege.[19] Captains general such as Luis de Las Casas (1790–1796),
who had been awarded his own plantation by expectant *habaneros*, and
the Marqués de Someruelos (1799–1812), who appreciated the advantages of cooperation with colonial interests, simply suspended royal
orders to return to the old mercantilistic system during peacetime or,
after brief interruptions, anticipated authorization to return to neutral
trade, while Cuban lobbyists worked at court to secure royal confirma-

16. The service records for the Cuban militia, 1801–11, are in AGI, PC, legs. 1770–73. It
was not unusual to find lieutenants who had served with the same militia unit for twenty to
thirty years or more. For commentary on the demoralized state of veteran officers, see
Mopos to Príncipe de la Paz, Havana, Sept. 6, 1797, MN, Mopos, vol. 1, fols. 187–209.

17. Juan Manuel Zapatero, "De la batalla del Caribe: El último ataque inglés a Puerto
Rico (17 de abril a 1 de mayo de 1797)," *Revista de historia militar* 3 (1959), 92–134.

18. Troop report, Mar. 13, 1807, Mopos to Someruelos, Havana, Mar. 8, 1800, both in
AGI, PC, legs. 1576, 1581.

19. The relationship between neutral trade and the military services of the planter
aristocracy has been treated in Allan J. Kuethe, "*Los Llorones Cubanos*: The Socio-Military
Basis of Commercial Privilege in the American Trade under Charles IV," in Barbier and
Kuethe, eds., *The North American Role*, 142–56.

tion of the inevitable.[20] The official vehicle for commercial petitions was the Havana Consulado which, significantly, had been constituted to ensure planter dominance. The first three priors were the Conde de Casa Montalvo, colonel of the Matanzas Dragoons; the Marqués del Real Socorro, colonel of the Havana Volunteer Infantry; and José Ricardo O'Farrill, lieutenant colonel of the Havana Volunteer Cavalry. It is evident that a connection emerged between military service and commercial lobbying that could not be escaped.[21]

Neutral trade meant access to the rich markets of the United States, which was quickly becoming the leading carrier in world shipping and which provided Cuba with flour and its sugar producers with wood for fuel and packing crates.[22] Exploiting the opportunities opened by the collapse of Saint Domingue, by the unrestrained access to the United States, and by high wartime prices, investment in the sugar industry reached a near frenzy.[23] The Spanish court, which was really powerless to do otherwise, continued thus, in the pattern established by Esquilache, Ricla, and O'Reilly, to repay Cubans for military services with commercial privileges.

Equally important, the Godoy government continued the practice of honoring deserving Cubans with appropriate military titles. At the top, stability prevailed in the politically sensitive command structure of the Havana-Matanzas militia.[24] When the Conde de Casa Montalvo, colonel of the Matanzas Dragoons, died shortly after returning from his fact-finding tour with Francisco Arango y Parreño, the second Conde de Gibacoa succeeded to a command that Gibacoa's father had long exercised. Juan Manuel O'Farrill, another son of Juan O'Farrill, advanced to lieutenant colonel. The second Conde de Casa Montalvo, after two years service as a cadet in the Royal Spanish Guards in Madrid, had just been named squadron commander in the volunteer cavalry. His brother, Juan Montalvo y O'Farrill, who was serving as second lieutenant in the Royal Guards, would soon become a veteran supernumerary lieutenant colonel in the Regiment of Cuba.

In 1796 the Conde de Buena Vista, colonel of the Volunteer Cavalry Regiment, died, like Casa Montalvo, at a young age. The Ministry of War replaced him with Martín de Ugarte, lieutenant colonel of the Regiment of Cuba and a bona fide veteran. The lieutenant colonel, José Ricardo O'Farrill, might have succeeded his cousin, for he, like Buena

20. Moreno Fraginals, *El ingenio,* 58.
21. Peter James Lampros, "Merchant-Planter Cooperation and Conflict: The Havana Consulado, 1794–1832," (Ph.D. dissertation, Tulane University, 1980), 58–68.
22. Barbier and Kuethe, eds., *The North American Role.*
23. Moreno Fraginals, *El ingenio,* I, 95–102.
24. The service records for the Havana and Matanzas militia for this period can be found in AGS, GM, legs. 1762–64, AGI, PC, legs. 1771–73.

Vista, held the honorary grade of veteran colonel, but Ugarte had the advantage of being at court at the time. He had been politicking for promotion to subinspector general of the army of Cuba, which post was currently vacant. The Ministry of War refused him that honor because he was a Cuban with strong local ties, but it awarded him command of the prestigious cavalry regiment, apparently to be rid of him.[25] O'Farrill later attempted to gain his own command through what proved to be an unsuccessful offer to raise a second cavalry regiment. He remained lieutenant colonel until ill health forced him to retire in 1809.[26] The Conde de Buena Vista left no sons, but his son-in-law, the Conde de O'Reilly, became a supernumerary colonel in the veteran infantry soon after his death.

The death in 1805 of the Marqués del Real Socorro, colonel of the Volunteer Infantry Regiment, led to the promotion of the third Conde de Casa Bayona to the position that his father had previously held. José Manual Zaldívar y Murguía, the first Conde de Zaldívar (1798) became lieutenant colonel. Zaldívar had begun as a cadet in 1769 and had subsequently advanced through all the appropriate ranks. Real Socorro left three sons as captains in his regiment. The eldest, José Francisco de Beitía y O'Farrill, who inherited his title, already held the grade of lieutenant colonel. A striking degree of continuity thus continued to prevail as the Cuban militia entered the nineteenth century.

As discussed in the last chapter, however, the pressure to manufacture military titles had intensified as the size of the Havana patriciate grew. Reluctant to expand the militia, the crown met this demand through makeshift means. As already seen, deserving officers might be awarded regular army grades, usually without salary, while remaining in the militia. Others were promoted upon retirement.[27] A few received habits in crusading orders.[28] The Marqués del Real Socorro had two sons accepted into the Royal College of Nobles in Madrid, one of whom married the daughter of the *corregidor* of Madrid. Two of the Conde de Casa Montalvo's sons also entered the Royal College of Nobles, and they went on to be accepted in the Royal Guards.[29] Other Cuban officers also received consideration for their sons in the Spanish army. The most prominent of these was Gonzalo O'Farrill, yet another son of

25. File on Martín de Ugarte, 1794–95, AGS, GM, leg. 6859.
26. Representation, José Ricardo O'Farrill, Havana, Jan. 13, 1800, AGI, PC, leg. 1576.
27. Files on Conde de Lagunillas, 1789, and Miguel Antonio de Herrera, 1791, both in AGS, GM, legs. 6870–71.
28. File on José Francisco Beitía, 1797, AGS, GM, leg. 6876; Interim Subinspector General Manuel Artazo to Someruelos, Havana, Sept. 1, Dec. 14, 1807, AGI, PC, leg. 1581.
29. File on petitions of the Conde de Casa Montalvo, June 30, 1790, Marqués del Real Socorro, 1788–96, royal order, Aranjuez, May 8, 1799, all in AGS, GM, legs. 6844, 6855, 6878.

Juan, who became a lieutenant general in Spain and eventually minister of war.[30]

More common was the promotion of officers to grades higher than their functional (*propietario*) rank, or the attachment of supernumeraries (*agregados*) to the officer corps. These practices were not unique to the reign of Charles IV, but they were far more common. By 1795 the Volunteer Infantry Regiment of Havana had five lieutenant colonels commanding companies while the Volunteer Cavalry Regiment had a colonel and a lieutenant colonel acting in the same capacity. The infantry also had two supernumerary captains. As the 1790s progressed, the supernumerary positions became increasingly popular, for they afforded all the honors of rank without any real responsibilities. By 1801 the Havana Infantry Regiment had two extra colonels, one lieutenant colonel, and five captains; by 1805 another captain had been added. The cavalry had two supernumerary captains and one lieutenant colonel—two by 1805. Meanwhile, both units possessed abundant numbers of officers functioning below their official grade.[31] Significantly, these practices were essentially peculiar to Havana.[32] The lust for martial honors was clearly weaker outside the central sugar zone and, in any event, the families of Cuatro Villas, Puerto Príncipe, and Santiago-Bayamo lacked both the kind of distinction and the kind of access to the political system that served the Havana patriciate so well.

The officer corps of the regular army underwent a similar transformation during the 1790s. By the end of the decade, the infantry regiments possessed one creole supernumerary colonel and two lieutenant colonels, the dragoons one colonel and one lieutenant colonel (a Floridian). Two creole lieutenant colonels held company commands. Moreover, Colonel Conde de O'Reilly, who had married the Condesa de Buena Vista, was attached to the infantry. The regular army thus presented the absurd spectacle of adding on officers at the very time its effective soldiery was declining precipitously.[33]

The means *habaneros* employed to acquire the new colonelcies and captaincies varied. Some received promotions as the reward for years of faithful service. Others combined previous military service with social and political "merit" that usually included contributions or loans they had made to the royal treasury. Still others secured military honors through outright purchase, or *beneficio.*

The systematic sale of military offices in America dated to at least

30. Jacobo de la Pezuela, *Diccionario geográfico, estadístico, histórico de la Isla de Cuba* (Madrid, 1863), IV, 159–62.

31. Service records, 1795, 1801, 1805, AGS, GM, leg. 7262, AGI, PC, legs. 1770-B, 1771-B.

32. The service records for these units, 1799–1811, are in AGI, PC, legs. 1770–73.

33. Service records, Cuban garrison, 1799, AGS, GM, leg. 7264.

1780 when José de Gálvez instructed his nephew Bernardo to raise
funds by that means to help finance the establishment of a second
veteran battalion for Louisiana.[34] Gálvez extended this practice to Cuba
during the expansion of the Regiment of Havana to three battalions and
the establishment of the Regiment of Cuba. At that time, at least four
captaincies were sold for five thousand pesos each, one lieutenancy for
three thousand, and four sublieutenancies for fifteen hundred each.[35]
During the 1790s, as the financial position of the royal treasury deteriorated and the clamor for military titles intensified, other offices were
sold both in the regular army and the disciplined militia, despite the
explicit prohibition of the latter practice in O'Reilly's 1769
regulation.[36]

The crown, uncomfortable with the idea of these purchases, attempted to ensure that buyers were reasonably well qualified for their
offices. Yet as financial woes mounted and the tempting sums that
creole planters were willing to pay became evident, the Ministry of War
tended to overlook more. No official legislation governed standards and
procedures for sales. The unspoken rule was that the price of an office
increased in rough proportion to the amount that the crown had to
forgive, and overall prices rose as the extent of creole demand became
evident. Thus, while a veteran captaincy sold for five thousand pesos in
1788, the crown was thinking in terms of fifteen thousand or more for a
large jump by 1799.[37] That year, Adriano de la Cruz paid six thousand
pesos for a supernumerary captaincy in the volunteer cavalry.[38] Also in
1799 the Conde de Casa Bayona paid ten thousand pesos to purchase
the promotion to supernumerary colonel in the Volunteer Infantry
Regiment for his son, Francisco, who was a captain.[39] Joaquín de Santa
Cruz, a sublieutenant, jumped to the same rank, also in the infantry, for
the identical price. José Ortega y Ozeguera had offered twelve thousand
pesos for the office but was refused; the crown considered the figure too
low to compensate for his family's relative lack of distinction. Joaquín
and Francisco, however, had impeccable social credentials. In 1795 the
Marqués de San Felipe y Santiago purchased a veteran supernumerary
colonelcy with salary for his son, Juan Francisco Núñez del Castillo, in
the Veteran Infantry Regiment of Havana at the price of thirty
thousand pesos. The father of Anastasio Francisco de Armenteros y
Zaldívar, of less distinction than the Marqués de San Felipe, paid the

34. Dabán to Navarro, Havana, Aug. 31, 1780, AGI, PC, leg. 1235.
35. Troop review, Infantry Regiment of Havana, 1790, AGS, GM, leg. 6872. These
prices were lower than those established in Mexico because they carried a smaller salary.
36. Reglamento para las milicias, 1769, ch. 2, art. 1.
37. Petition, Juan Valdéz y Navarrette, Havana, AGS, GM, leg. 6863.
38. File on beneficio of Manuel José de la Cruz, 1799, AGS, GM, leg. 6878.
39. File on beneficio of Franciso Chacón, 1799, AGS, GM, leg. 6861.

same price in 1798 for his son's colonelcy in the more prestigious Dragoon Squadron of America, but it carried no salary.[40] The Conde de Casa Barreto, about whom more will be heard later, offered forty thousand pesos that year for a colonelcy with salary in that same unit but was refused because he lacked previous military experience. Later negotiations established the price at fifty-five thousand, but for reasons not clear, perhaps second thoughts about the cost, the conde never delivered the money.[41]

Seen as a business proposition, the sale of militia offices was preferable to the sale of veteran offices because they entailed no salary unless the individual happened to suffer mobilization, and even so, the graceful, indeed expected, gesture for men of condition was to forgo that remittance. The sale of veteran offices without salary entailed much the same advantage, but those carrying a wage could be profitable as well. A colonelcy priced at thirty thousand pesos, for example, obligated the royal treasure to an annual salary of twenty-four hundred pesos, a reasonable 8 percent, with no obligation to repay the principal. The sale of military offices was thus one more source of income for the hard-pressed treasury.

The total number of sales does not appear to have been great.[42] The Ministry of War, although desperate for revenue, consistently showed both concern for the effect that promotion by purchase would have upon unit morale and uneasiness about the size of the upper officer corps. Far more offers were refused than accepted. Yet purchase was another means by which those craving military rank might find fulfillment at the right price, and doubtless it contributed a degree of flexibility to a system in which special arrangement of one type or another was a regular feature.

Hastened by sales, the Americanization of the regular army's officer corps quite naturally continued. By 1799 Cubans held 91 of the 179 offices in the two infantry regiments, the light infantry, and the dra-

40. These transactions are summarized in the file on the petition of Joaquín José de Orta y Ozaguera, 1799, AGS, GM, leg. 6863.

41. File on petition of the Conde de Casa Barreto, 1799, AGS, GM, leg. 6863.

42. Apart from the original sales that occurred during the expansion of the veteran garrison, 1787–89, I have been able to document the purchase of two colonelcies and one captaincy in the militia and two colonelcies, one captaincy, one lieutenancy, one sublieutenancy, and ensigncies in the veteran garrison. These figures are not exclusive. The circumstances surrounding purchases could be murky; for example, sales could be made conditionally. Moreover, the archives of the Ministry of War after 1800 were moved to the Archivo Histórico Militar in Segovia, where most of the Cuban documents burned in a nineteenth-century fire. See also file of José María and José Manuel Sotolongo, AGS, GM, leg. 6874; service records of Pedro Calvo, Dragoon Squadron of America, Dec. 31, 1801, José Zúñiga and Francisco Lamadriz, Regiment of Havana, June 30, 1803, all in AGI, PC, legs. 1770-B, 1771-A.

goons; creoles from other colonies, principally Florida, Mexico, and
Santo Domingo, held another eleven. Although Americans were more
concentrated in the lower ranks, over half of the captaincies of the
Regiment of Havana belonged to Cubans, as did half of the proprietary
colonelcies of that unit and the Regiment of Cuba. Brigadier Francisco
Montalvo, son of the first Conde de Macuriges, commanded the Regiment of Havana, and Juan Lleonart the Regiment of Cuba. The Marqués
de Casa Calvo commanded the latter unit's Second Battalion.[43] By 1803
Cubans held 100 of 177 offices; other creoles, including three Florid-
ians, held 8. Both infantry regiments were still commanded by Cubans;
Lleonart remained in place and Casa Calvo had transferred to the
Regiment of Havana to replace Montalvo who advanced to the governor's general staff.[44] By 1809 the percentage of Europeans had slipped
further, declining to 58 of 166 officers. Cubans numbered 102, other
creoles 6.[45] Both colonelcies, however, had reverted to Spaniards.
Lleonart had retired, and Casa Calvo, after an absence as governor of
Louisiana to effect the transfer of that colony to the French and later as
the head of a survey commission to define its western boundary,
journeyed to Spain in 1807, where he was made field marshal.[46] The
new colonel of the Regiment of Havana was the Conde de O'Reilly,
who, as discussed previously, had strong local connections.

The most spectacular figure to adorn the Cuban military during this
period was undoubtedly Joaquín Beltrán de Santa Cruz y Cárdenas, heir
to the Condado de San Juan de Jaruco, a title that he would inherit in
1804. A major figure in the sugar aristocracy and married in 1786 to
María Teresa Montalvo y O'Farrill, daughter of the first Conde de Casa
Montalvo and granddaughter of Juan O'Farrill, Beltrán de Santa Cruz
had begun his military career in a rather ordinary fashion. At age
sixteen, he had entered the volunteer infantry as a sublieutenant, rising
to captain two years later.[47] In 1788 he made an outlandish attempt to
purchase an active colonelcy in the new veteran Regiment of Cuba that
failed both because he lacked military merit and because the Ministry
of War was loath to sell an office of that importance, at least for the

43. Service records, army of Cuba, Dec. 1799, AGS, GM, leg. 7264. These figures
contain a slight distortion for they include the officers of the Third Battalion of the
Regiment of Cuba which held a much higher percentage of Spaniards. Administratively, the
regiment was treated as a single unit with promotions crossing battalion lines. In practice,
however, Cubans seldom accepted promotions to the Florida battalion.
    44. Service records, army of Cuba, June 30, 1803, AGI, PC, leg. 1771-A.
    45. Service records, army of Cuba, Dec. 1809, AGI, PC, leg. 1772-A.
    46. Holmes, *Honor and Fidelity*, 72–73; Artazo to Someruelos, Havana, Sept. 1, 1807,
Someruelos to Artazo, Havana, Mar. 2, 1808, both in AGI, PC, legs. 1581, 1582; file on
defense of the Florida frontier, 1804, AGMS, Ultramar, leg. 225.
    47. Service records, Volunteer Infantry Regiment of Havana, Dec. 1789, AGS, GM, leg.
7260.

niggardly sum of twenty thousand pesos that he offered. Journeying to court with Teresa the following year to enhance his opportunities, he failed to gain a habit in a military order for want of service merit but, owing to his social status, managed to become a gentleman of His Majesty's Bedchamber with entrance in 1792. In the meantime, Beltrán de Santa Cruz flooded the Ministry of War with petitions for promotion to militia lieutenant colonel; he was willing to accept appointment in any of the white regiments of Havana or Matanzas. Incredibly, he invoked his time at court, away from his command, as evidence of sacrifice and merit. He nevertheless remained a militia captain as late as 1794, his ambitions unfulfilled.[48]

The fortune of Beltrán de Santa Cruz changed dramatically when he somehow became an intimate of Manuel Godoy, possibly in connection with his service with the Royal Spanish Guards against the French.[49] Once he had secured Godoy's friendship and patronage, little seemed impossible. Although he had been refused a militia lieutenant colonelcy as late as 1793, the Ministry of War named him subinspector general of the army of Cuba in 1795, a position that no creole had ever held, and accorded him the rank of brigadier—all of this after the recent failure of the more qualified Martín de Ugarte to obtain the same post because of his local ties![50] Moreover, he became the first Conde de Santa Cruz de Mopos *con grandeza* and, in addition to his now heavy military responsibilities, won authorization to undertake various ambitious scientific and development projects, including schemes for cataloging plants and insects, opening roads, building ports in Nipe and Mariel Bays, populating Guantánamo, and constructing a transinsular canal near Havana.[51]

The Conde de Santa Cruz de Mopos returned to the island to assume his military duties and to begin his far-flung projects in February 1797, but Teresa Montalvo y O'Farrill, a woman of captivating charm and beauty, remained at court where she lobbied for her husband's interests and established herself as a prominent hostess, counting among the regular guests at her *tertulias* Spain's leading writers and artists, including Francisco de Goya. Known on a first-name basis by Minister of Finance Miguel Cayetano Soler and presumably others, she was in-

48. File on applications of Beltrán de Santa Cruz, 1788–93, AGS, GM, leg. 6874.

49. For biographical data, see Nieto, *Dignidades nobiliarias*, 496–99, 520–22, and Santa Cruz, *Historia de familias*, I, 336–45.

50. File on petitions of the Conde de Santa Cruz de Mopos, 1795, AGS, GM, leg. 6874.

51. The best documentation on Santa Cruz de Mopos' development projects can be found in the Museo Naval, Madrid, under his name. See also, Iris H. W. Engstrand, *Spanish Scientists in the New World: The Eighteenth-Century Expeditions* (Seattle, 1981), 161–72; Francisco de las Barras, "Noticias y documentos de la expedición del Conde de Mompox [*sic*] a la Isla de Cuba," *AEA* 9 (1952), 513–48.

strumental in protecting her husband's privilege of importing a hundred thousand barrels of flour into Cuba on monopoly terms and in securing transport for his sugar to Spain on royal warships during the First British War.[52] Despite his duties in Cuba, the conde himself again journeyed to court in 1802 to pursue his interests, leaving Cayetano Fantini as interim subinspector until his return two years later. Preoccupation with his multifaceted undertakings, not to mention the sugar and flour businesses, undoubtedly detracted from Mopos' work as subinspector general and may in part explain the woeful condition of the Cuban armed forces as the island entered the nineteenth century. He also contracted to provide tobacco for the royal monopoly, but despite his many enterprises, or perhaps because of them, he owed the royal treasury over a million pesos upon his premature death at age thirty-eight in 1807. This debt was forgiven his heirs![53] The case of the Conde de Santa Cruz de Mopos and San Juan de Jaruco, albeit unique in its dimensions, illustrates the access that Cubans had to the politics at court and the cronyism that was so much a part of the Godoy government.

The configuration of the military meant that Cubans firmly controlled their own destiny when word arrived on July 14, 1808, that Napoleon had installed his brother Joseph as king of Spain and that Ferdinand VII, who had succeeded to the throne upon his father's abdication in March, had been taken captive. The Havana and Matanzas militia, which had just had its defective weapons replaced during late winter and early spring, was probably the most potent fighting force on the island.[54] Roughly two-thirds of the officers of the depleted veteran units were native sons, and in any event, most of the remaining Spaniards had been in Cuba so long that many must have become Cubanized. Finally, the two withered regiments from New Spain that lingered in Havana were dominated by Mexicans with substantial Cuban penetration at the lower ranks.[55] The gamble that Charles III had made in 1763 when he resolved to arm Americans and the subsequent compromises that had evolved regarding the composition of the vet-

52. Mopos to Miguel Cayetano Soler, Havana, July 28, 1806, AGI, Ultramar, leg. 198; Lampros, "Merchant-Planter Cooperation," 292–99, 327–35; Condesa de Mopos to the Príncipe de la Paz, Madrid, Dec. 1, 1796, Feb. 3, Nov. 14, 1797, all in MN, Mopos, book 1.

53. Intendant Rafael Gómez Roubaud to Soler, Havana, July 30, 1806; Roubaud to Príncipe de la Paz, Havana, Mar. 29, 1807; Príncipe de la Paz to Soler, Madrid, June 20, 1807; petition, Condesa Viuda de Mopos y de Jaruco, Madrid, Sept. 30, 1807, all in AGI, Ultramar, leg. 198.

54. The correspondence for the equipping of the Havana and Matanzas militia is in AGI, PC, leg. 1582.

55. The last set of service records for these regiments was made in 1801. See AGS, GM, leg. 7277, and compare to the personnel reports for 1810 in AGI, PC, leg. 1762.

eran officer corps had produced their logical consequences.[56] The question now was whether the political accommodation that had been nurtured so carefully by Charles III and sustained by his son would be enough to hold Cuba in the fold.

The traditional explanation for Cuban loyalty during the dynastic crisis—that the fear of a slave revolt persuaded the elite to pursue politics as usual under most unusual circumstances—and the more recent view—that Cubans also enjoyed a uniquely satisfying access to the imperial political system—are indisputably correct in a general sense. In this book I have reinforced and expanded upon the latter proposition, and the former is an ever apparent theme in the documentation of Cuban affairs after 1791. Moreover, a series of limited but violent slave rebellions had shaken the Havana district and Puerto Príncipe in the late 1790s, heightening general concern. Subinspector General Mopos went so far as to organize *"legiones rurales,"* a kind of rural guard to ensure tranquility in the hinterland.[57] Yet these considerations do not explain everything.

On July 26, less than two weeks after news of the royal captivity had arrived, a petition passed through Havana urging the formation of a Junta Suprema de Gobierno and claiming for Havana equal authority with the juntas that were springing up in Spain. The petition was carried by the *síndico procurador* of the ayuntamiento, Tomás de la Cruz Muñoz, at the instigation of Francisco Arango y Parreño with the collaboration of Deputy Governor José Ilincheta and the Conde de O'Reilly. Arango obviously did not find the fear of a slave rebellion compelling enough to prevent an attempt to reorganize the colonial government. Captain General Someruelos had issued a proclamation demanding obedience to the Supreme Junta in Seville upon the arrival of the news of the royal tragedy, but on July 22, obviously under pressure, he reversed his position, asserting that Cuba had as much right as any other kingdom of Spain to form a provisional government pending the return of the legitimate monarch.[58] Someruelos, who had cultivated close connections with the Havana patriciate during his long tenure in Cuba, was plainly inclined to bend with the political tide rather than risk losing control. Moreover, according to an earlier denunciation by Intendant Rafael Gómez Roubaud, he was party to a

56. In the face of this evidence, the contention of Foner, *A History of Cuba*, I, 81–82, that a major factor determining Cuban fidelity was the intimidating presence of the Spanish military must be dismissed.

57. Accounts of these rebellions can be found in AGS, GM, leg. 6865. Documentation for the organization of the rural legions can be found in AGI, PC, leg. 1668

58. Someruelos to the Ayuntamiento of Havana, Havana, July 22, 1808, AGI, PC, leg. 1627.

clique led by Arango and Ilincheta that operated in the murky, ill-defined waters of Havana's inner politics.[59] The pretext for the formation of a Junta Suprema was the need to strengthen royal authority in the face of an unprecedented crisis. This step, the ayuntamiento later explained, would have consolidated colonial administrative power, "so divided... among various political officials" into a single "government that would unite all the authority . . . necessary to protect our existence."[60] Seventy-three men signed, but when Arango took stock of the number and quality of the signers two days later, he prudently withdrew the petition and the movement died.[61]

The meaning of the events of July has escaped the historians of the period. Most have ignored the event or passed lightly over it, presumably with the obvious justification that it bore no visible consequences. One exception is Vidal Morales y Morales, who dared state that had it continued this movement "probably would have resulted in the independence of this island." Another exception, Francisco J. Ponte Domínguez, in the sole monographic treatment of the subject asserted that the junta was "legally conceived," was not a covert rebellion against royal authority, and was inspired solely by patriotic considerations.[62] On most of these points, it is difficult to quarrel with either man, despite the distance that separates them. As Ponte Domínguez argued, the movement was not in fact an explicit rebellion against royal domination, but on the other hand the formation of a Junta Suprema would most certainly have begun a new political process whose consequences cannot be judged. Hence, Morales y Morales, while overstepping the limits of his evidence, cannot be faulted too much for projecting that the results of a self-constituted government might have resembled what happened later in other colonies. In this sense, Cuba would, as usual during the Bourbon period, have been in the vanguard of imperial change. The problem with their interpretations is that neither Morales y Morales nor Ponte Domínguez has asked the right questions concerning the meaning of the events in 1808. The movement was in fact quite revolutionary, although at the same time it most certainly was not an immediate threat to the traditional ties between Cuba and Spain.

Although pampered as a matter of royal policy, Cubans possessed

59. Representación, Intendant Roubaud, Havana, Sept. 2, 1805, AGI, Ultramar, leg. 200.

60. Ayuntamiento of Havana to Someruelos, Havana, Dec. 1, 1808, AGI, PC, leg. 1627.

61. The petition with signatories has been reproduced in Francisco J. Ponte Domínguez, *La junta de La Habana en 1808: Antecedentes para la historia de la autonomía colonial en Cuba* (Havana, 1947), 61, 119–21, and in Vidal Morales y Morales, *Iniciadores y primeros mártires de la revolución cubana* (Havana, 1931), I, 22–23.

62. Morales y Morales, *Iniciadores*, I, 21; Ponte Domínguez, *La junta*, 109.

specific grievances against the royal administration and in particular against the three autonomous branches of the local colonial government—the Commandancy General of Marine, the Royal Tobacco Factory, and the Intendancy. All three to some degree represented obstacles to economic expansion, and Marine Commandant Juan Villavicencio was the most unpopular man in Havana. The July 26 movement, had it succeeded, would have overthrown the autonomous powers of these officials, bringing them under the authority of the Junta Suprema. To this extent Arango's movement was revolutionary indeed.

The marine commandant held responsibility for protecting Cuba's forests from the wanton cutting of timber. Certain areas called *montes* were set aside for the exclusive use of the royal shipyard, but to cut trees of any sort required authorization from the marine commandant, a most annoying encumbrance for the sugar aristocracy. Since Minister of Finance Pedro López de Lerena's economy drive in the late 1780s, moreover, royal investments in shipbuilding had tapered off substantially.[63] This recession particularly damaged those who supplied lumber from their lands, while the *montes*, owned in part by private individuals, presented tempting prizes for planters. As the sugar industry grew, the demand for lumber intensified both for packing materials and especially for fuel. To clear wood from their own lands, whether for their own consumption, to supply Havana, or simply to make space for additional plantings, Cubans were required to obtain permission from the commandant. Although such authorization was regularly provided, the very fact that Cuba was a major importer of wood from Louisiana and the United States shows the restraint that these procedures had on deforestation.[64] Petitions to reconstitute the authority of the marine commandant, many of them from the Consulado, accumulated in Madrid, but an uncertain royal administration had not resolved the problem by 1808.[65]

It cannot be assumed, however, that all planters were affected the same way. The lands of many had long since been cleared, and outside imports were probably as cheap a source of timber as long-distance procurement from within the island. José Ricardo O'Farrill, for example, published a tract in 1806 pleading for the conservation of Cuba's

---

63. Barbier and Klein, "Revolutionary Wars and Public Finances," 331.

64. For the United States, see Lampros, "Merchant-Planter Cooperation," 317–19, 325–26; for New Orleans, AGI, PC, legs. 112, 188C.

65. The documentation on the struggle over cutting rights can be found in AGI, Ultramar, leg. 9. Moreno Fraginals, *El ingenio*, I, 159 asserts that a concession of Aug. 30, 1805, liberalized owners' rights to cut on their own land. The file on this subject records no such change until the file is interrupted by the French invasion.

forests.[66] Francisco Arango, as perpetual syndic of the Consulado, on the other hand, led a persistent assault on the powers of the marine commandant.[67]

The tobacco monopoly had never been popular in Cuba. People with the ability to do so had long before abandoned that product. The destruction of the monopoly, nevertheless, would open new opportunities for investment diversification. On another level, the officials of the royal tobacco monopoly had resisted encroachments by sugar against the lands of the small growers who had taken over tobacco production.[68] Again, Arango led the criticism of the monopoly, although, among his many portfolios, he also occupied the position of assessor of the Royal Tobacco Factory.[69]

During its history, the Intendancy had not necessarily provoked conflict with the Havana patriciate, although its mission to curtail contraband in conjunction with the Commandancy of Marine was an underlying irritant. Intendant Juan Pablo Valiente (1792–1798), for example, was a model of cooperation with planter-merchant interests, perhaps because he was the co-owner with Arango y Parreño of the plantation La Ninfa. Indeed, when informed of his pending recall to Spain, both the Consulado and the Havana ayuntamiento petitioned the king to permit him to remain. By contrast, Rafael Gómez Roubaud (1804–1808), a creature of Godoy and close friend of the Conde de Santa Cruz de Mopos y San Juan de Jaruco, was a persistent, bitter critic of Arango, Someruelos, and Ilincheta. An opponent of the repeated concessions that Havana exacted in the interest of neutral trade, Roubaud also served as superintendant of the Royal Tobacco Factory in 1808.[70]

Apart from recasting the colonial administration, a Junta Suprema would have offered other advantages. The continued need to deflect the mercantilistic pretenses of Spanish interests, albeit almost invariably successful, was an ongoing annoyance to the planter elite. Moreover, Jefferson's embargo, which had produced a sharp slump in sugar prices

66. "Sobre la conservación de Montes por Coronel de Milicias José Ricardo O'Farrill, presentado a la Sociedad Económica de la Havana," Oct. 22, 1796, AGI, Ultramar, leg. 9.

67. For Arango's numerous assaults on the Commandancy of Marine, see AGI, Ultramar, leg. 9.

68. H.E. Friedlander, *Historia económica de Cuba* (Havana, 1944), 123–25.

69. See, for example, Francisco Arango y Parreño, "Abolición de la Fábrica: Libertad en la siembra, fabricación y comercio del tabaco," in Raúl Maestri, ed., *De la factoría a la colonia* (Havana, 1936), 114–28.

70. Moreno Fraginals, *El ingenio*, I, 58–59, 61; Pierson, "Institutional History," 110–11; Pierson, "Francisco de Arango," 473–74; Lampros, "Merchant-Planter Cooperation," 336, 340, 347, 362–72; representación, Intendant Roubaud, Havana, Sept. 2, 1805, AGI, Ultramar, leg. 200. Roubaud was replaced by Juan de Aguilar y Amat on July 18, 1808, but remained *intendente graduado*. Ponte Domínguez, *La junta*, 44; *Calendario manual y guia de forasteros en la Isla de Cuba . . .* (Havana, 1809), 172.

and sales, reminded planters of their dependency on access to the broad markets they had enjoyed since 1793.[71] The political autonomy implied by a junta would have affirmed the ability to control commercial policies during a perilously uncertain time.

A final issue was colonialism itself. If juntas could be formed in the several provinces of Spain, were not Cubans entitled to the same right? Word that such juntas had in fact been formed provided the constitutional justification for Someruelos' about-face regarding the proper course of Cuban behavior.[72]

To state the obvious, few people in July 1808 could have realistically expected the return of Ferdinand VII to the throne. Napoleon, fresh from victories at Austerlitz, Jena, Auerstädt, and Friedland, was the master of much of Europe, and Spanish resistance seemed in disarray. The behavior of three prominent Cubans in Spain well expresses the tide of the times. Gonzalo O'Farrill, son of Juan, brother of two lieutenant colonels in the Havana militia, and brother-in-law of the Conde de Casa Bayona, went over to the French in October 1808 while still minister of war. He was followed by his cousin the Marqués de Casa Calvo, who was the former colonel of the Regiment of Havana and who currently enjoyed a command in Spain. In casting their lot with what seemed to be a winner, both men left extensive properties in Cuba, which were confiscated as they most surely must have anticipated.[73] Finally, Teresa Montalvo y O'Farrill, widow of the Subinspector General Conde de San Juan de Jaruco y Santa Cruz de Mopos, niece of Gonzalo O'Farrill, and an intimate of the inner circles at court, carried her lobbying to the royal couch, becoming the mistress of José Bonaparte.[74] Political opportunism had long been the style in Cuba and these three patricians plainly saw the future in Bonapartist terms. Havana was in no way prepared to accept a French monarch, but it also could not have anticipated the restoration of Ferdinand. The divisions that emerged in Havana in 1808 derived essentially, albeit not exclusively, from local politics and within that framework came down to the leadership of Arango and Ilincheta.

Given the realities of 1808, Arango y Parreño would superficially appear to have been the ideal leader of a reconstituted colonial government. Intellectually a disciple of Adam Smith and an implacable enemy of mercantilism, he had led the campaign for a liberalization of

---

71. Lampros, "Merchant-Planter Cooperation," 357ff.

72. Someruelos to the Ayuntamiento of Havana, July 22, 1808, AGI, PC, leg. 1627.

73. Someruelos to the Marqués de las Hormazas, Havana, Mar. 1, 1810, Someruelos to Varea, Jan. 17, 1811, both in AGI, SD, legs. 1282–83. Ponte Domínguez erred in stating that Casa Calvo was the nephew of Gonzalo O'Farrill. He was in fact the son of Catalina O'Farrill, sister of Juan.

74. Moreno Fraginals, *El ingenio*, II, 121; Barras, "Noticias y documentos," 515.

trade regulations both as Havana's representative at court and subsequently as syndic of the Consulado. He had, moreover, taken the lead in attacking the obstacles posed to the free market by the timber laws and the tobacco monopoly. He was a modernizing force within the Cuban elite.[75] Yet Arango and his coconspirator José Ilincheta were unable to marshal sufficient support to carry forward with their plan.

Morales y Morales, who called Arango's supporters a "Junta of notables," attributed this failure to the "many enemies of the great patrician don Francisco de Arango y Parreño."[76] Ponte Domínguez asserted that Arango was arrested by the opposition of the Conde de Casa Barreto who exercised what he called a kind of "liberum veto," forcing the ever prudent patrician to withdraw his plan rather than foment division.[77] In yet another interpretation, Ramiro Guerra attributed the failure of the movement to the fierce opposition of the three autonomous branches of the colonial administration supported by Spanish-oriented merchants.[78] The two latter explanations are unconvincing. In terms of the realities of 1808, the men blamed by Ponte Domínguez and Guerra for Arango's failure wielded very little real power. Casa Barreto was an outsider within the elite who was never once elected to an office in the municipal government or the Consulado or in the Patriotic Society of Friends of the Nation. His effort to mount a counter petition failed to obtain a single signature.[79] Roubaud and Villavicencio did indeed combat Arango's scheme, but it was not they who defeated the plan, for they commanded no troops. The missing element in Arango's coalition was sufficient creole military support, as historian closest to these events, Jacobo de la Pezuela, recognized. In a conference at the governor's palace on the evening of July 27, Pezuela wrote, opposition to Arango crystallized around Villavicencio, Roubaud, Barreto, and "among many military men, Brigadier [Francisco] Montalvo. Upon their hearing for the first time this plan, Montalvo interrupted Arango during his discourse and, slamming his fist upon the conference table, protested that neither a supreme nor provincial junta would be installed as long as he was alive and wielded a sword."[80]

Although Arango had persuaded Spanish Brigadier Agustín de Ibarra, commander of the veteran artillery brigades, to edit the July 26 petition and although he enjoyed the support of the Conde de O'Reilly,

75. Pierson, "Francisco de Arango," 451–78.
76. Morales y Morales, *Iniciadores*, I, 22–23.
77. Ponte Domínguez, *La junta*, 56–60.
78. Guerra, *Manual de historia de Cuba*, 223–25.
79. Ponte Domínguez, *La junta*, 71; Someruelos to Nicolás María de la Sierra, Havana, Sept. 7, 1810, AGI, SD, leg. 1282.
80. Jacobo de la Pezuela, *Historia de la Isla de Cuba*, (Madrid, 1878), III, 384–85.

commander of the Fixed Infantry Regiment of Havana, he managed to bring only four creole officers into his movement.[81] They included the Conde de Gibacoa, colonel of the Matanzas Dragoons; the Conde de Casa Bayona, colonel of the Volunteer Infantry Regiment; his son, Supernumerary Colonel Francisco Chacón of the same regiment; and Juan de Montalvo y O'Farrill, supernumerary colonel of the Fixed Infantry Regiment of Cuba. All four, about whom more will be said later, were unquestionably significant figures in the planter-officer corps, but they represented only a small portion of the Havana command structure.

The militia officer corps had traditionally counted the elite of Havana society among its members, and it still did.[82] Among the officers then assigned to the prestigious Volunteer Cavalry Regiment were the Condes de Casa Montalvo and de Vallellano, Colonel Martín de Ugarte, Lieutenant Colonel José Ricardo O'Farrill, and members of the Basabe, Cárdenas, Chacón, Cruz, Herrera, Morales, and Sotolongo families. Not one signed the petition. From the Volunteer Infantry Regiment, Casa Bayona was able to persuade only his son. Those who abstained included Lieutenant Colonel Conde de Zaldívar and many members of the Zaldívar family, the Marqués del Real Socorro and his two brothers, Supernumerary Colonel Joaquín de Santa Cruz, four more Cárdenas, another O'Farrill, and members of the Armenteros, Camacho, Herrera, Meyreles, Menocal, Morales, Pita, and Pozo families. Lieutenant Colonel Juan Manuel O'Farrill of the Matanzas Dragoons, like his brother, José Ricardo, remained aloof. Moreover, apart from Juan de Montalvo y O'Farrill, the entire creole contingent of the veteran officer corps abstained, including Juan Francisco Núñez del Castillo, son of the Marqués de San Felipe y Santiago; Pedro Calvo, the future Marqués de Casa Calvo; and as noted by Pezuela, Brigadier Francisco Montalvo, the highest ranking creole on the general staff of Havana.

It is possible, of course, that Cruz Muñoz did not reach all of these people. Some may have been away, ill, or otherwise unavailable. Yet most of the nobility congregated in the aristocratic district of the city. Thus many of the officers lived in close proximity to each other and could easily have been approached.[83] Arango plainly had reached the conclusion that he lacked sufficient military support when he withdrew his petition. No combat occurred. Given the social equation, such an eventuality would have been unthinkable. Arango was above all a

81. Ponte Domínguez, *La junta*, 48.

82. The service records for the army of Cuba are complete for the year 1809, in AGI, PC, leg. 1772, and can be compared to the roster of signatories published in Ponte Domínguez, *La junta*, 60–62, 119–21, and in Morales y Morales, *Iniciadores*, I, 22–23.

83. *Calendario*, 101–2.

political realist, and he was fully aware that a division in the elite of Saint Domingue had opened the way for slave rebellion.

Historians of Cuba have yet to complete a comprehensive analysis of the proponents of the Arango-Ilincheta movement. It is evident, nevertheless, that Morales y Morales' description of them as a "junta of notables" is an exaggeration, if for no other reason than the impressive number of prominent abstainers identified above. Forty-six of the signatories were Spaniards, many of them apparently merchants. A number of prominent planters, including the Condes de Casa Bayona and Gibacoa, the Marqués de Casa Peñalver and two other Peñalvers, Gonzalo de Herrera, and two Armenteros, did sign, of course. At least three, Pedro Pedroso, Bonifacio González Larrinaga, and Bernabé Martínez de Pinillos, were leading Cuban merchant–money lenders and real estate investors. Two others—Pedro María Ramírez and Francisco Hernández—can definitely be identified as merchants, and there were a number of clerics.[84] Most, however, were obscure figures, not notables.

Arango's political weakness arose from his lack of identification with the planter officer corps. Associated with the progressive, enlightened element of Havana, he had never established close ties with the creole military, showing no personal interest in titles of rank or privileges. In notes to his 1792 discourse on the development of Cuban agriculture, he had stated, "Honors should only be awarded for merit based on talent and virtue and not by reason of birthright," a conviction that he practiced when he refused a title of nobility offered him by the Havana ayuntamiento years later.[85] The leadership of his movement was closely associated with the Patriotic Society of Friends of the Nation, which had become a vehicle for the dissemination of enlightened thought. Arango, Ilincheta, O'Reilly, and Ibarra had all held offices in that organization in 1804, an association that explains much about the orientation of the July movement.[86]

Within this context, Arango's coconspirator, José Ilincheta, had done much to alienate the planter officer corps with its strong allegiance to traditional honors and privileges. Unlike New Spain and New Granada where jurisidictional clashes were commonplace, Cuba had experienced little such controversy during the early history of the reform. This harmony can in part be explained by the fact that the Cuban militia was well defined as were its prerogatives, but the inter-

84. Ponte Domínguez, La junta, 50; Moreno Fraginals, El ingenio, I, 69, 71; Lampros, "Merchant-Planter Cooperation," 374.

85. Quoted in Moreno Fraginals, El ingenio, I, 128. See also Pierson, "Francisco de Arango," 460. The title, Marqués de la Gratitud, was eventually assumed by Arango's grandson. Nieto, Dignidades nobiliarias, 125–60.

86. Junta ordinaria celebrada por la Sociedad Patriótica, Havana, July 13, 1804, AGI, PC, leg. 1734; Calendario, 97.

locking nature of the Havana directory and its common interests regarding the larger reform package most certainly militated against damaging contests for corporate prestige. This pattern changed during the 1790s, however, as the colony grew in complexity and as fashionable enlightened ideas disdaining traditional corporatist values penetrated Havana. Ilincheta was a leader in this movement and was known to host *tertulias* in his home where he delighted in ridiculing military honors and privileges.[87]

In 1791, shortly after becoming deputy governor of Havana and hence the custodian of ordinary justice, Ilincheta raised the first major legal challenge to the militia's *fuero*. In a protest to Captain General Las Casas, the deputy governor complained that the military jurisdiction as defined by the royal decree of April 15, 1771, was unreasonably broad and constituted an undue imposition upon the Havana community, as from an enlightened perspective it most surely did. The royal declaration, it will be recalled, had confirmed the active *fuero* for militia officers and sergeants. By challenging this privilege, Ilincheta struck directly at the planter-officer corps. He also revealed a practical motive for this attack when he lamented that he was deprived of fees to which he should otherwise be entitled as an ordinary justice because most of the nobility was enlisted in the militia.[88] Las Casas had little choice but to forward Ilincheta's complaint to Spain.

Matters were soon complicated by the arrival of a royal order of February 9, 1793, addressed to New Spain but also sent to Cuba. In a sweeping attempt to reduce jurisdictional conflicts, this legislation defined the army's *fuero* as absolute except in cases involving the disposition of entailed estates and the division of inheritances derived from civilians.[89] The order, acording to Auditor de Guerra Julián Francisco de Campos, was received to "the applause of all. The echo of their gratitude resounded in honor of His Majesty, repeated *vivas al Rey* being heard in the streets and plazas, and it caused such an emotional commotion that even retired soldiers yearned to return to royal service." Although Campos' statement, made in the midst of a jurisdictional conflict, can hardly be accepted at face value, the February order, by eliminating numerous instances of *desafuero*, seemingly placed the crown on the side of traditional corporatist arrangements and, in view

87. Lieutenant Governor Domingo Cabello to the Duque de Alcudia, Havana, Oct. 5, 1793, AGS, GM, leg. 6854. For an analysis of the relationship between commerce and the spread of enlightened ideas, see Peggy K. Liss, *Atlantic Empires: The Network of Trade and Revolution, 1713–1826*, (Baltimore, 1983).

88. Ilincheta to the Marqués de Bajamar, Havana, Nov. 11, 1791, AGI, PC, leg. 2142.

89. For a translation of this order and a description of the controversy that it raised in New Spain, see McAlister, *The "Fuero Militar,"* ch. 7.

of Ilincheta's challenge, was certainly welcome news to Cuba's volunteer officer corps.[90]

Ilincheta, however, boldly refused to honor the order because it had been issued through the Ministry of War. With strained and mischievous logic, he claimed in a letter of April 25 to Las Casas that, pending formal notification of the royal decision through the Council of the Indies, he could not act upon it in his capacity as an ordinary justice. In conjunction with this ploy, which was apparently designed to attract attention in Spain, he went on to question the meaning of the February order. Assuming that proper notification would eventually reach him, Ilincheta nimbly inquired whether the royal order encompassed the militia or simply applied to the regular army, a point of interpretation not at all clear in the reading although the crown had in fact intended that the disciplined militia be included. The deputy governor further observed that the new legislation seemed to entail only the passive *fuero*, which was in fact the limit of the privilege in New Spain, and then, bringing the order to bear on his challenge to the active *fuero*, asked if this was to be the future construction of the militia's privilege in Cuba as well. Las Casas sent Ilincheta's objection and inquiries to Spain where they did indeed attract official attention. In a blistering order of September 25 the Ministry of War severely reprimanded the deputy governor and demanded immediate compliance with the February order, but Ilincheta's tactic worked, for his request for clarifiction was joined to his earlier litigation against the active *fuero*.

In Madrid, Charles IV referred these questions to a special four-man committee comprising two officials from the Council of the Indies and two from the Ministry of War. In part because of problems arising from deaths and occupational transfers, this commission would vacillate for five years before bringing forth a recommendation. In the meantime, the Cuban officer corps marshaled its political forces to justify the preservation of the active *fuero*. The Conde de Buena Vista and the Marqués del Real Socorro, the colonels of the two Havana militia regiments, led a spirited rebuttal to Ilincheta in which they advanced the traditional corporatist argument that those who sacrificed to bear arms for the king were entitled to be honored with privileges in every respect.[91] Moreover, both men successfully petitioned for the right to come to court; Buena Vista pleaded for a change of climate to improve his health, and Real Socorro claimed pressing personal business. Buena Vista was indeed a sick man, suffering from hydrocele, an infirmity that had recently led to the death of his uncle, Juan O'Farrill. Unlike

90. The files for this case are in AGI, SD, leg. 2142 and AGS, GM, leg. 6865.
91. The militia response can be found in AGI, PC, leg. 1486.

O'Farrill, Buena Vista survived surgery in Havana for the disorder, but the ailment lingered, and he hoped for better results in a more healthful climate. Arriving in Spain in October 1793, he would die immediately upon his return to Cuba in 1796. Yet despite his illness, the conde managed to lobby at court for promotions to brigadier (1794) and to field marshal (1795), smoothing the path by generous contributions to the hard-pressed treasury. A man who could win two major promotions within two years could surely also find the means to make his views heard on the matter of military privilege. Real Socorro traveled to Madrid in 1796 where it seems likely that he also personally attended to a defense of the Cuban *fuero*.[92] Moreover, the newly appointed subinspector general of the Cuban army and intimate of Godoy, the Conde de Santa Cruz de Mopos, was himself still at court preparing for his triumphal return to Cuba. What specific influence these people, Mopos' wife, Teresa, or others may have exerted is unknown, but the events that developed make it clear that substantial pressure was brought to bear in the Ministry of War.

The crown had recently codified its latest thinking on the matter of military privilege through the 1794 regulation for the disciplined militia of New Granada. Originally organized under the Cuban regulation, New Granada's volunteers had enjoyed the active *fuero* since 1773, but precedent notwithstanding, the 1794 codification had struck the privilege as excessive.[93] In early 1798, shortly before issuing its findings on the Ilincheta complaint, the special commission was expanded to ten men, including Lieutenant General Gonzalo O'Farrill, the brother or brother-in-law of many of Havana's colonels, including Real Socorro. The commission, nevertheless, held to recent policy, recommending that the definition established for New Granada be extended to Cuba. In an abrupt and unusual rejection of a select committee report, however, Minister of War Juan Manuel Alvarez, Godoy's uncle, overruled the recommendation, stating "His Majesty does not presently [wartime] wish to curtail privileges"! Cuba's planter-officer corps thus retained a privileged position within the empire. Although the commission continued to meet for a number of years to resolve points of interpretation stemming from the February 9 order, the question of the active *fuero* did not arise again.[94] A royal order of December 17, 1804, reaffirmed the traditional arrangement.[95] In the meantime, following

92. Files on Conde de Buena Vista, 1792–96, Marqués del Real Socorro, 1789–96, both in AGS, GM, legs. 6855–56.
93. *Reglamento para las milicias disciplinadas de infantería y dragones del Nuevo Reino de Granada, y provincias agregadas a este virreynato* (Madrid, 1794); Kuethe, *Military Reform and Society,* 162.
94. File on militia privileges, AGI, SD, leg. 2142.
95. See Zamora, comp., *Biblioteca de legislación,* III, 326.

the establishment of the Consulado, the instances of military *de-safuero* were redefined to include causes arising from mercantile pursuits, which had been the customary practice and which also reflected the premium that the crown placed on commerce as a means to reestablish Spanish grandeur.[96]

During this period, the military and ordinary jurisdictions clashed at the local level. Lieutenant Governor Domingo Cabello and Ilincheta got into a dispute over the right to assume the governorship in Las Casas' absence, and during the fracas the lieutenant governor accused his rival of "trampling" upon militiamen.[97] And Alcalde Mayor Miguel Ciriaco Arango, Francisco's father, challenged the military jurisdiction in a frivolous action where the passive *fuero*, which was not at question in the larger dispute, applied.[98] In the end, all this litigation failed to alter the definition of the Cuban militia's privileges, except to confirm new limitations on the instances of *desafuero*, but it did define an important polarization in the Havana community. Ilincheta emerged clearly identified as an enemy of military corporate privilege and, at least to a lesser degree, so too did Arango, whose father had been in the deputy governor's camp, when he became Ilincheta's political intimate following his return from Spain. The crown, for its part, remained quite willing to honor its traditional commitments. This issue goes far to explain the refusal of Havana's creole officers to support the Arango-Ilincheta initiative of July 1808. The fundamental difference lay between an enlightened, progressive view of society, critical of privilege and special arrangement, on the one hand, and the traditional corporatist values so precious to the volunteer officer corps, on the other.

On a separate level, Francisco de Arango y Parreño's own earlier actions also weakened his political position in 1808. In his famous 1792 tract on Havana's agriculture and its development, Arango strongly urged the disbandment of Cuba's *pardo* and *moreno* battalions because, he alleged, they posed a threat to social stability. Although unaware that the 1792 census already recorded a combined slave and free black and mulatto majority, Arango foresaw the day when whites would become a minority, provided, of course, that sugar continued its expansion as he believed it must.[99] To his mind, all blacks, whether free or slave, possessed essentially the same grievances, and he believed that in the event of an occurrence similar to that of Saint Domingue none

96. Royal order, Aranjuez, May 13, 1799, AGS, GM, leg. 6864.

97. File on complaint of Lieutenant Governor Domingo Cabello, 1794, AGS, GM, leg. 6854.

98. File on jurisdictional conflict, 1798, AGS, GM, leg. 6861.

99. The 1792 census is discussed in Las Casas to Campo de Alange, Havana, Dec. 23, 1794, AGS, GM, leg. 6854. A breakdown of the 272,141 inhabitants showed 84, 965 slaves and 53,561 freedmen.

could be trusted. Arango, it was evident, respected the fighting quality of the black and mulatto battalions, and for that very reason he feared them. Were it possible to limit their role in society strictly to coastal defense, he would have viewed them as an asset; but such a limitation was not possible, and he dreaded the military knowledge they acquired through militia training. He lamented, moreover, that retired volunteers often turned up in the countryside where they had the opportunity to influence the slaves. He therefore urged the crown to replace the *pardo* and *moreno* units with whites.

The Consejo de Estado, which received Arango's report, referred the question to the Ministry of War, which in turn asked Las Casas for an opinion. Las Casas, who under normal circumstances was most amenable to the wishes of Havana's planters and who had earlier ridiculed the complaint of the *moreno* officers against Subinspector Seidel, showed no sympathy whatever for Arango's reasoning. The interests of free blacks and mulattoes, he argued were not the same as those of the slaves. The former customarily viewed those in bondage with a kind of contempt, seeking to maximize the social distance between themselves and their own origins, and blacks, he noted, sometimes owned slaves themselves. He believed that to deny the colored estate military responsibilities and honors would provoke useless discontent while costing the island some of its best fighting men. On the whole, he believed, *pardo* and *moreno* militiamen were satisfied with their privileges and with the incentive provided by the medals they could earn for good service.

Responsible for the defense of Cuba, Las Casas was keenly aware of the combat record of the *pardo* and *moreno* battalions and plainly had no intention of giving them up during wartime, especially since much of the regular army was currently operating outside of the island. The fate of Juan de Prado still lingered in the bureaucratic memory, and Las Casas obviously put his own career advancement first. In an usually cutting observation, he suggested that, if Arango were truly concerned about the emerging social imbalance in Cuba, he should work to limit slave imports and to encourage white immigration. The Ministry of War in reviewing this controversy observed that Arango had no firsthand knowledge of military affairs; the ministry therefore found no reason to quarrel with the captain general's vigorous defense of the black units and forwarded his report to the Consejo de Estado.[100] The consejo, with the king presiding, accepted the captain general's viewpoint, putting an end to the question for the immediate future.[101] Arango refused to let the matter rest and persuaded the Consulado to

100. File on Arango proposal, AGS, GM, leg. 6854.
101. Minutes, Consejo de Estado, July 6, 1795, AHN, Estado, book 10.

advance his argument anew in 1798, but the crown could not be budged.[102] Given his attack on their existence, there could be little doubt where Havana's *pardo* and *moreno* battalions stood in 1808; it was a further, dangerous complication for Arango, who was unable to win over the mass of the white militia or the regular army.

But what of the four officers who supported the petition? Unanimity within a large group is rare and, given the complexity of the issues that faced Cuba in 1808, could hardly have been expected. None of the four ever explained his motives, but some clues help account for their deviation from the norm. The behavior of José María Espinosa de Contreras y Jústiz, Conde de Gibacoa, is the most easily explained. Although he lived in Havana, Gibacoa owned vast tracts of land near Matanzas, whose dragoon regiment he commanded. His father, the first conde, originally made much of his fortune in shipbuilding and by providing lumber for the royal shipyard in Havana. The family, however, soon found itself embroiled in controversy with the Marine Commandancy over the right to cut the royally protected forests on their land.[103] Just prior to the turn of the century, moreover, in an effort to curtail illegal cutting, the marine commandant ordered an end to private shipbuilding in Matanzas, which was surely a severe blow to Gibacoa.[104] Under these circumstances, the prospect of a Junta Suprema under the influence of Arango and Ilincheta must have been attractive. Both had clashed earlier with the Marine Commandancy, and Arango ranked as its primary critic.[105] As leaders in a new junta of "unity," they would have been in a strong position to bring the marine commandant under their control, most likely to the benefit of Gibacoa, a consideration that probably outweighed corporate military considerations.

The only veteran creole officer who supported Arango was Juan Montalvo y O'Farrill, supernumerary lieutenant colonel of the Regiment of Cuba. As a youth, Montalvo, as discussed earlier, had been placed in the Royal College of Nobles in Madrid by his father, the Conde de Montalvo, and he was later admitted to the Spanish Royal Guards. During the French War, he had fought in the peninsula where he had been captured by the French and held prisoner. Although he was exchanged and sent back to Cuba after the conflict, one might speculate that he had absorbed enough enlightened ideas to associate com-

102. The Consulado's statement, July 10, 1799, can be found in AGS, GM, leg. 6865.

103. De la Torre to Arriaga, Havana, Feb. 24, 1775, AGI, SD, leg. 1223; file on colonelcy of the Dragoon Regiment of Matanzas, 1787, AGS, GM, leg. 6868.

104. Consulado of Havana to Francisco de Saavedra, Havana, May 22, 1798, AGI, Ultramar, leg. 9.

105. Domingo Cabello to Campo de Alange, Havana, Oct. 4, 1793, AGS, GM, leg. 6854; Guerra y Sánchez, et al. *Historia de la nación cubana*, III, 20, 25.

fortably with men of Arango and Ilincheta's ideological persuasion. Moreover, it is likely that the two men were friends. Both had been at court during the same period and were later joined by Montalvo's father. The conde, it will be recalled, had accompanied Arango on his foreign tour as the second representative of the Patriotic Society.[106]

The behavior of the Conde de Casa Bayona and his son, Francisco Chacón, is more difficult to explain. Whether they had grievances similar to those of the Conde de Gibacoa is unknown. Perhaps of significance was Casa Bayona's current status as *regidor perpetuo* of the Havana ayuntamiento, a position that most likely would have propelled him into a leadership role in the new government.[107]

On the other hand, to assert that every officer who declined to sign the petition did so solely in protest of Arango and Ilincheta's anticorporatist orientation would overstate a most important but certainly not exclusive point of motivation. Surely, many simply feared change at any level, and others had strong personal reasons to support the status quo. Gonzalo O'Farrill had just become minister of war, a circumstance that must have influenced his brothers and perhaps others. They had, of course, no way of anticipating his upcoming desertion to the French and at the moment were secure in their access to the political system on both sides of the water.[108]

Despite the potential consequences, the divisions that emerged in 1808 should not be overestimated. The two sides shared much common ground, including strong familial connections. Although Arango may not have been an acceptable leader for Havana, the city government would nevertheless elect him one of its representatives to the Cortes, reaffirming his customary role as the mouthpiece of the Havana patriciate. The Conde de Casa Bayona was the brother-in-law of the O'Farrill colonels. The Conde de O'Reilly was married to the Condesa de Buena Vista. And Ilincheta was betrothed to María Gabriela O'Farrill, daughter of Colonel José Ricardo O'Farrill, and would marry her the following September.[109] Only one individual sought to exploit the events of July for personal advancement, Casa Barreto, who, in a letter to the Supreme Junta in Spain, attempted to villify Arango and Ilincheta and claimed a major role in arresting the movement. His letter won him a royal commendation, but Governor Someruelos re-

106. File on Conde de Casa Montalvo, 1790–93, AGS, GM, leg. 6850; royal order, Aranjuez, May 8, 1799, AGS, GM, leg. 6878; Santa Cruz, *Historia de familias*, III, 309; Pierson, "Francisco de Arango," 465.

107. *Calendario*, 108–9.

108. Escudero, *Los cambios ministeriales*, 42–43.

109. File on marriage authorization for José Ilincheta and María Gabriela O'Farrill, 1803, AGI, Ultramar, leg. 12; Santa Cruz, *Historia de familias*, III, 341.

fused to publish it on the grounds that nothing revolutionary had in fact occurred and that the conde was a shameless opportunist.[110]

In response to a royal inquiry about the events in July, the ayuntamiento was anything but apologetic. Its actions, it reported, had resulted from legitimate confusion arising from knowledge that numerous juntas had been raised in Spain, a development that implied for Havana a responsibility to defend the royal interest as well. When it became apparent, however, that differences of opinion over Havana's proper course of action might imperil stability, all agreed that the status quo should be maintained pending the establishment of a national government in Spain. In a typical *habanero* ploy, the ayuntamiento also seized the opportunity to state its grievances and aspirations forcefully. The marine commandant was harshly denounced, and the city made plain its expectation that the crown further reform the commercial system or, in other words, that it permit Cuba to retain its access to markets in the United States.[111] The Council of the Regency, established early in 1810, had little choice but to tolerate neutral trade and in January 1812 acceded to planter demands by approving "absolute liberty" for the owners to cut trees in the *montes*.[112] Again Havana succeeded in exacting special concessions in return for services to the crown—in this instance overcoming the temptation to reorganize the colonial government!

No criminal charges ever resulted from the July movement, for Someruelos, the ayuntamiento, and the patriciate, with the exception of Casa Barreto, maintained silence. Although repeatedly forced to defend himself against allegations of treason, Arango served in the Cortes called by the Council of the Regency, where he worked successfully to frustrate an attempt to abolish the slave trade. In subsequent years, he assumed various official positions including a place on the Council of the Indies.[113] The Regency soon moved Ilincheta out of Havana, naming him *oidor* of the Audiencia of Guadalajara.[114] Steps to recall Someruelos to Spain began in 1810, although his replacement, Juan Ruíz de Apodaca, did not arrive until April 14, 1812.[115] Significantly, Francisco Montalvo was named subinspector general of the army of Cuba and in 1813 was promoted to viceroy of New Granada.

Events from within soon worked to close any political divisions that

110. Someruelos to Pedro Rivero, Havana, Feb. 5, 1810, Someruelos to Sierra, Havana, Sept. 7, 1810, both in AGI, SD, leg. 1282; Juan Ruíz de Apodaca to Antonio Caro Manuel, Havana, Mar. 3, 1813, AGI, SD, leg. 1285.
111. Havana ayuntamiento to Someruelos, Havana, Dec. 1, 1808, AGI, PC, leg. 1627.
112. Apodaca to Caro Manuel, Havana, Aug. 31, 1812, AGI, SD, leg. 1284.
113. Pierson, "Francisco de Arango," 461–62; Ponte Domínguez, *La junta*, 67–96.
114. Petition, Ilincheta, Sept. 10, 1810, Havana, AGI, SD, leg. 1282.
115. Royal order, Cádiz, Sept. 16, 1810, AGI, PC, leg. 1593.

may have lingered within the elite. In March 1809 when the colonial authorities, as a precautionary measure, expelled the French immigrants suspected of questionable loyalty, many free blacks and mulattoes joined in the action, looting French property and otherwise engaging in disorderly activities that Cuban creoles soon came to fear might widen to threaten the interests of all whites. Someruelos mobilized the militia, including the *pardo* and *moreno* battalions, to restore order. These events, which sent a shiver through the creole community, served as a reminder that instability at the top might well invite turmoil from below, and with the exception of a minor Masonic conspiracy in 1810, the patriciate closed ranks in the face of a common threat.[116]

Soon after, the Aponte Conspiracy reinforced this fear. During late 1811, José Antonio Aponte, a free black carpenter who saw himself as a modern-day Moses, secretly established a central revolutionary junta in Havana, determined to destroy slavery and burn the sugar plantations to revolutionize the economy. Aponte's junta established sister cells at various other points on the island as well. Although Captain General Someruelos uncovered the plot and arrested Aponte and eight of his collaborators, rebellions erupted in a number of localities, including the jurisdictions of Puerto Príncipe, Bayamo, Holguín, and the Peñas Altas plantation just east of Havana. Again the authorities called upon the disciplined militia to restore order. Aponte and his Havana conspirators were hanged amid "public applause," the bodies of Aponte and three others mutilated, and their heads and hands placed on public display. Additional executions occurred in Puerto Príncipe, and in the fall the Havana authorities constructed a garrote to throttle the Peñas Altas insurgents. Others were flogged and imprisoned. The incredible brutality of these spectacles, of course, reflected the panic that had gripped the slave society.[117]

In what was in some ways an even more frightening development,

116. Someruelos to Benito Hermida, Havana, Mar. 31, Apr. 28, 1809, both in AGI, SD, leg. 1281; Intendant Juan de Aguilar to Someruelos, Havana, Apr. 18, 1809, AGI, PC, leg. 1596. See also Anne Perotin, "Deux situations révolutionnaires en pays colonial: La Guadeloupe (1793)–Cuba (1809). Etude comparative des innovations institutionnelles locales: Comités de surveillance et juntas de vigilancia," *Bulletin de la Société d'Histoire de la Guadeloupe* 24 (2nd trimester 1975), 51–69. The Masonic conspiracy has been treated in Franciso Morales Padrón, "Conspiraciones y masonería en Cuba (1810–1826)," *AEA* 29 (1972), 343–77.

117. A brief overview of the Aponte conspiracy can be found in Foner, *A History of Cuba*, I, 91–94. For documentation on the military response and the subsequent punishments, see Someruelos to Aguilar, Havana, Mar. 13, Apr. 3, 6, 1812, all in AGI, PC, leg. 1600; Someruelos to Ignacio de la Pezuela, Havana, Feb. 14, Mar. 5, Apr. 12, 1812, Apodaca to Pezuela, Havana, June 11, 1812, Apodaca to Caro Manuel, Havana, Oct. 28, 1812, all in AGI, SD, leg. 1284.

the officers of the Havana Battalion of Morenos, denouncing dis-
crimination on the basis of the "accident of color," petitioned the
crown for what amounted to equal status, asking for effective command of their unit, the honor of enlisting their sons as cadets, improved
salaries, and the right to wear their hats in the presence of white
officials. They also renewed the 1789 request that a second battalion be
established under the authority of black officers, showing that the
demand for offices remained high among blacks. The petition, dated
May 25, 1812, was timed to greet the new captain general soon after his
arrival and came while the hunt for the Peñas Altas conspirators was
still underway. Distressingly, two of the men apprehended in connection with the latter incident were soldiers from the Moreno Battalion, a
chilling development that brought to mind Arango's warning many
years before. Bypassing Subinspector General Montalvo, the *morenos*
placed the petition in Apodaca's hands, hoping that he would send it
directly to Spain where the Cortes was currently debating the future of
the slave trade. The new governor, however, prudently sent it to Montalvo for an opinion.

The Cuban subinspector viewed the *moreno* initiative with the
utmost gravity, warning that "one false step can endanger the tran-
quillity of the island." Montalvo, who in terms of social theory had no
sympathy whatever for the petition, emphasized that public opinion
would not tolerate the proposed changes. Moreover, he loathed the
long-term implications of granting black officers full rights, for with
the *morenos* "obtaining equal status with the officers of the army, the
pretense of enjoying the same honors and prerogatives as the rest of the
citizens follows [as does] the inability to deny them equal access to
the premier positions in government which are the military ones." On
the other hand, Montalvo feared the Moreno Battalion, especially in
light of the crisis that beset the island, and he lamented that it had ever
been created. Offending its leadership would be risky, but he urged
Apodaca to phase out the unit gradually by permitting enlistments to
lag and by delaying the replacement of officers. The captain general
simply stalled, holding the petition in Havana rather than advancing it
to court, but he prudently transferred three of the *moreno* companies to
Florida when a border crisis flared with the United States.[118] The *pardo*
and *moreno* militia would endure until 1844 when a change of political
climate would lead to its abolition; it would then be reestablished in
1854.[119]

The restoration of Ferdinand VII in 1814 brought to a conclusion the
period of crisis. The monarch, who fully understood the meaning of the

118. File on *moreno* petition, 1812, AGI, PC, leg. 1798.
119. Klein, "The Colored Militia of Cuba," 24–25.

Havana petition of 1809, responded in a manner consistent with the behavior of his grandfather and father. His first major concession to Cuban demands came by royal order of August 30, 1815, which, confirming the action of the Regency in 1812, resolved the volatile issue of the royally protected forests to the complete satisfaction of the Havana patriciate. "Owners shall have," the order stated, "liberty to cut their trees and sell their wood to whomever they please; and neither the state nor any organization or individual may interfere with these sales."[120] In September 1814 the crown, in an abortive attempt to restore the mercantilistic structure, had ordered an end to neutral trade. Captain General Apodaca, however, like his predecessors, simply suspended implementation of the directive. Ferdinand capitulated in February 1818, opening the ports of Cuba to unrestricted world trade. Finally, in 1817, after an existence of a full century, the tobacco monopoly was abolished.[121]

These decrees brought to a conclusion yet another cycle of royal concessions to planter interests in return for military services. Cubans had manned the defenses of their island during a tortuous period when Spain could do little itself, and they had held fast during the dynastic crisis precipitated by the French occupation. Cuba, Spain's "ever faithful isle," was also Spain's "ever favored colony." After half a century, the bargain struck between Havana and the crown through Esquilache, Ricla, and O'Reilly still retained its essential features.

120. Royal order, Madrid, Aug. 30, 1815, AGI, Ultramar, leg. 9.
121. Between 1814 and 1819, the crown also enacted a series of land reform laws to the benefit of the sugar industry. These and the other concessions to Cuban planters are analyzed in Domínguez, *Insurrection or Loyalty*, 214–16. For contrasting commercial policy as applied elsewhere in the empire, see Timothy E. Anna, "Spain and the Breakdown of the Imperial Ethos: The Problem of Equality," *HAHR* 62 (May 1982), 268–69.

Conclusion

The Cuban military reform worked. The urgent need exposed by the Battle of Havana to broaden the manpower base of the army was met effectively through the introduction of the disciplined militia system and an expansion of the veteran garrison. Despite a rocky beginning, the enlarged regular army became a formidable force and remained so until circumstances beyond the control of the Spanish monarchy sapped its strength near the end of the eighteenth century. Cuba's volunteer regiments and battalions were faithfully maintained throughout the reigns of both Charles III and Charles IV. The several municipalities mustered their quotas of volunteers and funded their uniforms, while the crown, ever conscious of the militia's vital mission and assisted by Havana's money, equipped them. Under the guidance of veteran cadres, they drilled weekly, and top officers such as Antonio María Bucareli and Bernardo de Gálvez rated the Havana units as nearly equal to the veterans.

The militia system worked because the support apparatus functioned to the satisfaction of the creole directorate. From its inception, military reform was linked to commercial privileges, which were in turn shaped to the advantage of the Cuban patriciate and especially the emerging sugar aristocracy that came to command the regiments of Havana and Matanzas. In deference to the strategic importance of their island, the crown indulged these officers with honors and privileges that went well beyond the norm in other American colonies. And while they paid higher taxes and contended with tighter royal administration as a consequence of the decision to strengthen the military, Cubans stood as net beneficiaries of defense spending as the Mexican *situado* poured millions upon millions of pesos into the island. With overall

Bourbon policy working to their advantage, Cubans proved willing to render military service and did so repeatedly.

The most spectacular expression of Cuba's military readiness was the reconquest of Florida during the War of the American Revolution. Despite severe setbacks owing to an epidemic in the Army of Operations and to the October hurricane that scattered the first force destined to invade Pensacola, the Spanish were able to advance their campaigns because they could count upon the Cuban militia to man the home front while troops from the veteran garrison went on the offensive. Although beset by enormous hardships, Cuban militiamen also performed their role during the turmoil inflicted by the Wars of the French Revolution and Napoleon, when the veteran garrison quickly dwindled to a small fraction of its authorized complement. It is instructive that despite its earlier success in Cuba during the Seven Years' War, the United Kingdom did not attempt to invade Cuba again even though it conducted ambitious operations during the First and Second British Wars.

Cuban military contributions had their principal local impact in the economic transformation of the island. Although many factors promoted the sugar boom that set in after 1763, the commercial privileges that the planter-officers exacted in return for their services contributed in a major way to the establishment of an institutional structure favorable to the island's development. The trade regulation of 1765, the capstone on the reform program of Esquilache and Charles III, opened the way for the rapid growth of the sugar industry. When Saint Domingue collapsed in 1791, Cuba was poised to exploit its opportunities. Appreciative of the Cuban contribution during 1779–1783, moreover, the crown had permitted broad *habanero* access to the royal administration, both on the island and at court, where patricians lobbied for and received the concessions they needed to hasten economic expansion. This process continued during the wars of Charles IV when Cubans repeatedly used their military services to extract further privileges, principally in the area of neutral trade with the United States. By 1815 Cuba boasted a population of nearly 600,000 and stood on the threshold of world leadership in sugar production.[1]

The political outcome of the arrangement between the crown and the elite was fidelity during the French invasion and the captivity of Ferdinand VII. Owing to a relentless, if gradual, penetration of the veteran officer corps, Cubans had come to control the regular army as well as their traditional stronghold, the disciplined militia, but Hava-

---

1. Kenneth F. Kiple, *Blacks in Colonial Cuba, 1774–1899* (Gainesville, 1976), 38; Moreno Fraginals *El ingenio,* II, 172–74.

na's officers turned back a revolutionary movement headed by Francisco Arango y Parreño and José Ilincheta that, at the very least, plotted an ambitious reorganization of the Cuban government and that may well have led to far more serious consequences. Although personifying much of what the Havana elite sought commercially, Arango did not identify with the tradition-oriented corporatist values that the Old Regime had so carefully nurtured in the Cuban army and that meant so much to its officers, who imagined themselves to be modern-day feudal lords. These men blocked Arango's movement, and when the perils of political division became evident to all during the disorders that rocked the colony from below soon thereafter, political agitation quickly waned. The restored monarch continued the policy he inherited from his predecessors by repaying Cubans for their military services and loyalty with yet another round of major concessions to the sugar industry, thus cementing a tie with the planter elite that would endure well into the nineteenth century.

The events of 1808 suggest that Arango y Parreño's place in history must be reconsidered. Undoubtedly, he was a bright, capable spokesman for the Cuban elite, but to rank him, as most have, as the major figure in the Havana patriciate is off the mark. Although important, he was not a leading sugar producer, nor did he stand at the head of the planter aristocracy, a role that would be best ascribed to the O'Farrill, Montalvo, Beitía, Chacón, Núñez, Beltrán, and Calvo men. Arango overstepped his limits in 1808 and when reminded of his customary role returned to it without violence or bloodshed, permitting the royal administration to co-opt him with official positions and honors for the rest of his life. Had the Cuban army supported him, a Bolívar he might have been, but he died a royal bureaucrat.

The impact of the disciplined militia system upon the men who held offices in the *pardo* and *moreno* units is more difficult to assess. Efforts from within that estate to expand the black militia to provide more offices, not to mention the example of men uniforming companies in return for the prestige of title of rank and the *fuero militar*, show that in the ethos of Cuban society the quest for military honors was not resticted to whites. Corporate privileges, royal decorations, and the right to bear arms undoubtedly conveyed a level of distinction that many eagerly sought. Yet it is equally evident that the artisans who populated the colored officer corps, standing hat in hand before their white instructors, chafed at the humiliations inflicted upon them during their service for the king. Although militia office afforded a welcome measure of status, that status was confined within the colored estate and was not enough to satisfy.

Finally, a word is in order about the thousands of small farmers, shopkeepers, artisans, and laborers who served as soldiers in the Cuban militia. For most of them, the distinctions offered by their privileges and the honor of the uniform was enough to sustain their interest in weekly drills during normal times. They mastered military skills in impressive numbers and performed effectively when called upon. Havana's *pardos* and *morenos* seem to have been particularly responsive to the opportunities conveyed by military service, showing a proficiency that came to be feared within the upper estate. It is also evident that the price of soldiery was difficult, at times insufferable, during the seemingly endless wars unleashed by the French Revolution. But enlisted men had little choice. The patricians who controlled the political and economic structures supported the system, permitting them little room for protest or escape. It should be remembered, however, that those wars created trying times throughout the Western world and suffering was by no means unique to the Cuban army.

To generalize from Cuba's experience would be perilous in the extreme. The island was a unique colony where special military needs and a ready access to the royal administration produced unusual results. Cuba was the beginning point for much of the reform legislation that transformed the late Bourbon empire, but to assume that the application of this legislation in other settings was the same or that in different circumstances it produced similar results would be to invite error. The Cuban military reform produced an example of how the disciplined militia system was supposed to work but seldom did in the mainland colonies. Its history underscores the complexity that characterized Bourbon America.

Appendix 1

UNIT ORGANIZATION IN THE ARMY OF CUBA

Table A-1. **Organization of a Veteran Infantry Regiment**

Grade	Number in Each Grenadier Company (1 per battalion)	Number in Each Fusilier Company (8 per battalion)	Total in the Regiment
Captains	1	1	18
Lieutenants	1	1	18
Second Lieutenants	1	1	18
First Sergeants	1	1	18
Second Sergeants	1	2	34
First Corporals	3	4	70
Second Corporals	3	4	70
Drummers	1	2	34
Soldiers	54	64	1,132
Totals*	63	77	1,358

Command and Staff Group

First Battalion	Second Battalion
1 colonel	1 lieutenant colonel
1 *sargento mayor*	1 adjutant major
1 adjutant major	2 ensigns
2 ensigns	1 chaplain
1 chaplain	1 surgeon
1 surgeon	1 corporal, *gastador*
1 corporal, *gastador*	6 *gastadores*
6 *gastadores*	1 master armorer
1 master armorer	2 fifers
1 drum major	
2 fifers	

SOURCE: *Ordenanzas de S.M.*, vol. I, trat. I, tit. i, arts. 1–6.

* Personnel totals do not include officers.

Table A-2.   **Unit Organization under the Regulation for the Disciplined Militia of Cuba, 1769**

White Infantry Battalion

Grade	Number in Each Grenadier Company *(1 per battalion)*	Number in Each Fusilier Company *(8 per battalion)*	Total
Captains	1	1	9
Lieutenants (vet.)	1	1	9
Second Lieutenants	1	1	9
Sergeants (vet.)	1	1	9
Sergeants (vol.)	2	2	18
Drummers (vet.)	1	1	9
First Corporals (vet.)	2	2	18
First Corporals (vol.)	4	4	36
Second Corporals	6	6	54
Soldiers	64	74	656
Totals	80	90	800

Command and Staff Group

1 colonel	1 *sargento mayor* (vet.)	1 adjutant (vet.)
2 ensigns	1 chaplain	1 surgeon
1 drum major	1 corporal, *gastador*	6 *gastadores*

Pardo Infantry Battalion

Grade	Number in Each Grenadier Company (1 per battalion)	Number in Each Fusilier Company (8 per battalion)	Total
Captains	1	1	9
Lieutenants	1	1	9
Second Lieutenants	1	1	9
First Sergeants	1	1	9
Second Sergeants	2	2	18
Drummers	1	1	9
First Corporals	6	6	54
Second Corporals	6	6	54
Soldiers	64	74	656
Totals	80	90	800

Command and Staff Group

White	Pardo
1 adjutant major (subinspector)	1 commander
4 adjutants	2 ensigns
5 *garzones*	1 drum major
	1 corporal, *gastador*
	6 *gastadores*
	8 fifers

Cavalry Regiment

Grade	Number in Each Carabineer Company (1 per regiment)	Number in Each Cavalry Company (12 per regiment)*	Total
Captains	1	1	13
Lieutenants (vet.)	1	1	13
Second lieutenants	1	1	13
Ensigns	1	1	13
Sergeants (vet.)	1	1	13
Sergeants (vol.)	1	1	13
Corporals (vet.)	2	2	26
Corporals (vol.)	2	2	26
Troopers	44	44	572
Totals	50	50	650

Command and Staff Group

1 colonel	1 lieutenant colonel	1 *sargento mayor* (vet.)
1 adjutant major (vet.)	1 chaplain	1 surgeon
4 trumpeters (vet.)		

*Three cavalry companies were comprised in a squadron.

Dragoon Regiment

Grade	Number in Each Foot Company (3 per regiment)	Number in Each Mounted Company (3 per regiment)	Total
Captains	1	1	6
Lieutenants	1	1	6
Second Lieutenants	1	1	6
Sergeants (vet.)	1		3
Sergeants (vol.)	2	2	12
Drummers (vet.)	1		3
First Corporals (vet.)	2		6
First Corporals (vol.)	4	3	21
Second Corporals	6	3	27
Soldiers/troopers	84	42	378
Totals	100	50	450

Command and Staff Group

1 colonel	1 adjutant major (vet.)	2 ensigns
1 chaplain	1 surgeon	

NOTE: Personnel totals do not include officers.

Appendix 2

PRESTIGE APPOINTMENTS IN THE HAVANA
AND MATANZAS MILITIA

Militia office		Age
	December 1763	
	Volunteer Cavalry Regiment	
Colonel	Martín Esteban de Aróstegui, brigadier of the army	43
Lieutenant colonel	Juan O'Farrill	42
Captains	Juan Tomás de Jáuregui	40
	José de la Torre	56
	Martín de Zayas	48
	Nicolás Chacón	47
	Ambrosio de Jústiz	39
	Felipe José de Zequeira	34
	Esteban José de la Barrera	32
	Juan Núñez del Castillo y Sucre, third Marqués de San Felipe	28
	Nicolás de Cárdenas	27
	Manuel Morales	25
	Miguel Antonio de Herrera	24
	José Garro	22
	Martín Tomás Aróstegui	18

Volunteer Infantry Regiment

Colonel	Luis de Aguiar, colonel of the army	43
Lieutenant colonel	Francisco José Chacón y Torres,	
	second Conde de Casa Bayona	51
Captains of the First Battalion	Francisco de Cárdenas	46
	José Zaldívar	42
	Melchor Armenteros	—
	Esteban Porlier	49
	Francisco Bruñón	36
	Rafael Cárdenas	44
	Ignacio Peñalver	26
	Miguel Coca	22
	Tomás Aróstegui	17
Sublieutenants of the First Battalion	Francisco Castellón	—
	Antonio Duarte	29
	Manuel Duarte	36
	Juan de Santa Cruz	19
	Juan de Jústiz	—
	Anastasio Arango	22
	Mauricio Molina	23
	Hubaldo de Coca	20
	Juan de Santa Cruz	19
Ensigns of the First Battalion	Manuel de Zayas	18
	Joaquín de Zayas	18

Matanzas Dragoons

Colonel	Jerónimo de Contreras y Jústiz	38

December 1781

Volunteer Cavalry Regiment*

Colonel	Juan Bautista Vaillant,	
	colonel of the army	45
Lieutenant colonel	Esteban José de la Barrera	50
Captains First commander	Ambrosio de Jústiz,	57
	lieutenant colonel of militia	
Second commander	Juan Núñez del Castillo y Sucre,	
	third Marqués de San Felipe and	
	lieutenant colonel of militia	46

*The company of carabineers had been recently dissolved and incorporated into the other companies, reducing the number of captains to twelve. Two of the captaincies were elevated to the rank of captain-commanders.

	Miguel Antonio de Herrera	42
	Martín Tomás Aróstegui, lieutenant colonel of militia	36
	José Ricardo O'Farrill	32
	Francisco Calvo de la Puerta y O'Farrill, second Conde de Buena Vista	31
	José de Arredondo y Ambulodi, first Conde de Vallellano	33
	Ignacio Montalvo y Ambulodi, first Conde de Casa Montalvo	33
	Miguel de Cárdenas	29
	Luis Basabe	27
	Sebastián de la Cruz	35
	Tomás Domingo de Sotolongo	31

Volunteer Infantry Regiment

Colonel	Francisco de Cárdenas	64
Lieutenant colonel	Antonio José de Beitía, second Marqués del Real Socorro	30
Captains of the First Battalion	José Zaldívar, lieutenant colonel of militia	60
	Juan Bruno de Zayas	36
	Juan de Santa Cruz	37
	Joaquín de Zayas	36
	Miguel Coca	46
	Manuel Duarte	54
	Anastasio Arango	40
	Mauricio Molina	41
	Hubaldo de Coca	38
Captain of the Second Battalion	José María Chacón y Herrera, third Conde de Casa Bayona	26
Sublieutenants of the First Battalion	Francisco Morales	37
	Pedro Armenteros	37
	Antonio García	31
	Lope Morales	33
	José Remigio Pita	32
	José Manuel Zaldívar	30
	Nicolás Viamonte	39
	Juan de Urra	35
	José Luis Meyreles	29
Ensign of the First Battalion	Manuel José Urrutia	30

Matanzas Dragoons

| Colonel | Jerónimo de Contreras y Jústiz, first Conde de Gibacoa | 56 |

December 1792

Volunteer Cavalry Regiment

| Colonel | Francisco José Calvo de la Puerta y O'Farrill, second Conde de Buena Vista and colonel of the army | 42 |
| Lieutenant colonel | José Ricardo O'Farrill, lieutenant colonel of the army | 43 |

Captains
First commander	José de Arredondo y Ambulodi, first Conde de Vallellano and lieutenant colonel of militia	43
Second commander	Luis Basabe	38
	Sebastián de la Cruz	44
	Tomás Domingo de Sotolongo	42
	Pedro Julián de Morales	43
	Rafael Ignacio de Morales	37
	Manuel Chacón	39
	Antonio de Garro y Zayas	26
	Ignacio Santa Cruz	26
	Pablo Molina	49

| Supernumerary captain | José Lorenzo Montalvo y O'Farrill | 20 |

Volunteer Infantry Regiment

| Colonel | Antonio José de Beitía, second Marqués del Real Socorro and colonel of the army | 41 |
| Lieutenant colonel | José María Chacón y Herrera, third Conde de Casa Bayona and colonel of militia | 37 |

Captains of the
First Battalion
	Miguel Coca, lieutenant colonel of militia	57
	Anastasio Arango, lieutenant colonel of militia	52
	Juan de Santa Cruz	48
	José Manuel Zaldívar	41
	Pedro Armenteros	48
	José Remigio Pita	43
	José Luis Meyreles	40
	Joaquín Beltrán de Santa Cruz	23
	José Francisco de Beitía y O'Farrill	19

Sublieutenants of the First Battalion	Manuel Urrutia, lieutenant of militia	32
	José Palomino	42
	Bartolomé Camacho	26
	Joaquín Camacho	25
	Joaquín Santa Cruz	24
	Francisco Zaldívar	18
	Juan de Cotilla	27
	Mateo de Cárdenas	26
Ensigns of the First Battalion	Rafael O'Farrill	24
	Nicolás de Cárdenas	19
Supernumerary Sublieutenant	Ciriaco Arango, lieutenant of militia	33

Matanzas Dragoons

Colonel	Ignacio Montalvo y Ambulodi, first Conde de Casa Montalvo	43
Lieutenant colonel	José María de Contreras y Jústiz, second Conde de Gibacoa	41

December 1809

Volunteer Cavalry Regiment

Colonel	Martín de Ugarte, colonel of the army	51
Lieutenant Colonel	José Ricardo O'Farrill, colonel of the army	60
Captains First commander	José de Arredondo y Ambulodi, first Conde de Vallellano and colonel of militia	60
Second commander	José Lorenzo Montalvo y O'Farrill, second Conde de Casa Montalvo and lieutenant colonel of militia	36
	Luis Basabe	55
	Tomás Domingo de Sotolongo	59
	Manuel Chacón	56
	Lope Morales	37
	Rafael Ignacio de Morales	36
	José Manuel Ponce	41
	Nicolás de Cárdenas	35
	Ignacio Herrera	44
	Manuel Morales	39
	Manuel José de la Cruz	19

Supernumeraries
   Lieutenant Colonel   José Félix de Córdoba   51
   Captain   Mariano Cabrera   41

                         Volunteer Infantry Regiment

Colonel   José María Chacón y Herrera,
                           third Conde de Casa Bayona
                           and colonel of the army   54
Lieutenant colonel   José Manuel Zaldívar,
                           first Conde de Zaldívar   58

Captains of the
   First Battalion   José Francisco de Beitía y
                           O'Farrill, third Marqués del
                           Real Socorro and lieutenant
                           colonel of militia   35
                         Pedro Armenteros   65
                         José Remigio Pita   60
                         José Luis Meyreles   57
                         Francisco Zaldívar   35
                         Bartolomé Camacho   43
                         Mateo de Cárdenas   43
                         Joaquín de Cárdenas   34
                         Francisco Menocal   35

Sublieutenants of
   the First Battalion   Pedro Armenteros   33
                         Agustín de Cárdenas   33
                         Miguel Pita   28
                         Ramón Meyreles   31
                         José Cayetano Zaldívar   25
                         Francisco López Ganuza   40
                         José Ramón Zaldívar   24
                         Pedro Celestino Sánchez   26
                         Domingo Armona y Lizundia   24

Captains of the
   Second Battalion   Vicente Pérez Justiniani   68
                         Rafael O'Farrill   41

Ensign of the
   First Battalion   Antonio José de Beitía   17
                         Agustín Xenes   26

Supernumeraries

Colonels	Joaquín de Santa Cruz	41
	Francisco Chacón y O'Farrill	32
Captains	Ramón Alderete	39
	Antonio José de Beitía y O'Farrill	28
	Antonio María de Cárdenas	32
	Francisco Javier de Beitía y O'Farrill	23
	Juan Cobarrubias	32
	Ambrosio Benito Morales	29
Sublieutenants	Ciriaco Arango, captain of militia	50
	Francisco Zepero	38
	José de Lima	25

Matanzas Dragoons

Colonel	José María de Contreras y Jústiz, second Conde de Gibacoa and colonel of the army	58
Lieutenant colonel	Juan Manuel O'Farrill, lieutenant colonel of the army	55

SOURCES: O'Reilly to Ricla, Havana, November 22, 1763, AGI, SD, leg. 2078; service records, disciplined militia of Havana and Matanzas 1765, 1771, 1781, 1792, 1809, in AGI, SD, legs. 2093, 2129, 2098, AGS, GM, legs. 7261, AGI, PC, legs. 1770–73.

NOTE: These ages should be taken as approximations, for the service records are unreliable on this point, showing considerable inconsistency.

Appendix 3

THE O'FARRILL OFFICERS
TO 1808

—María Josefa O'Farrill

Ignacio Montalvo y Ambulodi
first Conde de Casa Montalvo
b. 1749   d. 1795
Colonel, Matanzas Dragoons

—María Catalina O'Farrill

José María Chacón y Herrera,
third Conde de Casa Bayona
b. 1755   d. 1838
Colonel, Vol. Inf. Reg.

—María Luisa O'Farrill

Antonio José de Beitía,
second Marqués del Real Socorro
b. 1751   d. 1805
Colonel, Vol. Inf. Reg.

Juan O'Farrill y Arriola
b. 1721   d. 1779
Lieutenant colonel,
Vol. Cavalry Reg.

Luisa María Herrera y Chacón

—José Ricardo O'Farrill
b. 1749   d. 1842
Lieutenant colonel, Vol. Cavalry Reg.

—Gonzalo O'Farrill
b. 1754   d. 1831
Lieutenant general of the army,
and minister of war

—Juan Manuel O'Farrill
b. 1754   d. 1825
Lieutenant colonel, Matanzas Dragoons

—Rafael O'Farrill
b. 1768   d. 1845
Captain, Vol. Inf. Reg.

Catalina O'Farrill y Arriola,
first Condesa de Buena Vista

—Francisco José Calvo de la Puerta y O'Farrill,
second Conde de Buena Vista
b. 1750   d. 1796
Colonel, Vol. Cavalry Reg.

—Sebastian Calvo de la Puerta y O'Farrill,
first Marqués de Casa Calvo
b. 1751   d. 1820
Field marshal, Army of Spain

NOTE: This chart lists highest function by 1808 and does not include sons who were not officers and daughters who married civilians.

└─María Teresa Montalvo y O'Farrill
    |
  Joaquín Beltrán de Santa Cruz y Cárdenas,
    first Conde de Santa Cruz de Mopos and third Conde de San Juan de Jaruco
    b. 1769   d. 1807
    Field Marshal and Subinspector General of the Cuban Army

└─José Lorenzo Montalvo y O'Farrill,
    second Conde de Casa Montalvo
    b. 1773   d. 1814
    Captain, Vol. Cavalry Reg.

└─Juan Montalvo y O'Farrill
    b. 1778   d. 1844
    Supernumerary Lieutenant Colonel, Reg. of Cuba

─────Francisco Chacón y O'Farrill
    b. 1777   d. 1816
    Supernumerary colonel, Vol. Inf. Reg.

└─José Francisco de Beitía y O'Farrill,
    third Marqués del Real Socorro
    b. 1774   d. 1811
    Captain, Vol. Inf. Reg.
    |──────────────────────────────Antonio José de Beitía y Armona,
                             fourth Marqués del Real Socorro
└─Antonio José de Beitía y O'Farrill   b. 1792   d. 1864
    b. 1781   d. 1820   Ensign, Vol. Inf. Reg.
    Supernumerary captain, Vol. Inf. Reg.

└─Francisco Javier de Beitía y O'Farrill
    b. 1786   d. 1833
    Supernumerary captain, Vol. Inf. Reg.

─────María Calvo de la Puerta y del Manzano,
    third Condesa de Buena Vista
    |
  Pedro Pablo O'Reilly,
    second Conde de O'Reilly
    b. 1768   d. 1832
    Colonel, Regiment of Havana

Abbreviations

AAE, CE	Archives des Affaires Etrangères, Correspondance Politique Espagne
AEA	*Anuario de estudios americanos*
AGI	Archivo General de Indias
AGMS	Archivo General Militar de Segovia
AGS	Archivo General de Simancas
AHN	Archivo Histórico Nacional
GM	Guerra Moderna
Hac	Secretaría de Hacienda
HAHR	*Hispanic American Historical Review*
IG	Indiferente General
MN	Museo Naval
PC	Papeles de Cuba
SD	Santo Domingo
SHM	Servicio Histórico Militar

Bibliography

ARCHIVES

Archives des Affaires
Etrangéres, Paris
    Correspondence Politique
    Espagne
Archivo General de Indias,
Seville
    Consulado de Cádiz
    Indiferente General
    Papeles de Cuba
    Santo Domingo
    Ultramar
Archivo General Militar de
Segovia
    Ultramar

Archivo General de Simancas
    Guerra Moderna
    Secretaría de Hacienda
Archivo Histórico Nacional,
Madrid
    Estado
Archivo Nacional de Colombia,
Bogota
    Milicia y Marina
Museo Naval, Madrid
    Mopos
Servicio Histórico Militar,
Madrid

PRINTED MATERIALS

Aimes, Hubert H.S. *A History of Slavery in Cuba, 1511–1868.* Rpt. New York, 1967.

Aiton, A.S. "Spanish Colonial Reorganization under the Family Compact," *HAHR* 12 (Aug. 1932), 269–80.

Alden, Dauril. "The Undeclared War of 1771–1777: Climax of Luso-Spanish Platine Rivalry," *HAHR* 41 (Feb. 1961), 55–74.

Allahar, Antón L. "The Cuban Sugar Planters (1790–1820): 'The Most Solid and Brilliant Bourgeois Class in All of Latin America'" *The Americas* 41 (July 1984), 37–57.

Arango y Parreño, Francisco. "Abolición de la fábrica: Libertad en la siembra, fabricación y comercio del tabaco," in Raúl Maestri, ed., *De la factoría a la colonia*. Havana, 1936.

Archer, Christon I. *The Army in Bourbon Mexico, 1760–1810*. Albuquerque, 1977.

———. "Bourbon Finances and Military Policy in New Spain, 1759–1812," *The Americas* 37 (Jan. 1981), 315–50.

———. "Charles III and Defense Policy for New Spain, 1759–1788," in Gaetano Massa, ed., *Paesi mediterranei e America Latina*. Rome, 1982, pp. 190–200.

———. "The Royalist Army in New Spain: Civil-Military Relationships, 1810–1821," *Journal of Latin American Studies* 13 (May 1981), 57–82.

Arrate, José María Félix de. *Llave del nuevo mundo*, intro. by Julio J. Le Riverend Brusone. Rpr. México, 1949.

Artola, Miguel. "Campillo y las reformas de Carlos III," *Revista de Indias*, nos. 115–18 (1969), 685–714.

Barbier, Jacques A. "The Culmination of the Bourbon Reforms, 1787–1792," *HAHR* 57 (Feb. 1977), 51–68.

———. "Peninsular Finance and Colonial Trade: The Dilemma of Charles IV's Spain," *Journal of Latin American Studies* 12 (May 1980), 21–37.

———. "Indies Revenues and Naval Spending: The Cost of Colonialism for the Spanish Bourbons, 1763–1805," *Jahrbuch für Geschichte von Staat, Wirtschaft, und Gesellschaft Lateinamerikas* 21 (Cologne, 1984), 171–88.

———. *Reform and Politics in Bourbon Chile, 1755–1796*. Ottawa, 1980.

———. "Towards a New Chronology for Bourbon Colonialism: The *Depositaria de Indias* of Cadiz, 1722–1789," *Ibero-Amerikanisches Archiv* 6 (1980), 335–53.

———. "Venezuelan *Libranzas*, 1788–1807: From Economic Nostrum to Fiscal Imperative," *The Americas* 37 (Apr. 1981), 457–78.

Barbier, Jacques A., and Herbert S. Klein. "Revolutionary Wars and Public Finances: The Madrid Treasury, 1784–1807," *Journal of Economic History* 41 (June 1981), 315–39.

Barbier, Jacques A., and Allan J. Kuethe, eds. *the North American Role in the Spanish Imperial Economy, 1760–1819*. Manchester, Eng., 1984.

Barras, Francisco de las. "Noticias y documentos de la expedición del Conde de Mompox [sic] a la Isla de Cuba," *AEA* 9 (1952), 513–48.

Beerman, Eric. "Un bosquejo biográfico y genealógico del General Alejandro O'Reilly," *Hidalguía: La revista de genealogía, nobleza y armas* 24 (Mar.–Apr. 1981), 225–44.

———. "José de Ezpeleta," *Revista de historia militar* 21 (1977), 97–118.

Bergamini, John D. *The Spanish Bourbons: The History of a Tenacious Dynasty.* New York, 1974.

Beverina, Juan. *El Virreinato de las provincias del Río de la Plata: Su organización militar.* Buenos Aires, 1953.

Blanck, Guillermo de. Introduction to *Papeles sobre la toma de La Habana por los ingleses en 1762.* Havana, 1948.

Bobb, Bernard E. *The Viceregency of Antonio María Bucareli in New Spain, 1771–1779.* Austin, 1962.

Brading, D.A. *Miners and Merchants in Bourbon Mexico, 1763–1810.* Cambridge, 1971.

Burkholder, Mark A., "The Council of the Indies in the Late Eighteenth Century: A New Perspective," *HAHR* 56 (Aug. 1976), 404–23.

Burholder, Mark A., and D.S. Chandler. *From Impotence to Authority: The Spanish Crown and the American Audiencias, 1687–1808.* Columbia, Mo., 1977.

Calendario manual y guía de forasteros en la Isla de Cuba . . . Havana, 1809.

Campbell, Leon G. "The Army of Peru and the Túpac Amaru Revolt, 1780–1783," *HAHR* 56 (Feb. 1976), 31–57.

———. *The Military and Society in Colonial Peru, 1750–1810.* Philadelphia, 1978.

Caughey, John Walton. *Bernardo de Gálvez in Louisiana, 1776–1783.* Berkeley, 1934.

———. "The Panis Mission to Pensacola, 1778," *HAHR* 10 (Nov. 1930), 480–89.

Céspedes del Castillo, Guillermo. "La renta del tabaco en el Virreinato del Perú," *Revista histórica* 21 (1954), 138–63.

Christelow, Allen. "Contraband Trade between Jamaica and the Spanish Main, and the Free Port Act of 1766," *HAHR* 23 (May 1942), 309–43.

———. "French Interest in the Spanish Empire during the Ministry of the Duc de Choiseul, 1759–1771," *HAHR* 21 (Nov. 1941), 515–37.

Colón y Larriátegui Ximénez de Embún, Félix. *Juzgados militares de España y sus Indias* . . . , 2nd ed., 4 vols. Madrid, 1786–96.

Congreso Venezolano de Historia. *Memoria del Tercer Congreso Venezolano de Historia,* 3 vols. Caracas, 1979.

Cruz Hermosilla, Emilio de la. "Lorenzo Montalvo, figura señera de la Armada," *Revista general de marina* 202 (Jan. 1982), 17–23.

Delgado, Jaime. "El Conde de Ricla, capitán general de Cuba," *Revista de historia de América,* nos. 55–56 (1963), 41–138.

Deschamps Chapeaux, Pedro. *Los batallones de pardos y morenos libres.* Havana, 1976.

Díaz-Trechuelo Spinola, María Lourdes, María Luisa Rodríquez Baena, and Concepción Pajarón Parody. "Antonio María Bucareli y Ursua (1771–1779)," in José Antonio Calderón Quijano, ed., *Los virreyes de Nueva España en el reinado de Carlos III*, vol. I. Seville, 1967, 383–658.

Diggs, Irene. "Color in Colonial Spanish America," *Journal of Negro History* 38 (Oct. 1953), 403–27.

Domínguez, Jorge I. *Insurrection or Loyalty: The Breakdown of the Spanish American Empire*. Cambridge, Mass., 1980.

Engstrand, Iris H.W. *Spanish Scientists in the New World: The Eighteenth-Century Expeditions*. Seattle, 1981.

Escudero, José Antonio. *Los cambios ministeriales a fines del antiguo régimen*. Seville, 1975.

———. *Los origenes del Consejo de Ministros en España*, 2 vols. Madrid, 1979.

Estado militar de España. Madrid, 1799.

Farriss, N.M. *Crown and Clergy in Colonial Mexico, 1759–1821*. London, 1968.

Fernández Duro, Cesáreo. *La armada española desde la unión de los Reinos de Castilla y Aragón*, 6 vols. Rpr. Madrid, 1973.

Fisher, John. "Critique of Jacques A. Barbier's 'Culmination of the Bourbon Reforms, 1787–1792,'" *HAHR* 58 (Feb. 1978), 83–86.

———. "Imperial 'Free Trade' and the Hispanic Economy, 1778–1796," *Journal of Latin American Studies* 13 (May 1981), 21–56.

Foner, Philip S. *A History of Cuba and Its Relations with the United States*, 2 vols. New York, 1962–63.

Friedlander, H.E. *Historia económica de Cuba*. Havana, 1944.

Girón María, Francisco. *Espejo de gobernadores: Biografía de don Diego José Navarro*. Seville, 1942.

Goebel, Julius. *The Struggle for the Falkland Islands: A Study in Legal and Diplomatic History*. New Haven, 1927.

Guerra, Ramiro. *Manual de historia de Cuba desde su descubrimiento hasta 1868*, 2nd ed. Madrid, 1975.

Guerra y Sánchez, Ramiro, José M. Pérez Cabrera, Juan J. Remos, and Emeterio S. Santovenia. *Historia de la nación cubana*, 10 vols. Havana, 1952.

Guiteras, Pedro J. *Historia de la conquista de La Habana por los ingleses sequida de Cuba y su gobierno*. Havana, 1932.

Hellwege, Johann. *Die spanischen Provinzialmilizen im 18. Jahrhundert*. Boppard am Rhein, 1969.

Hernández Palomo, José Jesús. *El aguardiente de caña en México*. Seville, 1974.

Holmes, Jack D.L. *Honor and Fidelity: The Louisiana Infantry Regi-*

ment and the Louisiana Militia Companies, 1766–1821. Birmingham, 1965.

Hull, Anthony H. *Charles III and the Revival of Spain.* Washington, D.C., 1981.

Humboldt, Alejandro de. *Ensayo político sobre la Isla de Cuba,* intro. by Fernando Ortiz, 2 vols. Rpr. Havana, 1930.

Hussey, Roland Dennis. *The Caracas Company, 1728–1784: A Study in the History of Spanish Monopolistic Trade.* Cambridge, Mass., 1934.

Inglis, G. Douglas. "Cuban Settlement Systems and Demographic Patterns in the 1770s," in Margaret E. Crahan, ed., *Cuba: Social Transformations, 1750–1950.* Forthcoming.

———. "The Spanish Naval Shipyard at Havana in the Eighteenth Century," in *New Aspects of Naval History.* Baltimore, 1985.

Inglis, G. Douglas, and Allan J. Kuethe. "El consulado de Cádiz y el reglamento de comercio libre de 1765," in *Jornadas de Andalucía y América,* vol. IV. Seville, 1985, pp. 108–22.

King, James Ferguson. "Evolution of the Free Slave Trade Principle in Spanish Colonial Administration," *HAHR* 22 (Feb. 1942), 34–56.

Kinnaird, Lawrence, ed. *Spain in the Mississippi Valley, 1765–1794,* 3 vols. Washington, D.C., 1946–49.

Kiple, Kenneth F. *Blacks in Colonial Cuba, 1774–1899.* Gainesville, 1976.

Klein, Herbert S. "The Colored Militia of Cuba, 1568–1868," *Caribbean Studies* 4 (July 1966), 17–27.

Knight, Franklin W. "Origins of Wealth and the Sugar Revolution in Cuba, 1750–1850," *HAHR* 57 (May 1977), 231–53.

———. *Slave Society in Cuba during the Nineteenth Century.* Madison, 1970.

Kuethe, Allan J. "La batalla de Cartagena de 1741: Nuevas perspectivas," *Historiografía y bibliografía americanistas* 18 (1974), 19–38.

———. "The Development of the Cuban Military as a Sociopolitical Elite," *HAHR* 61 (Nov. 1981), 695–704.

———. *Military Reform and Society in New Granada, 1773–1808.* Gainesville, 1978.

———. "More on 'The Culmination of the Bourbon Reforms': A Perspective from New Granada," *HAHR* 58 (Aug. 1978), 477–80.

———. "Towards a Periodization of the Reforms of Charles III," *Bibliotheca americana* 1, no. 3 (Jan. 1984), 143–67.

Kuethe, Allan J., and Lowell Blaisdell. "The Esquilache Government and the Reforms of Charles III in Cuba," *Jahrbuch für Geschichte von Staat, Wirtschaft und Gesellschaft Lateinamerikas* 19 (Cologne, 1982), 117–36.

Kuethe, Allan J., and G. Douglas Inglis. "Absolutism and Enlightened
  Reform: Charles III, the Establishment of the *Alcabala*, and Com-
  mercial Reorganization in Cuba," *Past and Present: A Journal of
  Historical Studies*, no. 109 (Nov. 1985), 118–43.
Lafuente, Modesto. *Historia general de España desde los tiempos primi-
  tivos hasta la muerte de Fernando VII*, 25 vols. Barcelona, 1887–91.
Lampros, Peter James. "Merchant-Planter Cooperation and Conflict:
  The Havana Consulado, 1794–1832." Ph.D. dissertation, Tulane
  University, 1980.
Lavín, Arturo G. "El palacio de los Condes de San Juan de Jaruco,"
  Revista de la Biblioteca Nacional 2 (July–Sept. 1951), 45–70.
Levene, Ricardo, ed. *Documentos para la historia argentina*, vols. V and
  VI. Buenos Aires, 1915.
Lewis, James A. "Las Damas de La Habana, el Precursor, and Francisco
  de Saavedra: A Note on Spanish Participation in the Battle of York-
  town," *The Americas* 37 (July 1980), 83–99.
Liss, Peggy K. *Atlantic Empires: The Network of Trade and Revolu-
  tion, 1713–1826*. Baltimore, 1983.
Love, Edgar F. "Negro Resistance to Spanish Rule in Colonial Mexico,"
  Journal of Negro History 52 (Apr. 1967), 89–103.
McAlister, Lyle N. *The "Fuero Militar" in New Spain, 1764–1800*.
  Gainesville, 1957.
McNeill, John Robert. "Theory and Practice in the Bourbon Empires of
  the Atlantic: The Roles of Louisbourg and Havana, 1713–1763."
  Ph.D. dissertation, Duke University, 1981.
Marchena Fernández, Juan. "La financiación militar en Indias: Intro-
  ducción a su estudio," *AEA* 36 (1979), 81–110.
———. "Guarniciones y población militar en Florida oriental (1700–
  1820)," *Revista de Indias*, nos. 163–64 (Jan.–June 1981), 91–142.
———. *La institución militar en Cartegena de Indias, 1700–1810*.
  Seville, 1982.
———. *Oficiales y soldados en el ejército de América*. Seville, 1983.
Marqués del Real Transporte. *Defensa y satisfacción . . . a los cargos que
  se le han formado . . .* Madrid, 1764.
Marrero, Leví. *Cuba: Economía y sociedad*, to date 11 vols. Río Piedras,
  Puerto Rico, and Madrid, 1972–84.
Martínez Cardós, José. "Don José del Campillo y Cossío," *Revista de
  Indias*, nos. 119–22 (1970), 501–42.
Martínez-Valverde, C. "Operaciones de ataque y defensa de La Habana
  en 1762," *Revista general de marina* 164 (Apr. 1963), 487–503, and
  (May 1963), 706–27.
Medina Rojas, F. de Borja. *José de Ezpeleta, gobernador de la Mobila,
  1780–1781*. Seville, 1980.
Mijares Pérez, Lucio. "Programa político para América del Marqués de

la Ensenada," *Revista de historia de América*, no. 81 (Jan.–June 1976), 82–130.

Morales Padrón, Francisco. "Conspiraciones y masonería en Cuba (1810–1826)," *AEA* 29 (1972), 343–77.

Morales y Morales, Vidal. *Iniciadores y primeros mártires de la revolución cubana*, vol. I. Havana, 1931.

Moreno Fraginals, Manuel. "Iglesia e ingenio," *Revista de la Biblioteca Nacional José Martí* 5 (Jan.–Dec. 1963), 11–28.

———. *El ingenio: Complejo económico social cubano del azúcar*, 3 vols. Havana, 1978.

Navarro, Governor Diego José. "Bando sobre prohibir el uso de armas y capas a negros y mulatos," Havana, May 4, 1779, in *Boletín del Archivo Nacional* 28 (Jan.–Dec. 1929), 103–4.

Nieto y Cortadellas, Rafael. *Dignidades nobiliarias en Cuba*. Madrid, 1954.

———. Introduction to *Nuevos papeles sobre la toma de la Habana por los ingleses en 1762*. Havana, 1951.

Nowell, Charles E. "The Defense of Cartegena," *HAHR* 42 (Nov. 1962), 477–501.

Ordenanzas de milicias provinciales de España. Madrid, 1734.

Ordenanzas de S.M. para el régimen, disciplina, subordinación, y servicio de sus ejércitos . . . Madrid, 1768.

Pares, Richard. *War and Trade in the West Indies, 1739–1763*, 2nd ed. London, 1963.

Pérez Cabrera, José Manuel. "Don Luis de Las Casas, fundador de la 'Sociedad Ecónomica,'" *Revista bimestre cubana* 24 (Nov.–Dec. 1926), 891–913.

Pérez de la Riva, Juan. "Inglaterra y Cuba en la primera mitad del Siglo XVII [sic]: Expedición de Vernon contra Santiago de Cuba en 1741," *Revista bimestre cubana* 36 (July–Oct. 1935), 50–66.

———. Introduction to *Documentos inéditos sobre la toma de La Habana por los ingleses en 1762*. Havana, 1963.

Perotin, Anne. "Deux situations révolutionnaires en pays colonial: La Guadeloupe (1793)–Cuba (1809). Etude comparative des innovations institutionnelles locales: Comités de surveillance et juntas de vigilancia," *Bulletin de la Société d'Histoire de la Guadeloupe* 24 (2nd trimester 1975), 51–69.

Pezuela, Jacobo de la. *Diccionario geográfico, estadístico, histórico de la Isla de Cuba*, 4 vols. Madrid, 1863.

———. *Historia de la Isla de Cuba*, 3 vols. Madrid, 1878.

Phelan, John Leddy. "Authority and Flexibility in the Spanish Imperial Bureaucracy," *Administrative Science Quarterly* 5 (1960), 47–65.

———. *The People and the King: The Comunero Revolution in Colombia, 1781*. Madison, 1978.

Pierson, William Whatley, Jr. "Francisco de Arango y Parreño," *HAHR* 16 (Nov. 1936), 451–78.

———. "Institutional History of the *Intendencia,*" *James Sprunt Historical Studies* 19 (Chapel Hill 1927), 74–133.

Ponte Domínguez, Francisco J. *La junta de la Habana en 1808: Antecedentes para la historia de la autonomía colonial en Cuba.* Havana, 1947.

Priestley, Herbert Ingram. *José de Gálvez: Visitor-General of New Spain (1765–1771).* Berkeley, 1916.

Real declaración sobre puntos esenciales de la ordenaza de milicias provinciales de España . . . Madrid, 1767.

Reglamento para el comercio libre de España a Indias . . . Madrid, 1778.

Reglamento para la guarnición de La Habana, castillos, y fuertes de su jurisdicción, Santiago de Cuba, San Agustín de la Florida; y su annexo San Marcos de Apalache. México, 1753.

Reglamento para la guarnición de La Habana . . . 1719. Madrid, 1719.

Reglamento para la guarnición de la Plaza de Cartagena de Indias, castillos y fuertes de su jurisdicción. Madrid, 1736.

Reglamento para la guarnición de la Plaza de Puerto Rico, castillos, y fuertes de su jurisdicción. Madrid, 1741.

Reglamento para la guarnición de la Plaza de Santo Domingo, en la Isla Española, castillos y fuertes de su jurisdicción. Madrid, 1738.

Reglamento para la guarnición de la Plaza de Valdivia y castillos de su jurisdición [sic]. Lima, 1753.

Reglamento para la guarnición de la Provincia de Yucatán, castillos, y fuerte de su jurisdicción. México, 1754.

Reglamento para la guarnición de las plazas, y fuertes de la frontera de la Concepción, Valparaíso, y Chiloe del Reyno de Chile . . . Lima, 1753.

Reglamento para las milicias de infantería, y caballería de la Isla de Cuba. Havana, 1765.

Reglamento para las milicias de infantería, y caballería de la Isla de Cuba. Madrid, 1769.

Reglamento para las milicias disciplinadas de infantería y dragones del Nuevo Reino de Granada, y provincias agregadas a este virreynato. Madrid, 1794.

Restrepo Canal, Carlos. "El sitio de Cartagena por el Almirante Vernon," *Boletín de historia y antigüedades* 28 (1941), 447–67.

Rivero Muñiz, José. *Tabaco: Su historia en Cuba,* 2 vols. Havana, 1964–65.

Rodríguez, Amalia A., ed. *Cinco diarios del sitio de La Habana.* Havana, 1963.

Rodríguez Casado, Vicente. "Comentario al decreto y real instrucción de 1765 regulando las relaciones comerciales de España e Indias," *Anuario de historia del derecho español* 13 (1936–41), 100–135.

———. "O'Reilly en la Louisiana," *Revista de Indias*, no. 2 (1941), 115–38.

———. "La política del reformismo de los primeros Borbones en la marina de guerra española," *AEA* 25 (1968), 601–18.

———. *La política y los políticos en el reinado de Carlos III*. Madrid, 1962.

Roig de Leuchsenring, Emilio, ed. *Cómo vio Antonio de Valdés la toma de La Habana por los ingleses*. Havana, 1962.

———. ed. *Cómo vio Jacobo de la Pezuela la toma de La Habana por los ingleses*. Havana, 1962.

Rush, Orwin, ed. *The Battle of Pensacola, March 9 to May 8, 1781*. Tallahassee, 1966.

Russell Hart, Francis. *The Siege of Havana, 1762*. London, 1931.

Sanders, George Earl. "The Spanish Defense of America, 1700–1763." Ph.D. dissertation, University of Southern California, 1973.

Santa Cruz y Mallen, Francisco Xavier de. *Historia de familias cubanas*, 6 vols. Havana, 1940–50.

Servicio Histórico Militar, *Dos expediciones españolas contra Argel, 1541 y 1775*. Madrid, 1946.

Sevilla Soler, María Rosario. *Santo Domingo: Tierra de frontera (1750–1800)* Seville, 1980.

Shafer, R.J. *The Economic Societies in the Spanish World (1763–1821)*. Syracuse, N.Y., 1958.

Sharp, William Frederick. *Slavery on the Spanish Frontier: The Colombian Chocó, 1680–1810*. Norman, 1976.

Socolow, Susan Migden. *The Merchants of Buenos Aires, 1778–1810*. Cambridge, 1978.

Starr, J. Barton. *Tories, Dons, and Rebels: The American Revolution in British West Florida*. Gainesville, 1976.

Suárez, Santiago Gerardo, ed. *Las fuerzas armadas venezolanas en la colonia*. Caracas, 1979.

Suárez, Santiago Gerardo. "Conflictividad social de la reforma militar dieciochista," *Memorias del Congreso Bicentenario de Simón Bolívar*. Caracas, forthcoming.

———. *Las milicias: Instituciones Militares hispanoamericanas*. Caracas, 1984.

———. ed. *Las fuerzas armadas venezolanas en la colonia*. Caracas, 1979.

Suplemento de algunos particulares que quedaron omisos, y sin comprehenderse en el Reglamento para la Plaza de La Habana... México, 1754.

Syrett, David, ed. *The Siege and Capture of Havana, 1762*. London, 1970.

Tanzi, Héctor José. "La justicia militar en el derecho indiano," *AEA* 26 (1969), 175–277.

TePaske, John J. *The Governorship of Spanish Florida, 1700–1763.* Durham, 1964.

———. "La política española en el Caribe durante los siglos XVII y XVIII," in *La influencia de España en el Caribe, la Florida, y la Luisiana, 1500–1800.* Madrid, 1983, pp. 61–87.

Thomas, Hugh. *Cuba: The Pursuit of Freedom.* New York, 1971.

Thompson, Buchanan Parker. *Spain: Forgotten Ally of the American Revolution.* North Quincy, Mass., 1976.

Tornero, Pablo. "Hacendados y desarrollo azucarero cubano (1763–1818)," *Revista de Indias,* nos. 153–54 (July–Dec. 1978), 715–37.

———. "La participación de Cádiz en el comercio exterior de La Habana (1776–1786)," *Jornadas de Andalucía y América,* vol. I. Huelva, 1981, pp. 85–103.

Torres Ramírez, Bibiano. "Alejandro O'Reilly en Cuba," *AEA* 24 (1967), 1357–88.

———. *Alejandro O'Reilly en las Indias.* Seville, 1969.

Voelz, Peter Michael. "Slave and Soldier: The Military Impact of Blacks in the Colonial Americas." Ph.D. dissertation, University of Michigan, 1978.

Wortman, Miles. "Bourbon Reforms in Central America, 1750–1786," *The Americas* 32 (Oct. 1975), 222–38.

Ximeno, José Manuel de. "Los caballeros maestrantes de La Habana," *Revista de la Biblioteca Nacional* 4 (Oct.–Dec. 1953), 111–27.

Zamora y Coronado, José María. comp. *Biblioteca de legislación ultramarina en forma de diccionario alfabético . . .,* vol. 3. Madrid, 1845.

Zapatero, Juan Manuel. "De la batalla del Caribe: El último ataque inglés a Puerto Rico (17 de abril a 1 de mayo de 1797)," *Revista de historia militar* 3 (1959), 92–134.

———. "Las batallas por la Isla de Cuba, 'llave del nuevo mundo y antemural de las Yndias Occidentales,'" *Revista de historia militar* 8 (1961), 47–64.

———. "La heroica defensa de Cartagena de Indias ante el almirante inglés Vernon en 1741," *Revista de historia militar* 1 (1957), 115–52.

Index

Cuba, 1753–1815, has been set on the Linotron 202 in nine point Trump Medieval with two points of spacing between the lines. Trump Medieval was also selected for display. The book was designed by Jim Billingsley, composed by Modern Typographers of Florida, Inc., printed offset by Thomson-Shore, Inc., and bound by John H. Dekker & Sons. The paper on which this book is printed bears acid-free characteristics for an effective life of at least three hundred years.

THE UNIVERSITY OF TENNESSEE PRESS : KNOXVILLE